AF566826

Buddha

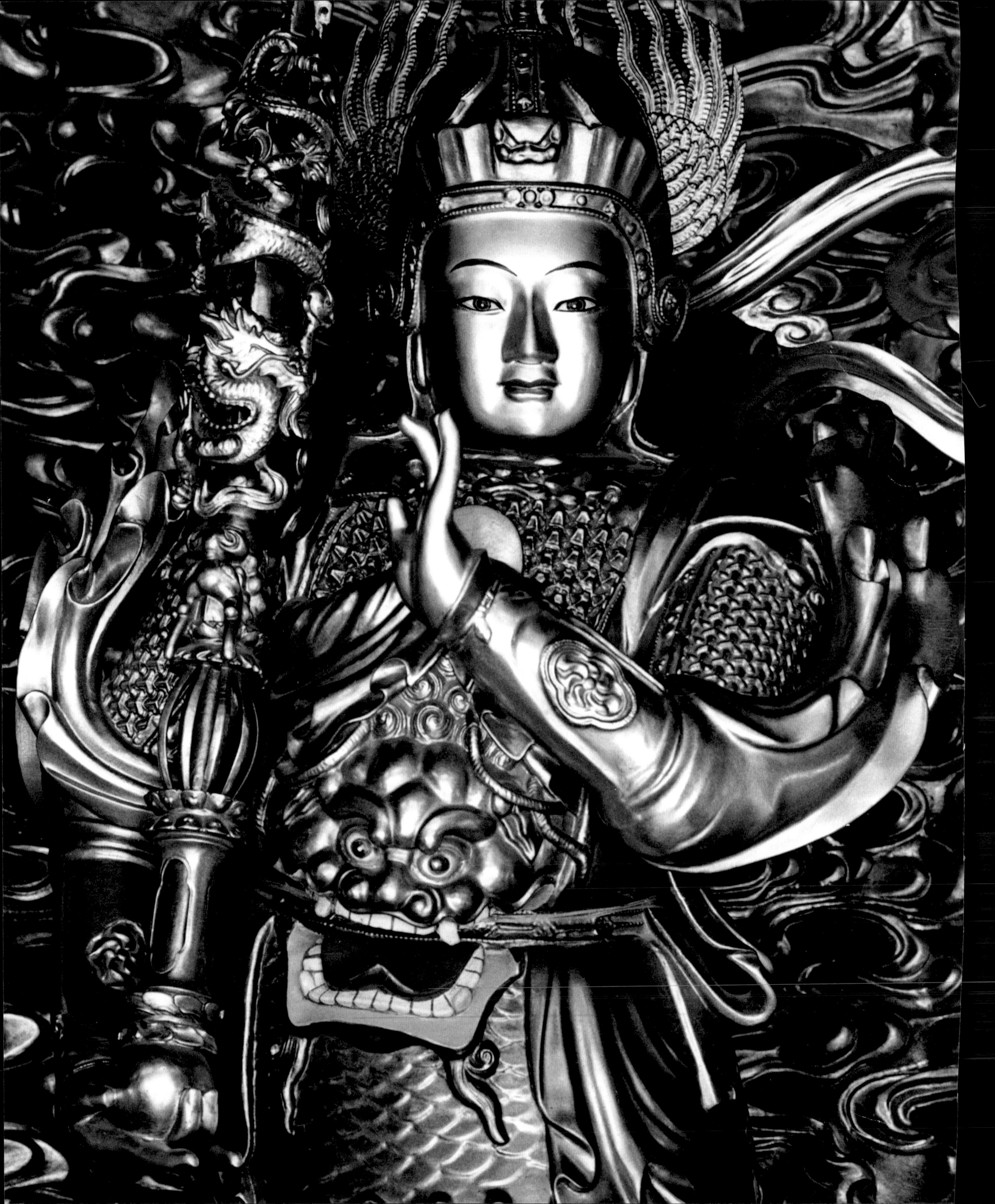

Buddha

PHOTOGRAPHS BY
MICHAEL KENNA

EDITED BY
IRA STEHMANN

WITH AN ESSAY BY
JENS-UWE HARTMANN &
GUDRUN MELZER

PRESTEL
Munich · London · New York

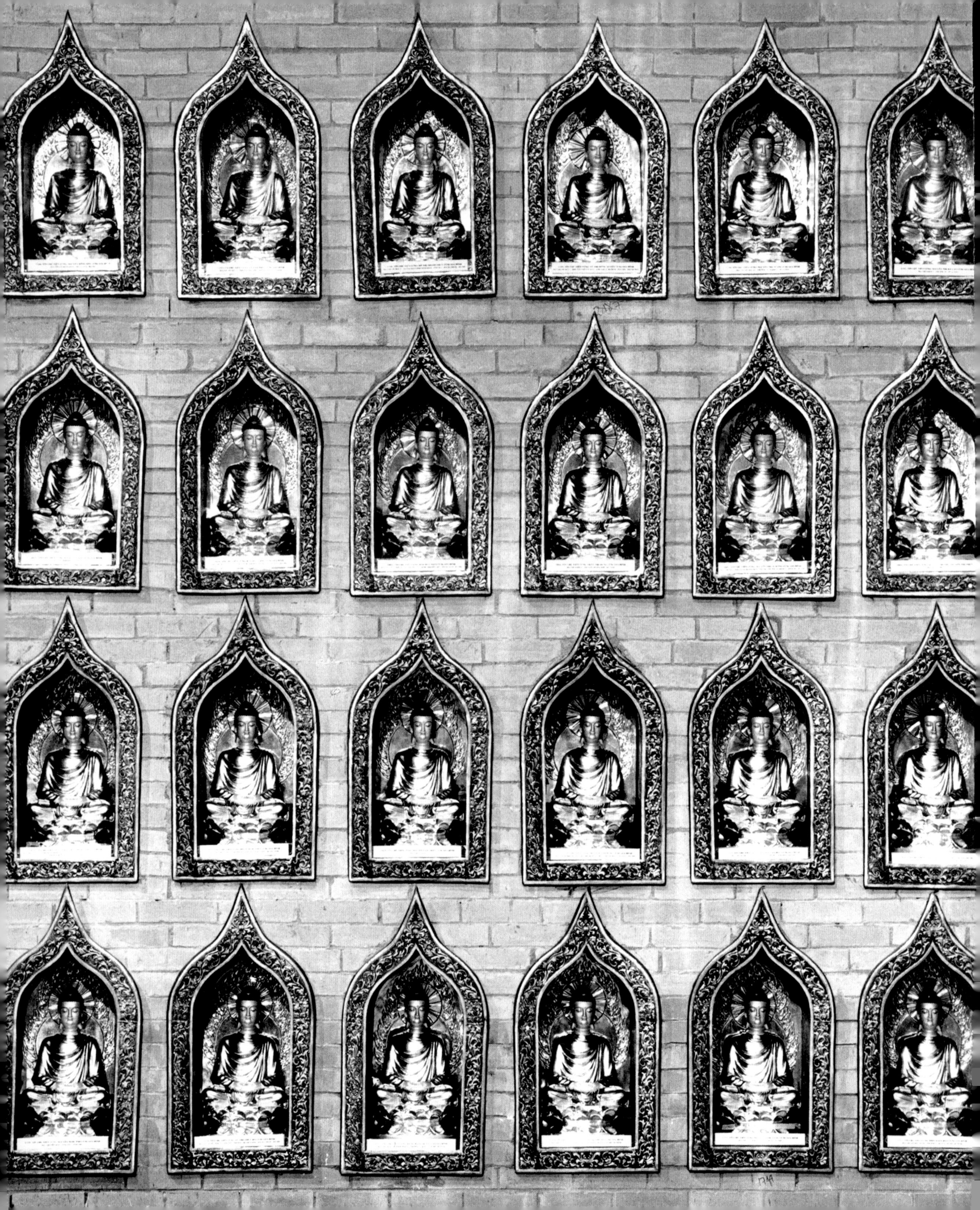

Wall of Buddhas, Bai Dinh Pagoda,
Ninh Binh, Vietnam, 2019

Unity and Diversity: The Image of the Buddha and Its Development

JENS-UWE HARTMANN
GUDRUN MELZER

No other symbol from any Asian religion is as prevalent as the depiction of the meditating Buddha. Whether the image is painted or carved from wood, chiselled from stone or cast in metal, it is instantly recognizable by anyone nowadays. We require no additional explanation in order to understand who is being depicted. The image of the Buddha is employed so often and so successfully in advertising simply because it is so well known. Tour operators capitalize on the fact that depictions of the Buddha are instantly recognizable, as do airlines and tea producers. In particular, references to the Buddha and his meditation posture somehow seem obvious in connection with recuperation and the intensive experience of the present moment. More surprisingly, even a coffee roasting company has fallen back on this by now tried-and-tested icon in order to associate its products with particular feelings.

All this shows that the Buddha, at least as an image, now occupies a position right at the centre of our society, exuding an aura of peace and serenity that relates well to our need for relaxation and well-being. Only a sitting Buddha—ideally with his eyes half-closed in meditation—is capable of conveying this impression of deep composure and the feeling of unshakeable self-repose. The fact that the historical Buddha lived and worked in India, and that his teachings have been disseminated across large parts of Asia, also adds a touch of exoticism. What all these images have in common is, indeed, an apparent lack of temporality and spatiality. In this respect, whether the image in question is of a modern concrete Buddha from a hardware store or a reproduction of a Japanese Buddha figure from the twelfth century is initially of secondary importance here.

In light of this, it is easy to forget that in many parts of Asia, Buddha images such as these convey a great deal more to the viewer than merely a vague feeling of wellness. They are, above all, charged with a range of religious messages that usually elude the Western viewer. These include—to give just one example—the various hand gestures conveying different meanings. However, such images also contribute to cultural identity, for the manner of representation, far from being arbitrary, is bound u with styles that have developed over time and are regionally inflected. Despite all their similarities, a Buddha in Bangkok differs significantly from its counterparts in Lhasa or in Seoul. There is a reason why Michael Kenna arranges his photographs by region. To the untrained eye, the initial impression is one of a surprisingly broad spectrum within the individual representations in terms of, for instance, the faces, coils of hair, proportions and clothing. At the same time, though, there are recognizable commonalities within a region that are not shared by any other region. This enables the photographs selected here to present the depiction of the Buddha as a kind of universal (which is what makes it so unmistakable), while also clearly showing that behind every depiction there is a historical development. That historical reference is preserved by the photographs, for the Buddhas are not detached from their locations.

Places and pictorial perspectives invite the viewer to contemplate the photographs in this book on a deeper level. The sculpted works appear in their natural context, often with allusions to their cultic veneration. They have not been selected on the basis of particular historical or aesthetic criteria; instead, each one stands for itself. On the one hand, we see Buddhas created by outstanding artists in the central sanctuary of a temple, and on the other, numerous Buddhas donated by ordinary people, figures that may have had an important personal meaning, perhaps as votive offerings. Such representations are ubiquitous at sacred sites, as mural reliefs or assembled in rows, and are often made from modern materials. At some locations, their clothing is repeatedly changed; others feature touches of colour from modern restoration work. Some of the sculptures chosen for this volume are damaged in many places or have weathered with age. The occasional inclusion of photographs of landscapes throughout the volume cleverly reinforces the regional references while also conjuring up powerful associations. The monochromatic images of mountains, trees and branches placed between the East Asian Buddhas are reminiscent of the ink illustrations from the landscape painting of that region, reduced to the essential and therefore all the more impressive. With only a few brushstrokes, as it were, they provide the perfect environment for the Buddhas in that they evoke the aesthetic of the very culture in which these Buddha figures were created.

The origins of the Buddha image remain surrounded by mystery. The current belief among scholars is that the Buddha lived in north-east India between the end of the sixth and the beginning of the fourth century BCE; it is not possible to narrow his dates down any further. The oldest preserved Buddhist buildings date from the third century BCE, when the famous ruler Aśoka united large parts of South Asia under one empire. These buildings, known as stūpas, are inaccessible ceremonial buildings (see pp. 132, 138, 142) often enclosed by a fence. The relics preserved in the stūpas were venerated through ritual circumambulation in a clockwise direction. Veneration also took the form of various offerings, such as flowers, garlands, incense, items of clothing and lamps, which in later periods were all presented as offerings to statues of the Buddha as well. Those who wished to invest greater time and effort could expand the ritual sites and adorn them with further architectural and sculptural decoration. Several popular Buddhist texts describe how immeasurably great the religious rewards may be for those who offer up gifts to stūpas or to effigies of the Buddha, or even create these themselves. We read, for example, in a work that answers the question of what veneration of Buddha statues and stūpas could bring the worshipper—a question posed by King Prasenajit, one of the rulers at the time of the Buddha—that in future existences within the cycle of rebirth, the devotee would have a well-proportioned, permanently healthy body, keen senses and a melodious voice, live a long and happy life, be born into a good and sufficiently wealthy family, or even be reborn as a divine being. It goes on to say that the offerings also make worshippers morally irreproachable, thus providing them with an opportunity for salvation from the cycle of existence. Although this work was certainly written after the death of the Buddha, it clearly demonstrates the perceptions that may have lain behind the offerings. Religious texts of this kind serve to glorify those who are generous with their donations, especially the laity, who are not themselves able to follow the ascetic, salvation-oriented lifestyle of Buddhist monks. Such texts can therefore also be recited as part of a devotional ritual, the aim being to ensure the greater efficacy of the commendable deed. This efficacy is substantiated by the belief that these are the authentic words of the Buddha and have permanent truth.

For the Buddhist laity, but also for the monks, a spiritual engagement with the Buddha himself, not only with his teachings (the Dharma) or his community (the Sangha), is of great importance. Lay people, for example, are therefore advised to devote themselves to the spiritual visualization of the Buddha on the regular Buddhist fast days, which follow the lunar calendar and thus fall on full-moon and new-moon days, as well as on the respective half-moon days in between. Meditation on the Buddha, his characteristics and merits, but also his stature, beauty and melodious voice—summarized in Indian tradition in the thirty-two attributes of a distinguished person and the eighty additional features of his body—has been an inherent part of Buddhist thought and behaviour since ancient times, and it is this practice which gave rise, early on, to the need to represent the Buddha in pictorial form.

The earliest examples of narrative Buddhist art come from the second century BCE. These are stone reliefs, early scenic depictions of the most important events in the life of the Buddha. The main character, however, is nowhere to be seen. At first, the person of the Buddha was not depicted, at least not in human form. He was represented through symbols standing for a particular event and showing where the viewer should imagine him to be within the image. The Buddha attained awakening under a particular tree, so an empty seat under the "Tree of Awakening" (the Bodhi Tree) marks this important event in his life. The reliefs depict numerous individuals, including

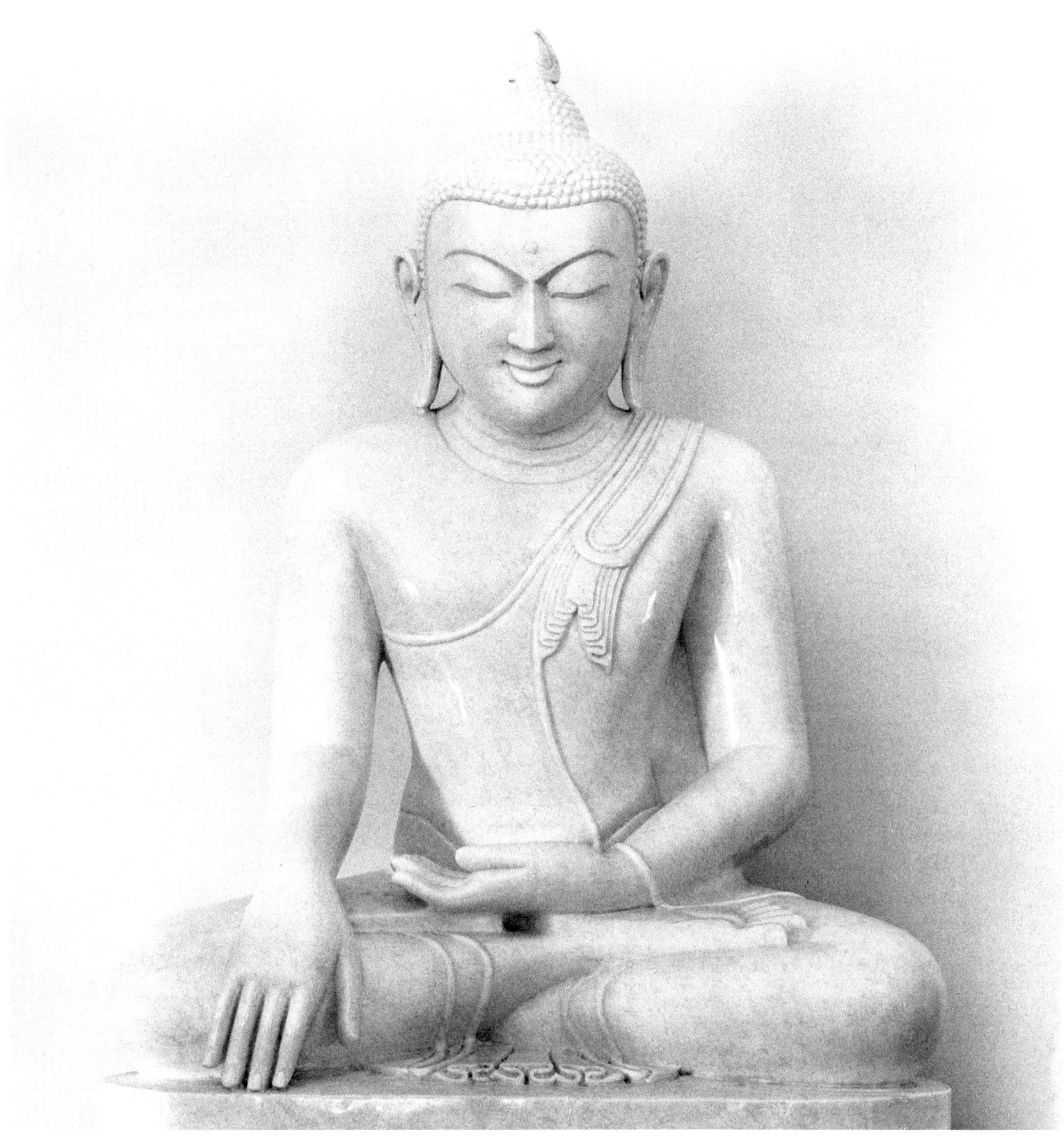

White Buddha,
Kalaw, Myanmar, 2019

divinities and other non-human beings, all of whom are represented in human form. Only the Buddha himself is missing, and this is true not only of his life since his awakening, but also of his life as a child. Even in the depiction of his supernatural birth, we see only his mother and various companions. This eschewal of figural representation of the Buddha is described as the aniconic phase in Buddhist art. Why believers and artists refrained from depicting the Buddha in human form remains unknown. Buddhism does not prohibit the making of images, so one may well ask whether the artists considered themselves incapable of representing an enlightened personality in pictorial form. Here, too, the answer has yet to be determined.

It would seem that the first stone reliefs depicting the Buddha in human form appeared out of the blue shortly after the beginning of the Common Era. Again, we do not know exactly why the shift from aniconic to iconic representation happened at this particular point in time. There is evidence, however, that the two other Indian religions, Hinduism and Jainism, also began to portray their central divinities and founding figures for the first time in this period. We may therefore assume that this was a religious development encompassing the whole of India.

Significantly, the region in which the first figural representations were produced was ruled by dynasties that did not originate from South Asia, and there was constant interaction with various ethnic groups of non-Indian origin who were assimilated to different degrees. The best-known of these dynasties were the originally nomadic Kuṣāṇas, who came from Central Asia and brought with them aspects of Iranian culture, but who also actively maintained trade and cultural contact with the entire ancient world. Scholars still disagree on where the first Buddha image was created. At about the same time, the first statues appeared in Mathura, in central northern India, and in Gandhara, in the extreme north-west of the Indian subcontinent. In antiquity, Gandhara was the name for the area around the city of Peshawar, in northern Pakistan. Nowadays, it is the name given to a very particular artistic style with visual elements which point not to India but rather to Rome and Greece. The geographical range of this striking artistic style extends, in the west, well beyond the Peshawar region and as far as the Bamiyan Valley in Afganistan.

Despite their geographical distance from one another, there are remarkable similarities between the earliest depictions of the Buddha from Mathura and Gandhara—but also interesting original differences, which can be understood as independent approaches to the search for a suitable form of representation. What characterizes the faces in both cases is the fact that they display no individual features at all. Instead, they depict an idealized type, a feature of all early religious art in India. What they also have in common is the posture, such as the ascetic, lotus-style sitting position, still characteristic today, with the soles of the feet pointing upwards: similar to, but not wholly identical with, sitting cross-legged. A further common feature is the clothing (a monk's triple robe), as are the pierced and lengthened earlobes, indicating that the Buddha was born a prince and grew up in a king's palace—in ancient India, men from the upper class wore large, heavy earrings. Both schools of art were already familiar with the type of representation in which the Buddha raises his right arm in front of his body, his palm turned upwards. This gesture, interpreted as "the granting of fearlessness", can also be found in depictions of the other religions. In principle, all later representations go back to the oldest visualizations from Mathura and Gandhara. In Mathura, there was a noticeably strong tendency to depict the Buddha as a ruler, but this was abandoned in favour of a more ascetic type, possibly because of the strong influence of the Gandhara school of art. Nonetheless, some elements of the iconography of the ruler, such as the lion throne, have remained, albeit much less conspicuously.

Another commonality worth noting is that the oldest figures, astonishingly enough, depict the Buddha's hair tied up in a topknot. Given that he cut his hair after leaving the palace, he should actually be portrayed with a shaven head. And yet the Buddha's hair also demonstrates one of the marked differences between the two artistic styles. Whereas in Mathura it was depicted as flat and waveless and distinguished primarily by its boundary, artists in Gandhara took their cue from their Greek and Roman models and depicted the hair initially as wavy and in separate strands. The topknot was, however, apparently regarded as inappropriate and very quickly transformed into the protuberance characteristic of the Buddha's head—the peculiar cranial bump—which itself is then shown as covered with hair.

As with the hair, the shape of the monk's robe exhibits characteristic differences. In the Buddha figures from Mathura, the robe is very close-fitting, like a damp cloth, and appears almost transparent; it leaves the right arm exposed and simply features a relatively schematic drape over the left upper arm (see p. 115 for a later example from the Gupta period, around the fifth or beginning of the sixth century). The Buddhas from Gandhara, on the other hand, are clad in a monk's robe that is clearly modelled on the Roman toga; the robe is characterized by an occasionally very elaborate arrangement of folds, and it covers the whole body (pp. 110, 117–119). Interestingly, both ways of representing the Buddha's clothing live on in Buddhist art today.

This cursory comparison alone makes very clear that although the Mathura and Gandhara modes of representation could not have developed entirely independently of one another, they did originally have their own approaches before a consistent type was established. Nonetheless, the oldest Buddha figures are easily recognizable, even if it is not possible to place them either in time or location.

The first representations depict a figure looking intently at the viewer with eyes wide open. The pivotal change in this regard occurred between the end of the Kuṣāṇa period and the beginning of the rule of the Indian Gupta dynasty. This is when the typical, idealized facial expression with lowered eyelids emerged, directing the Buddha's gaze downwards at a slant, his head slightly inclined. This attribute, which may have originated in Gandhara, gained acceptance in the ensuing period and remains a defining feature to this day. It gave rise to the characteristic meditative facial expression, radiating spiritual serenity and inner peace, which has been taken up so enthusiastically by the present-day wellness movement. It also accounts for the universality of the Buddha image across the whole of the Buddhist world.

At the same time as the lowered eyelids appeared in portrayals of the Buddha, the straight hair from Mathura and the curly hair from Gandhara converged into the characteristic short, tight curls spiralling to the right and covering the head. The ringlet of hair on the forehead, which can be seen in both Mathura and Gandhara depictions, remained, whereas the small moustache found on early Gandhara Buddhas disappeared completely.

Another factor contributing to the Buddha's high degree of recognizability is the set number of postures, which are very limited. It is in no way left to the artist to determine how the figure is presented. The Buddha is shown either sitting with his legs crossed in a meditating posture—by far the most common form—or standing upright. If he is sitting in a Western posture with legs hanging down, then it is usually not a portrayal of the historical Buddha Śākyamuni but of the future Buddha Maitreya. Reclining Buddhas are even rarer, but where they do exist, they are always lying on their right side, the head propped up by the right hand. This physical position is reserved exclusively to depict the process of dying and therefore for the entry into nirvana, one of the four main events in the life of the Buddha. The hand gestures (Sanskrit: mudrā) are more variable, but even these are reduced to a specific repertoire and cannot simply be varied as the artist sees fit. For example: the raised right hand with the fingers pointing upwards promises protection and assurance (pp. 18, 22–23, 29, etc.), whereas a hand with the tips of the fingers pointing down to the earth and the back of the hand facing the viewer suggests the awakening (pp. 9, 49, 52, 62–63, etc.). One hand placed on top of the other in the lap of the Buddha signifies meditation (pp. 26, 66, 77, 83, etc.), and one (p. 125) or two hands in an argumentative gesture represents the teaching Buddha (pp. 55, 69). The Buddha Vairocana has its own quite particular characteristic (p. 39). Theoretically, there are countless Buddhas over innumerable aeons. Some of these, however, have acquired a specific meaning and are also recognizable by their hand gestures, such as the aforementioned Vairocana or the Buddha Amitābha, who is inherently identifiable by his meditation gesture (pp. 26). A further attribute could be a begging bowl in the left hand (pp. 127, 137), and the monk's robe may cover both shoulders or leave the right shoulder exposed. Since ancient times, the depiction of the Buddha has been limited to this small number of possible variations, allowing the artist only very limited scope for creative input. Individualism has never been an aim or even a requirement, except when the decorative elements are involved.

In addition to Buddhas, we also find depictions of bodhisattvas: individuals who have advanced vary far along the path to enlightenment but have not quite reached the level of a Buddha. Some of them have attained a high degree of importance, such as Kṣitigarbha, who is depicted as a monk and therefore resembles the Buddha, yet does not possess the cranial protuberance so typical of the Buddha (pp. 14, 24, 27, 41). He is well known for having descended into the realms of hell in order to rescue the unhappy creatures reborn there. The most famous bodhisattva is Avalokiteśvara, who is believed to be the embodiment of compassion and may be appealed to for protection against any kind of worldly adversity. He is easily identifiable by the lotus flower in his hand (p. 65), whereas Vajrapāṇi, another bodhisattva, is identifiable by the vajra, a special ritual object, in his right hand (p. 123). Depictions of warlike or frightening figures are found in the entrance areas to Buddhist temples in particular, where they serve either as gatekeepers or as protectors of the Buddhist teachings (frontispiece).

The formal canon was therefore essentially already established when Buddhism began to spread beyond India and into the greater part of Asia. The standard formula for depictions of the Buddha reached both Java and Japan. It was exported to East Asia, and extended likewise into Sri Lanka, Tibet and Mongolia. This is why statues of the Buddha are relatively easy to recognize when they are found at the Borobudur, in Kamakura, Angkor Wat, Kandy or Lhasa, even though they are separated by great swathes of time and enormous distances. This does not, of course, mean that one could mistake a fifth-century Chinese Buddha for a Thai Buddha from the eighteenth century. As this volume impressively demonstrates, regional differences certainly do exist. Such differentiation, however, is always based on secondary features, such as the proportions or shape of the eyes, lips or hair. We must often also consider details that do not pertain to the Buddha figure itself, such as the shape of the throne, the halo, the accompanying figures, and the like. These factors certainly enable us to distinguish different styles depending on time and place. It is generally the case that the Buddha's facial expression was modified very early on in China: the face took on more obviously East Asian features, the eyes were represented as more closed, the lips more distinctive, and the hair more coiled. Changes such as these migrated with Chinese Buddhism to Japan and Korea and left their mark on modes of representation there, too.

To illustrate this with a further example: in South Asia as well, a detail such as the shape of the lips can help to make at least a rough distinction. Whereas Buddha statues in the Khmer art of Cambodia, for instance, are often characterized by a broad, almost sensual mouth, figures in the Sukhothai style in Thailand feature a delicately curved lip line. Again and again, we find reciprocities between different styles of art, which usually point to close political relations or economic ties between the respective regions. A good example of this is the Tibetan cultural area. Tibet came under the influence of Buddhism relatively late, that is to say, from the eighth century on. At this particular time, artists copied modes of representation from both the Pāla art of north-east India and the art of Kashmir in the north-west. From the twelfth or thirteenth century onwards, when Buddhism was gradually declining in northern India, we see the increasing influence of Chinese art. This ultimately resulted in the characteristic Tibetan mode of representation, which even today blends Indian models and Chinese influences in a unique way.

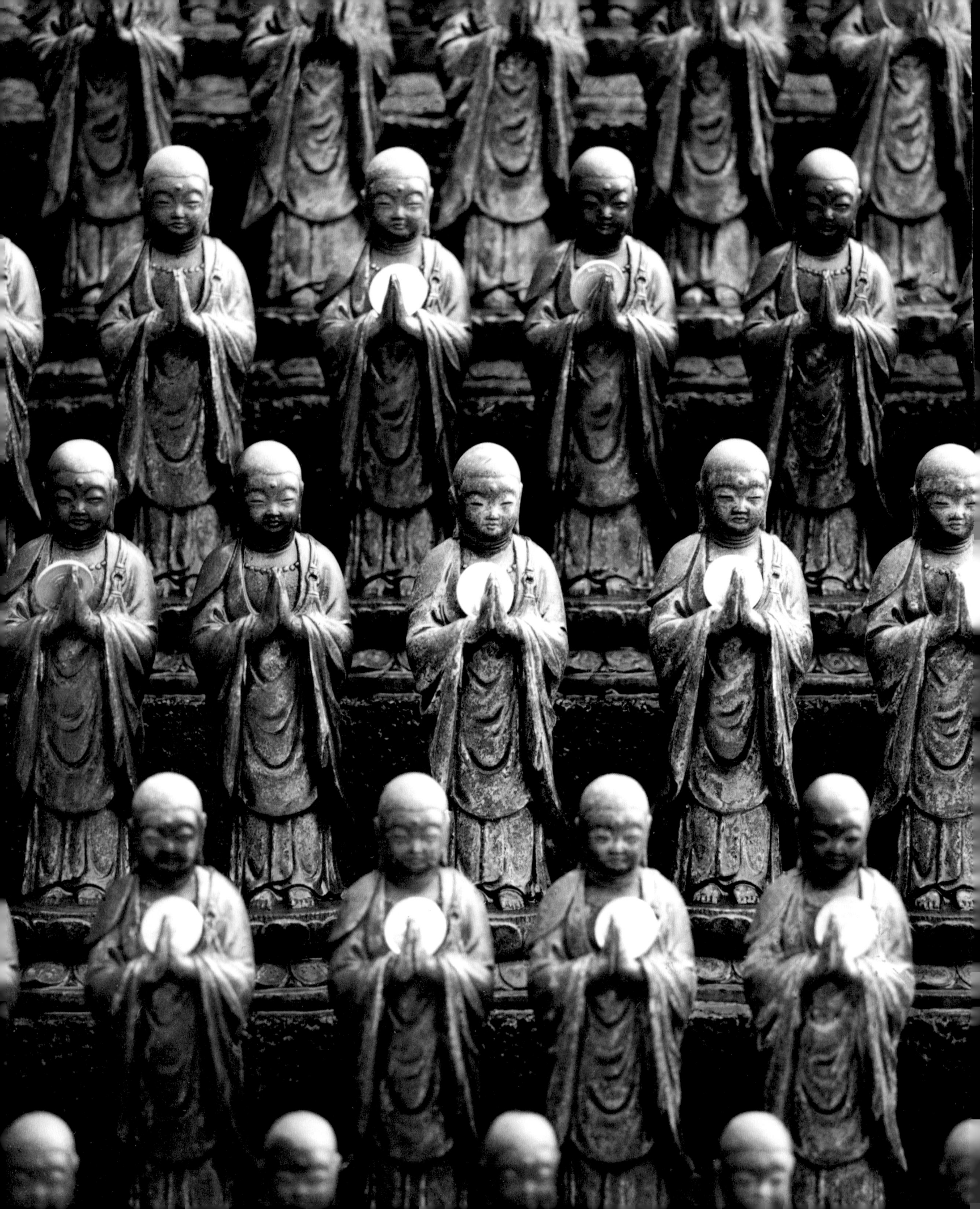

Japan

Jizo Protectors, Onzanji,
Tokushima, Shikoku, 2003

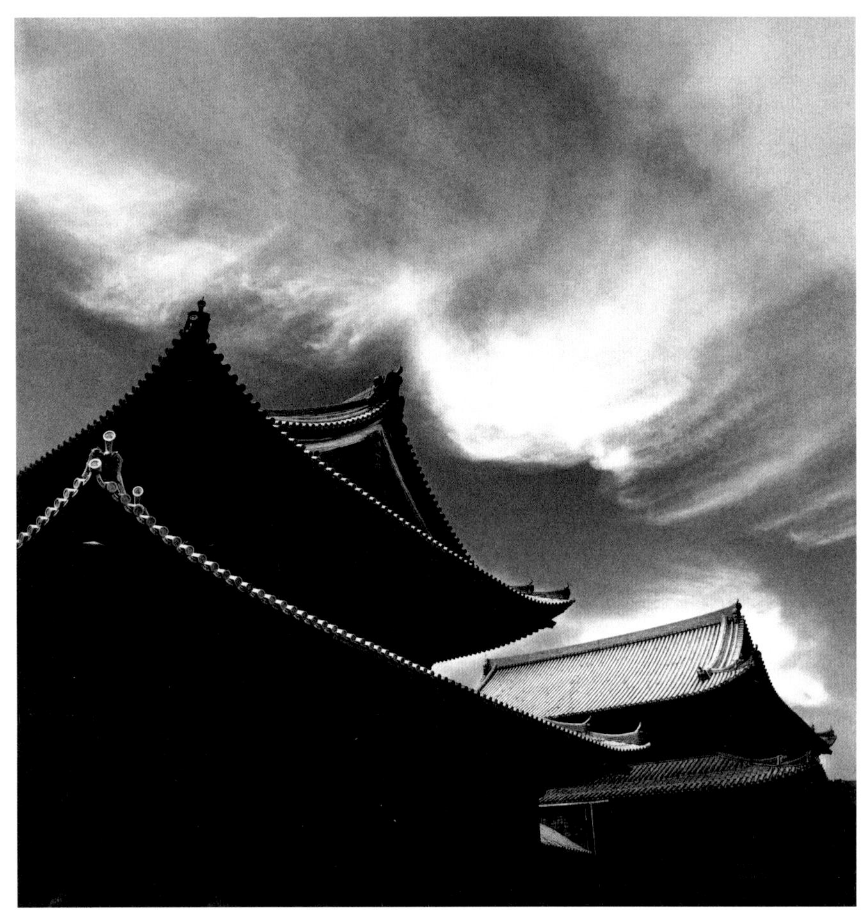

Afternoon Clouds,
Myoshi Temple, Kyoto, Honshu, 2001

Buddha Statues, Kyoto,
Honshu, 1987

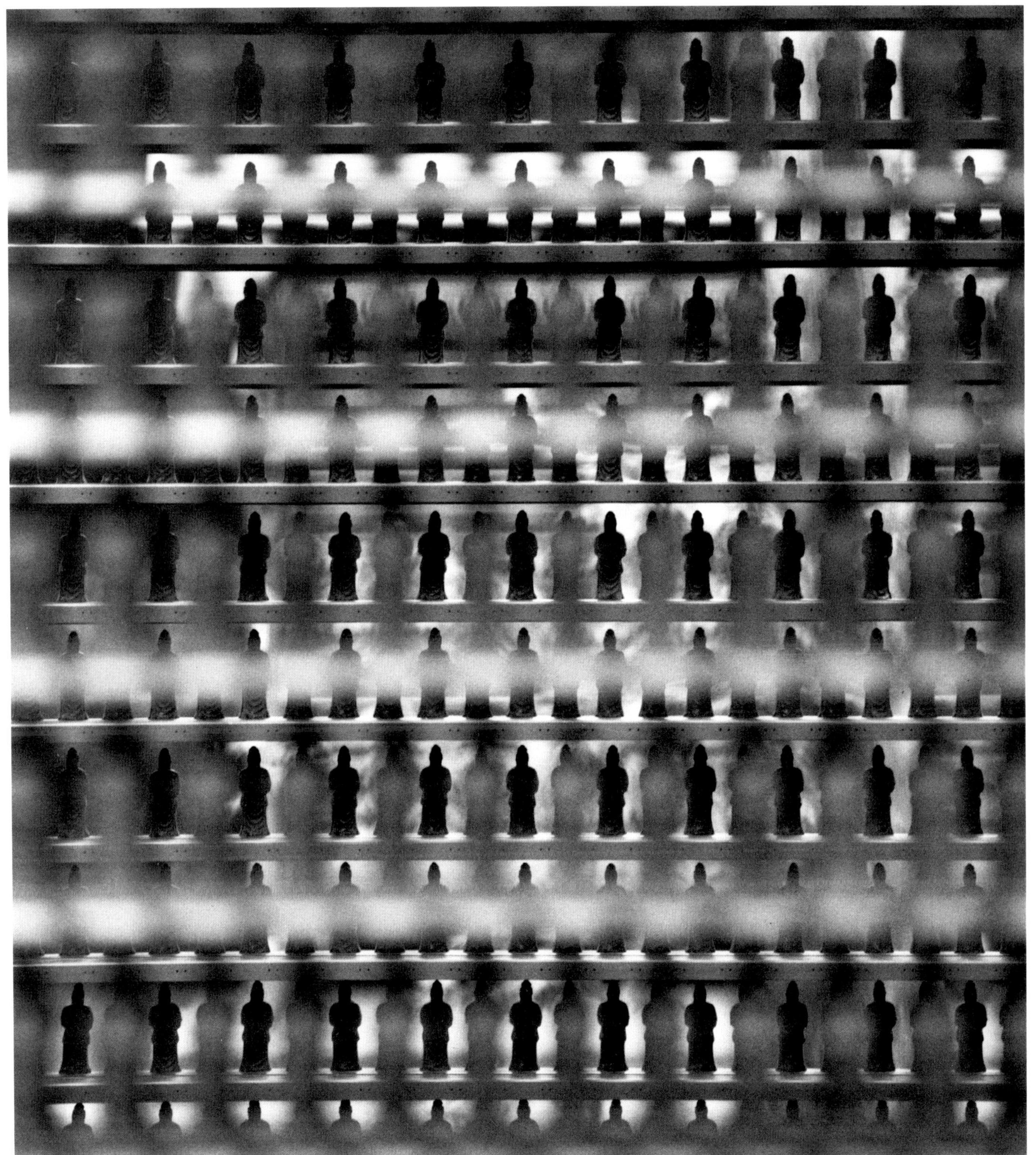

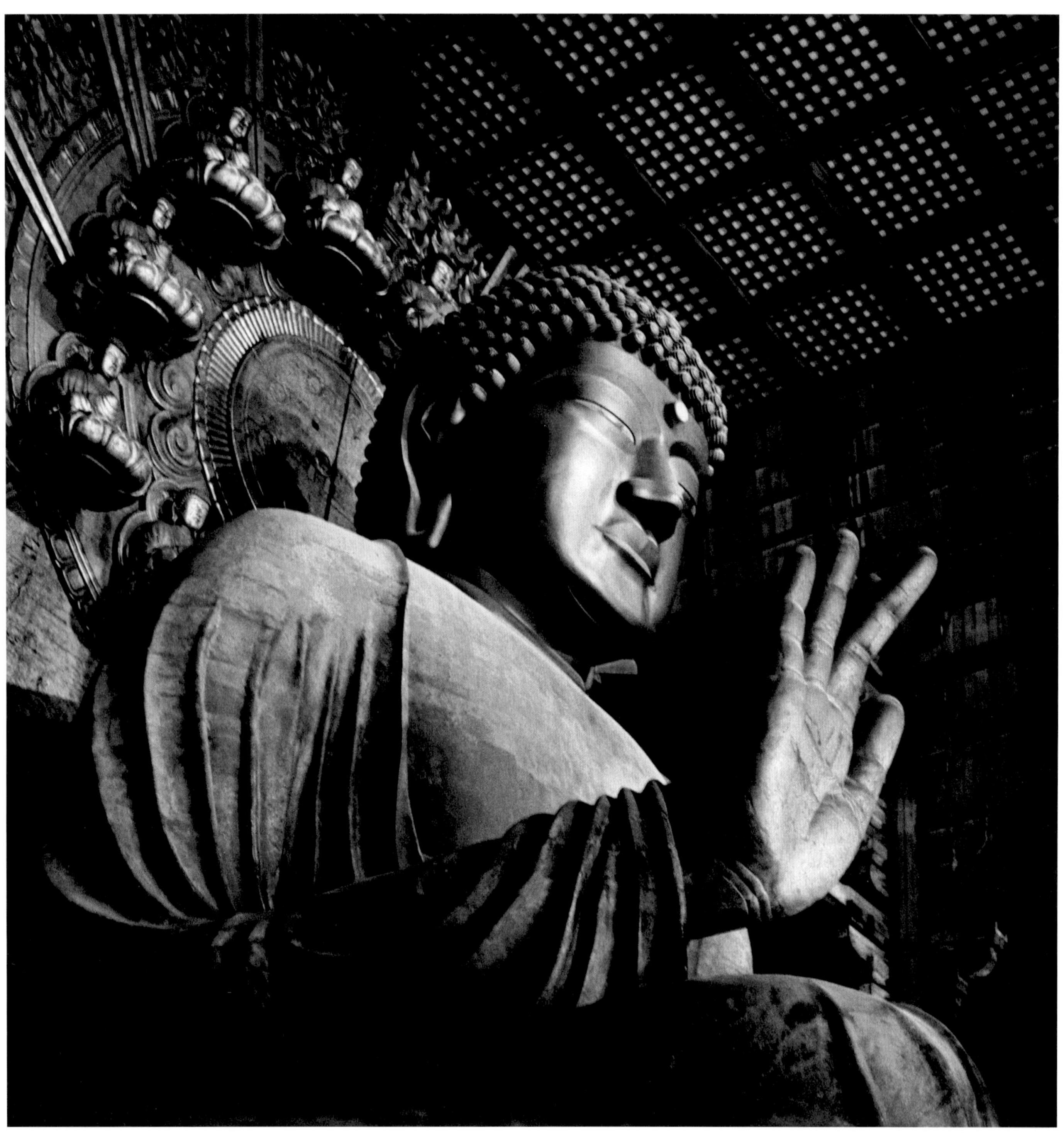

JAPAN

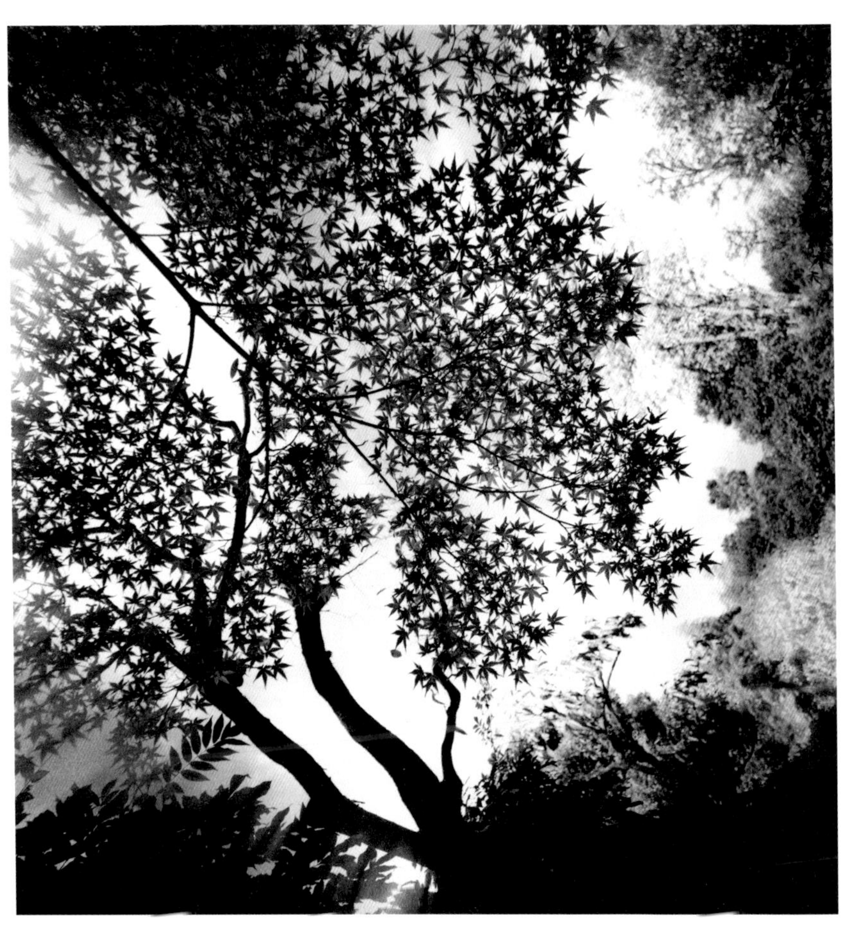

Todai-ji Daibutsu, Nara,
Honshu, 2003

Maple Leaves, Eikando Zenrinji,
Kyoto, Honshu, 2001

JAPAN

Dainichi Nyorai, Daito Pagoda,
Koyasan, Honshu, 2006

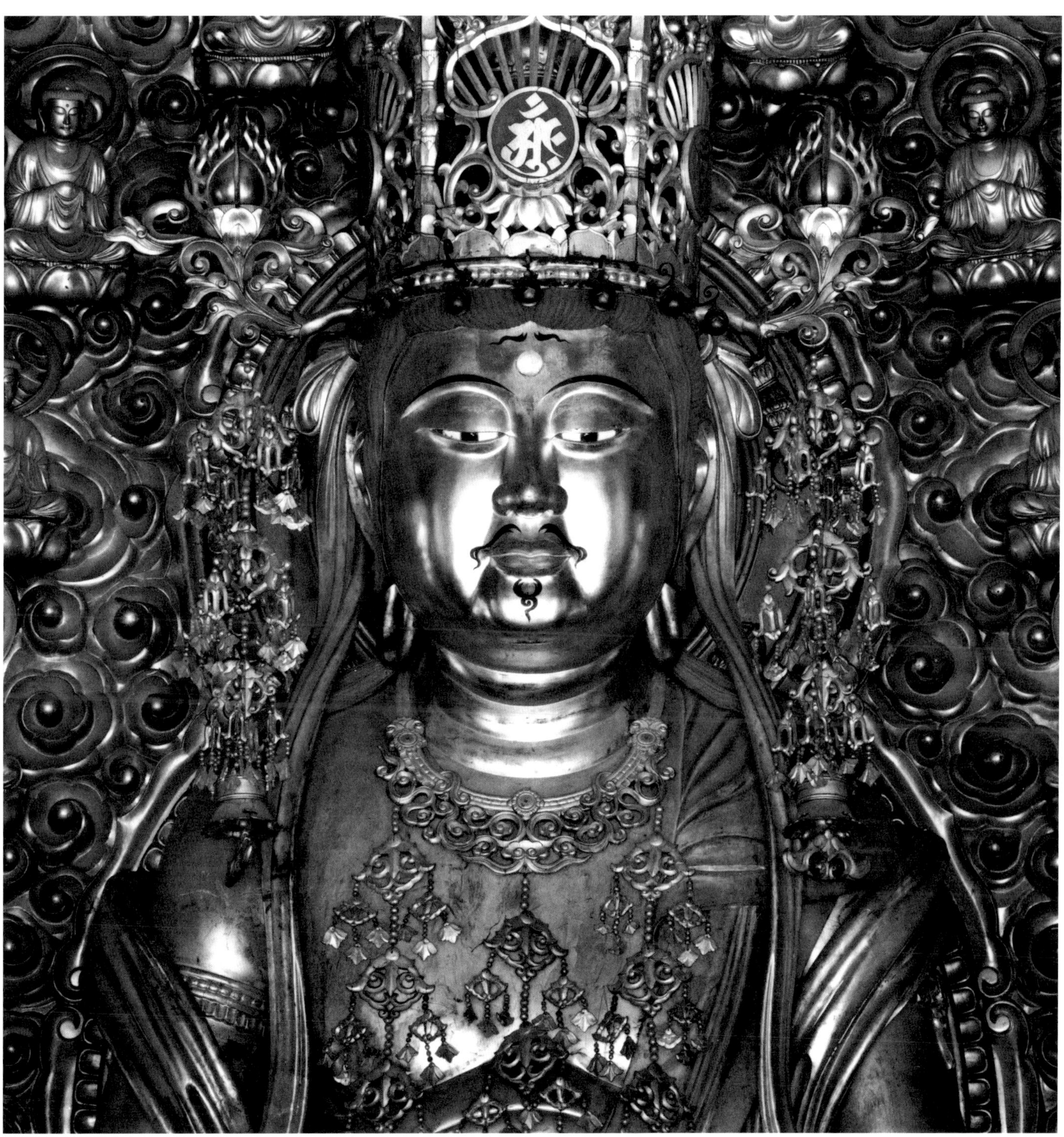

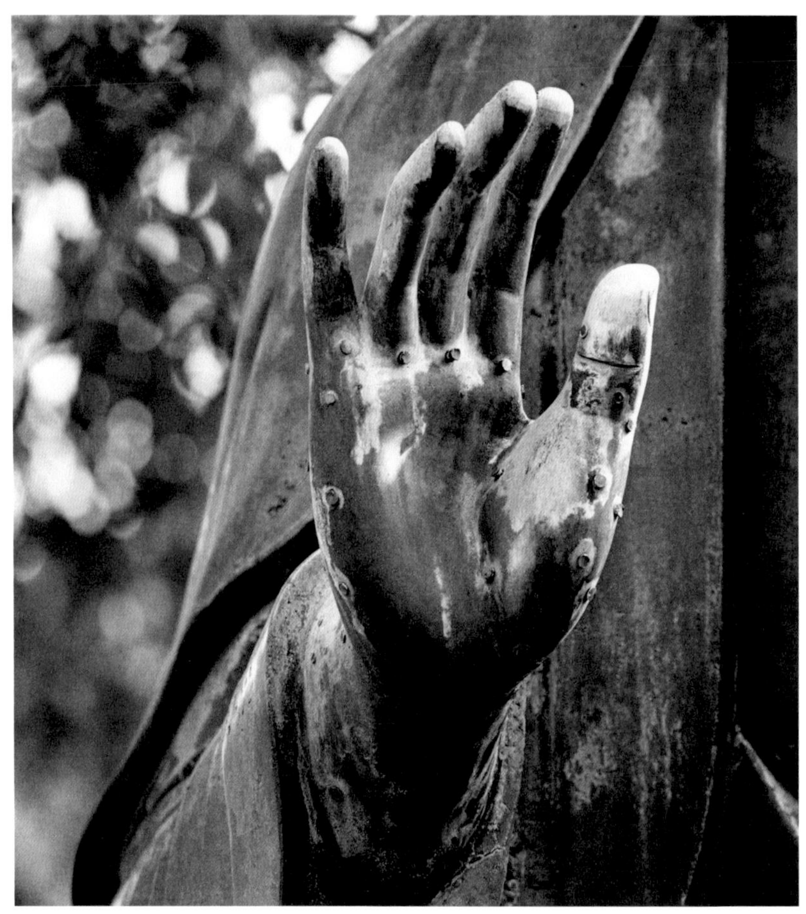

Blessing Mudrā, Shidoji,
Kagawa, Shikoku, 2002

JAPAN

Ushiku Daibutsu, Honshu, 2018

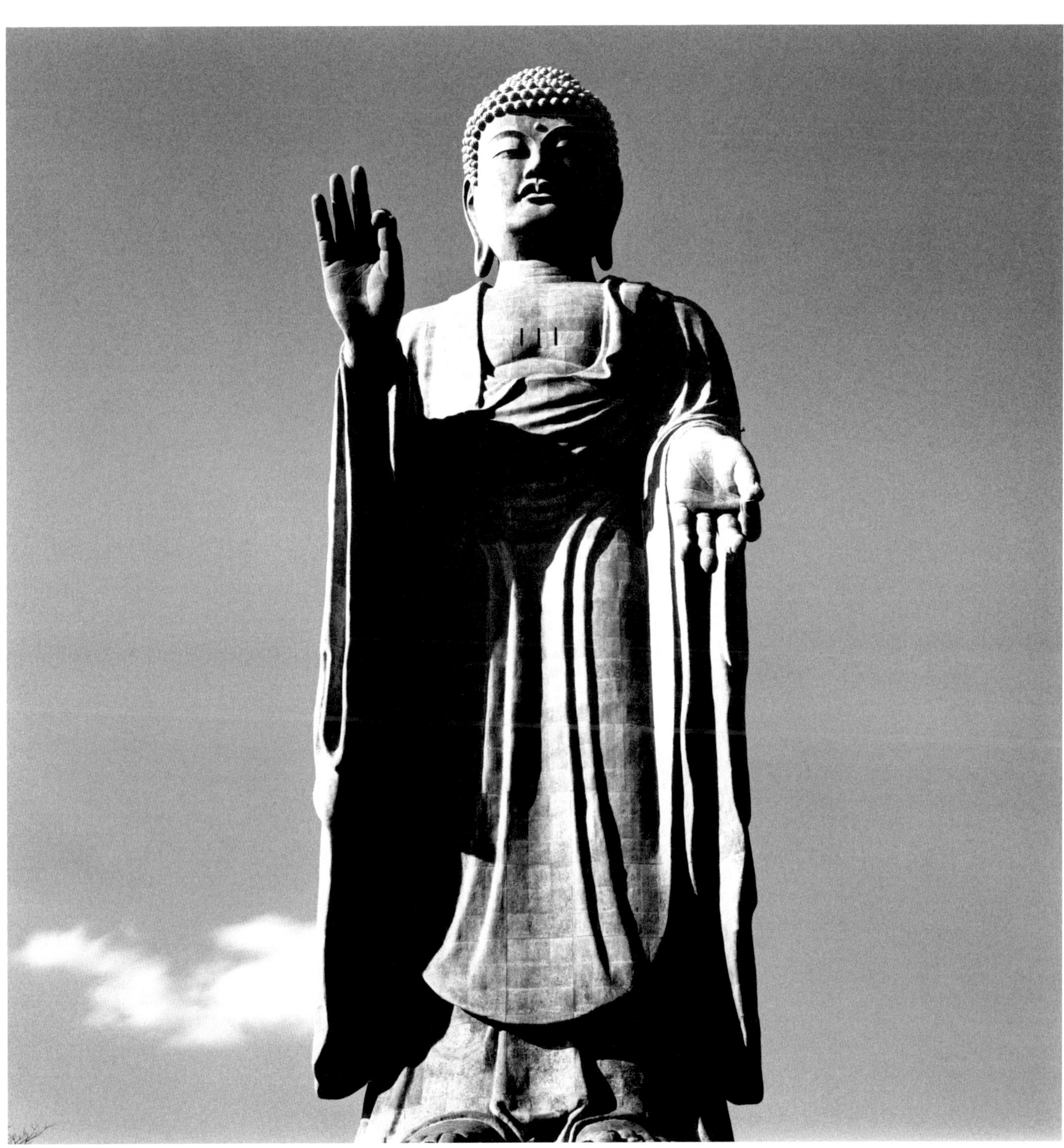

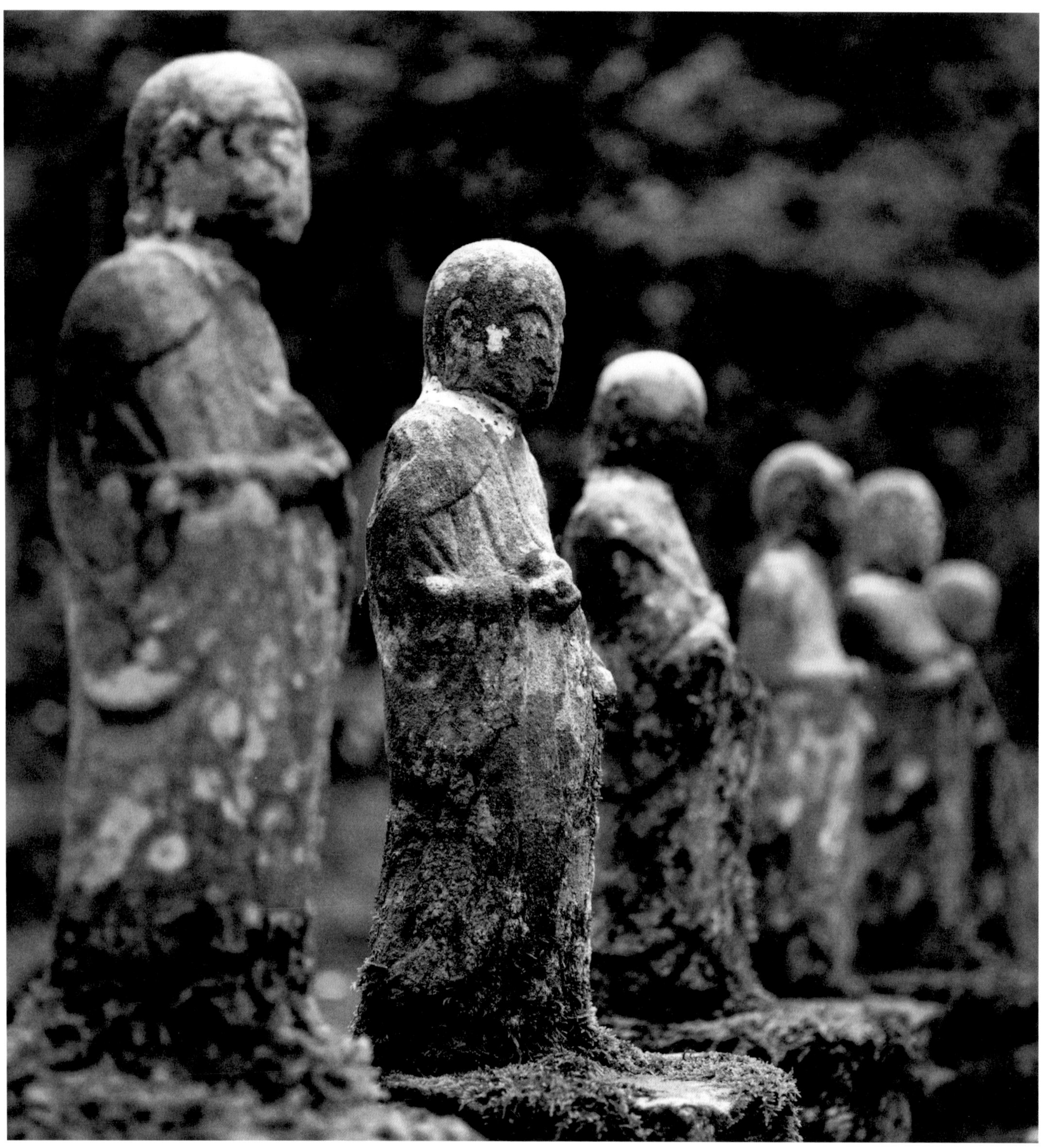

JAPAN

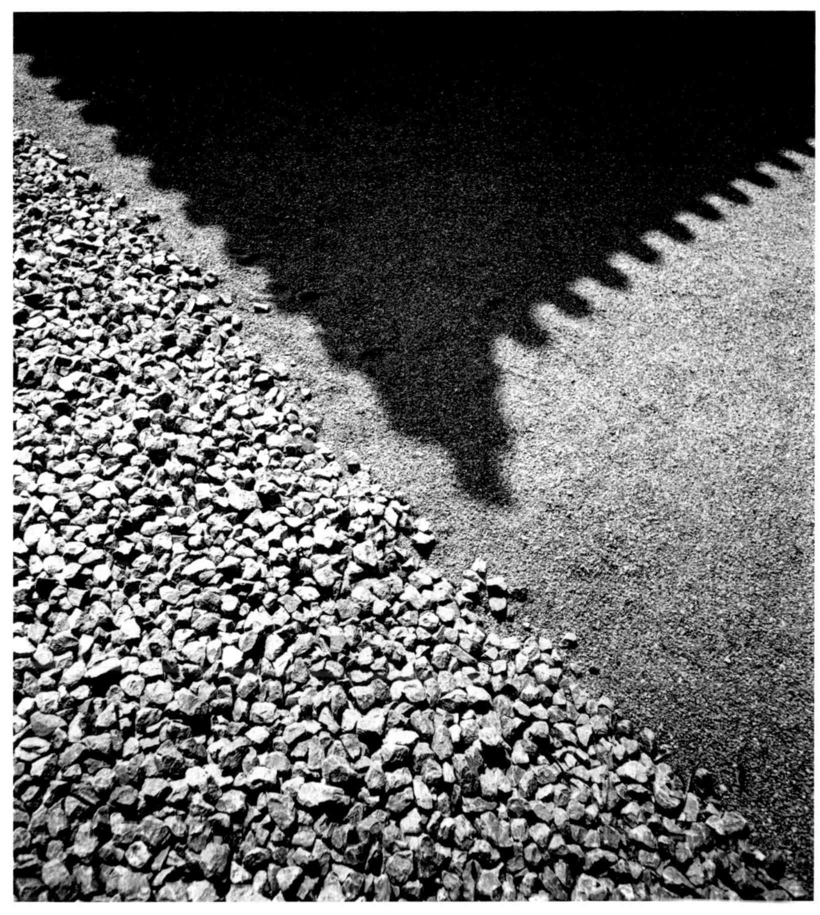

Six Protectors, Yakuki, Shikoku, 2001

Rock Garden and Roof Shadow,
Tosa Kokubunji, Kochi, Shikoku, 2012

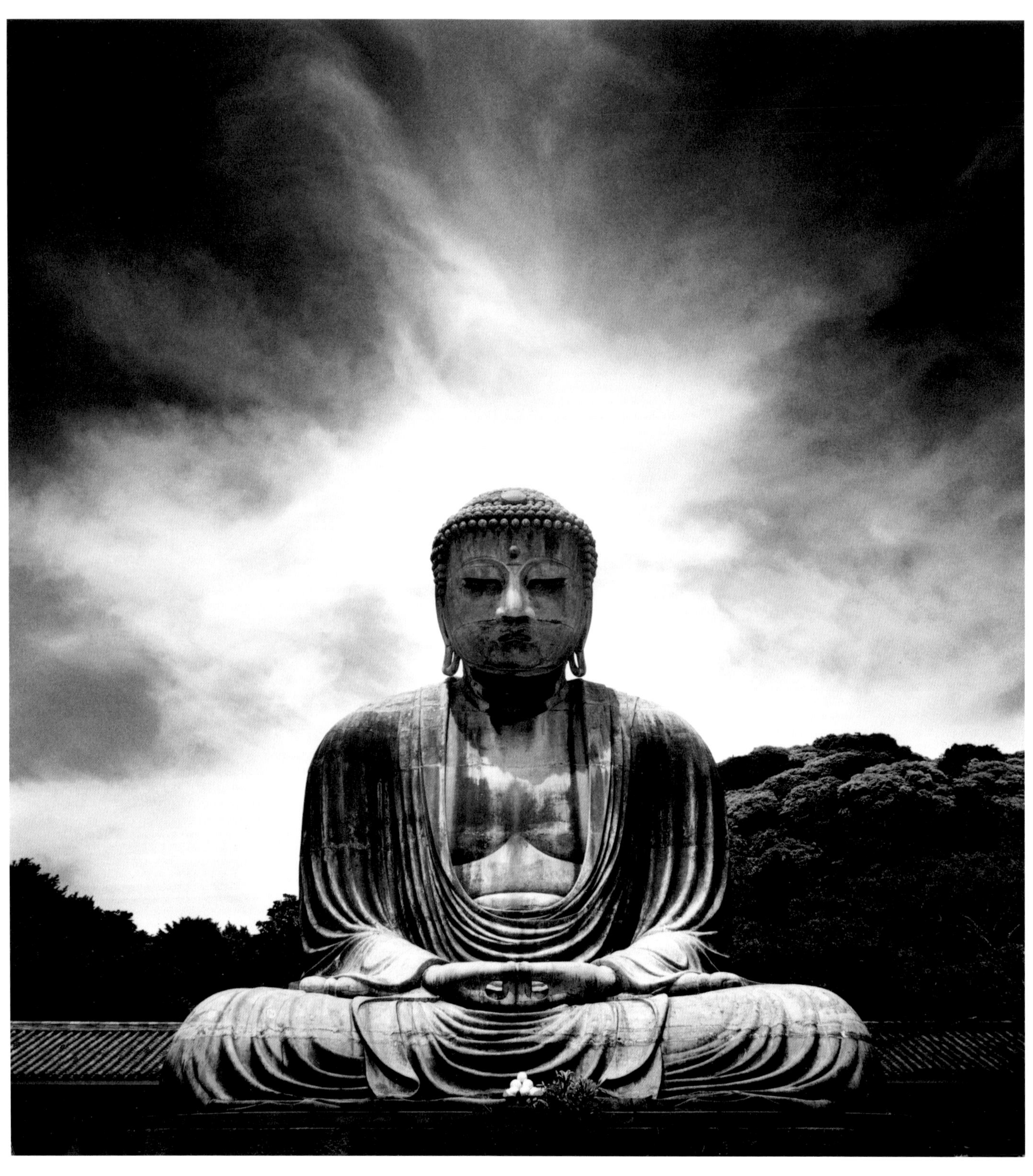

Amida Buddha, Kotoku-in,
Kamakura, Honshu, 2007

JAPAN

Jizo, Osorezan, Honshu, 2002

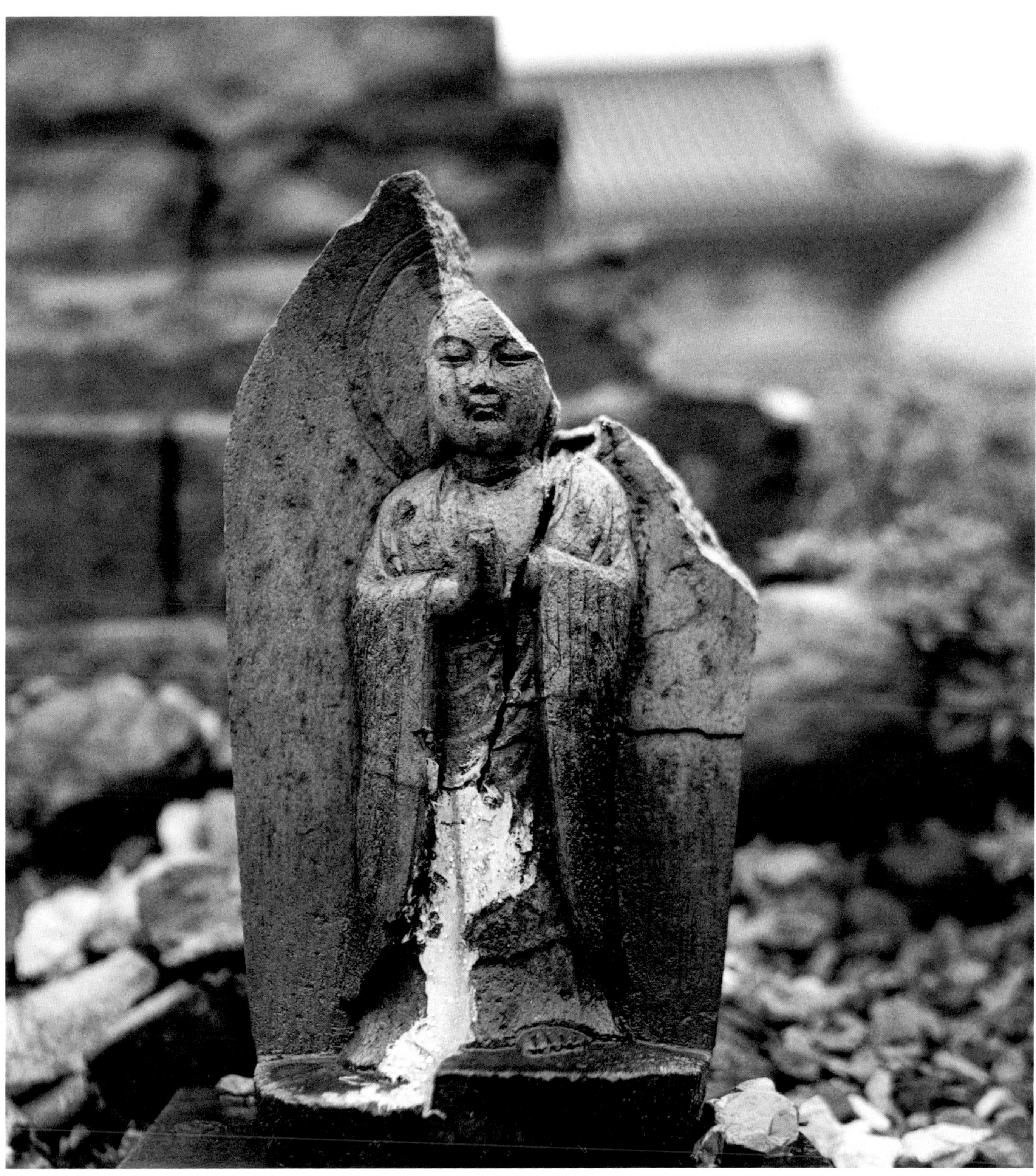

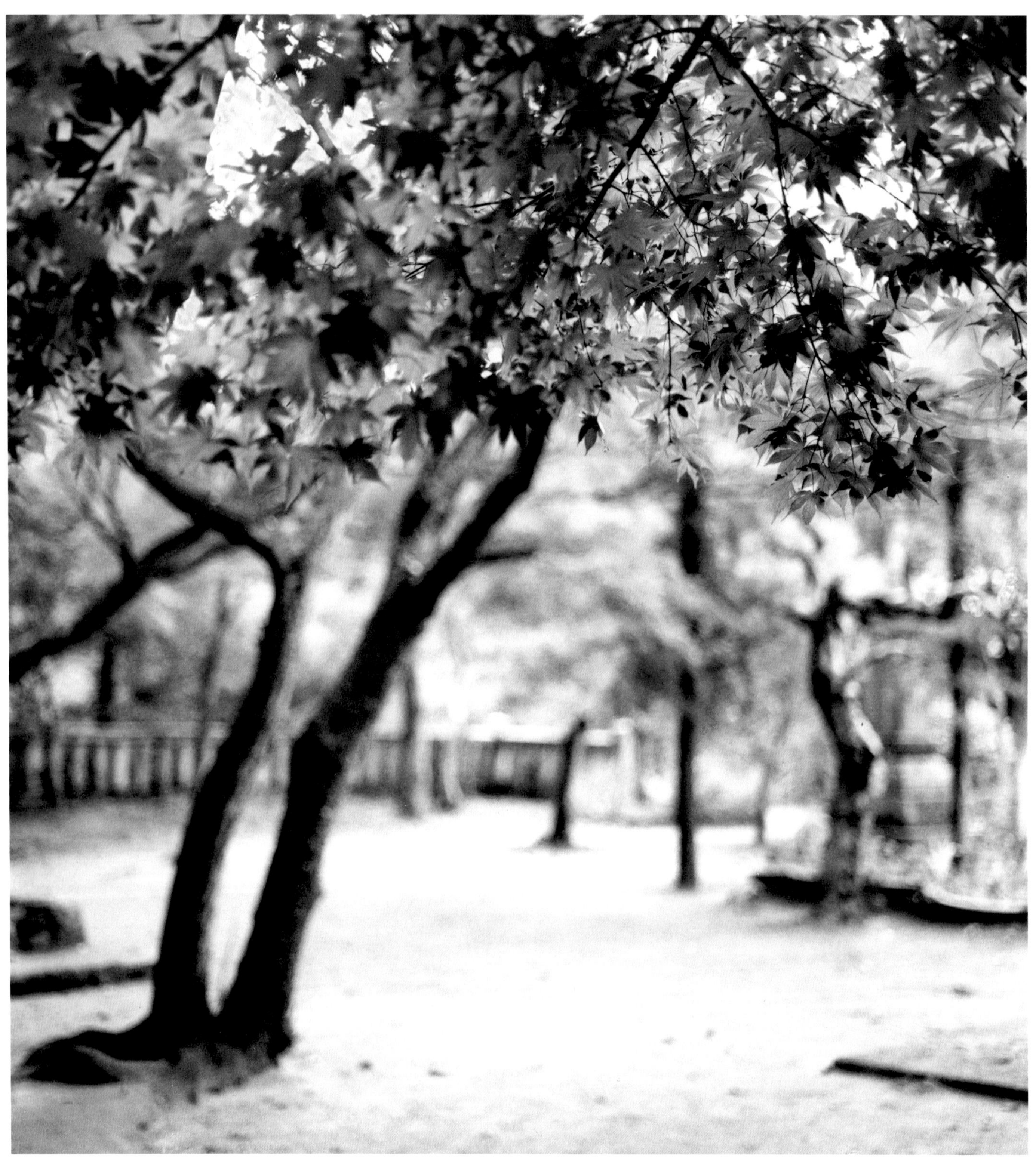

Temple Garden, Negoroji,
Kagawa, Shikoku, 2003

Seated Buddha
at the Musée Guimet,
Paris, 2018

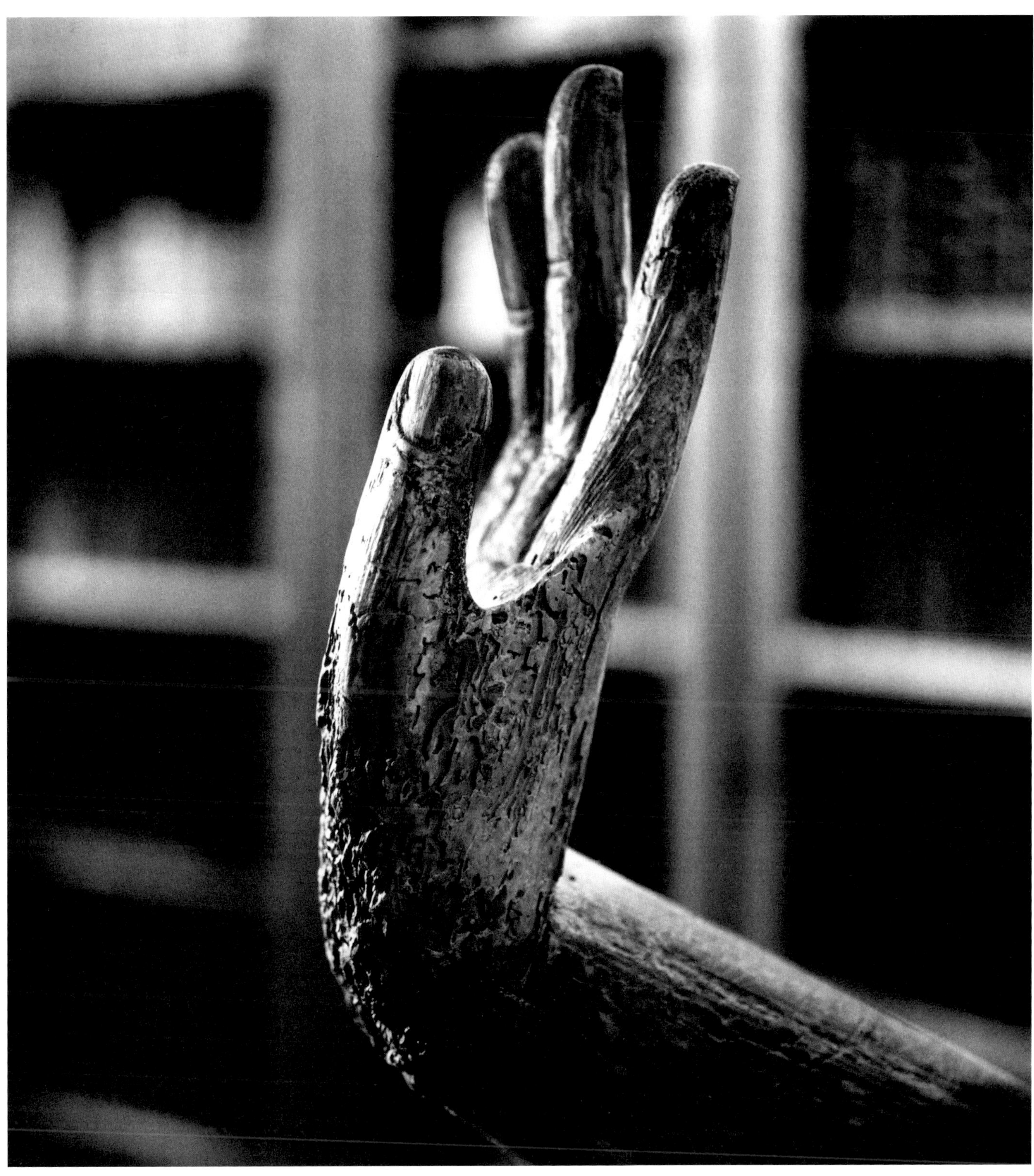

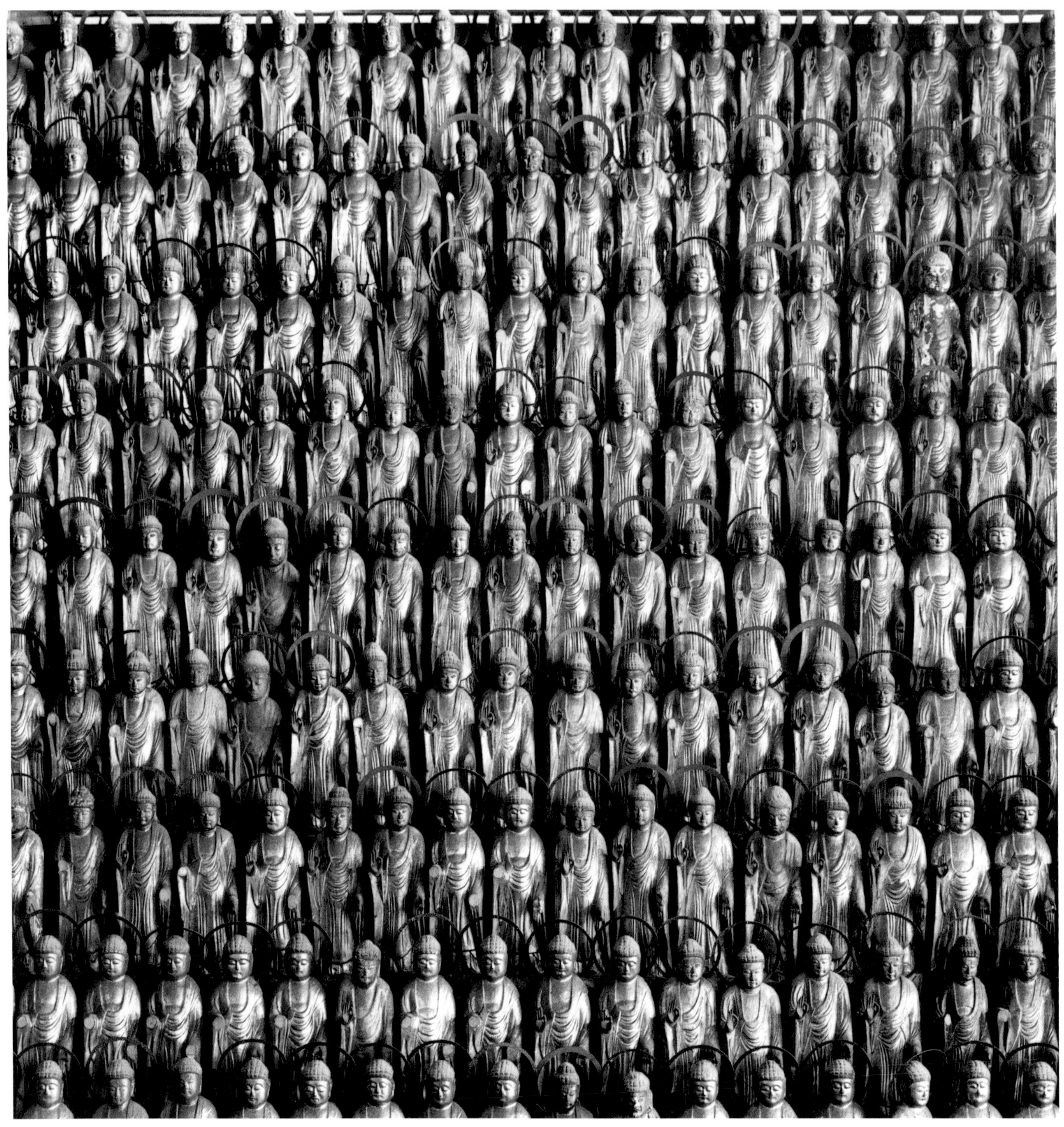

JAPAN

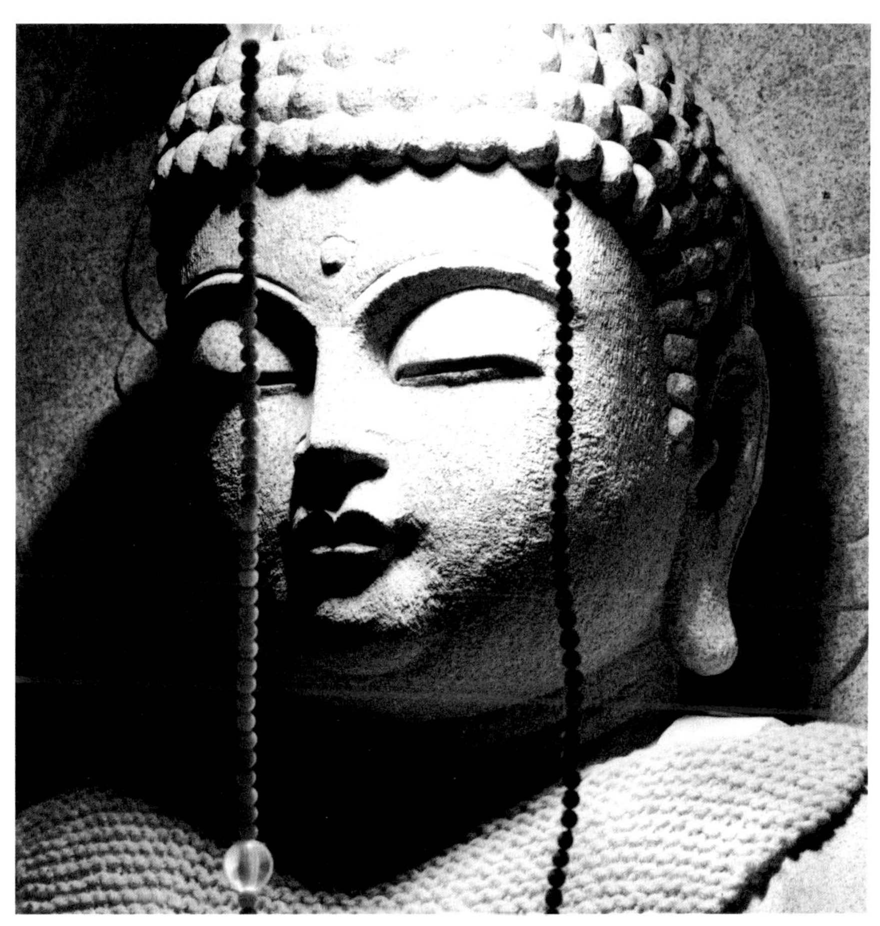

Buddha Statues, Prayer Hall,
Koyasan, Honshu, 2006

Jizo Bosatsu, Ishitej, Ehime,
Shikoku, 2003

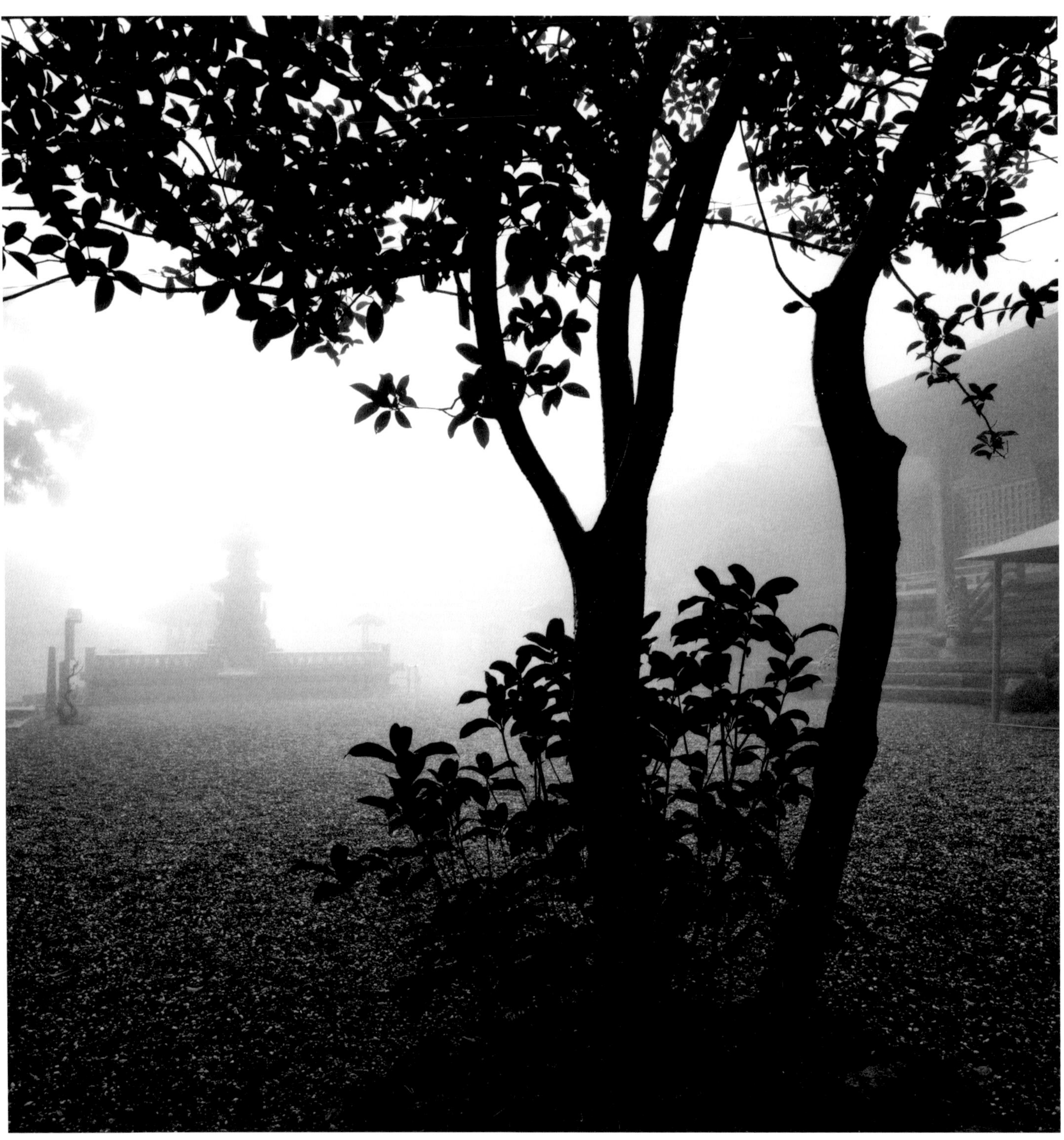

JAPAN

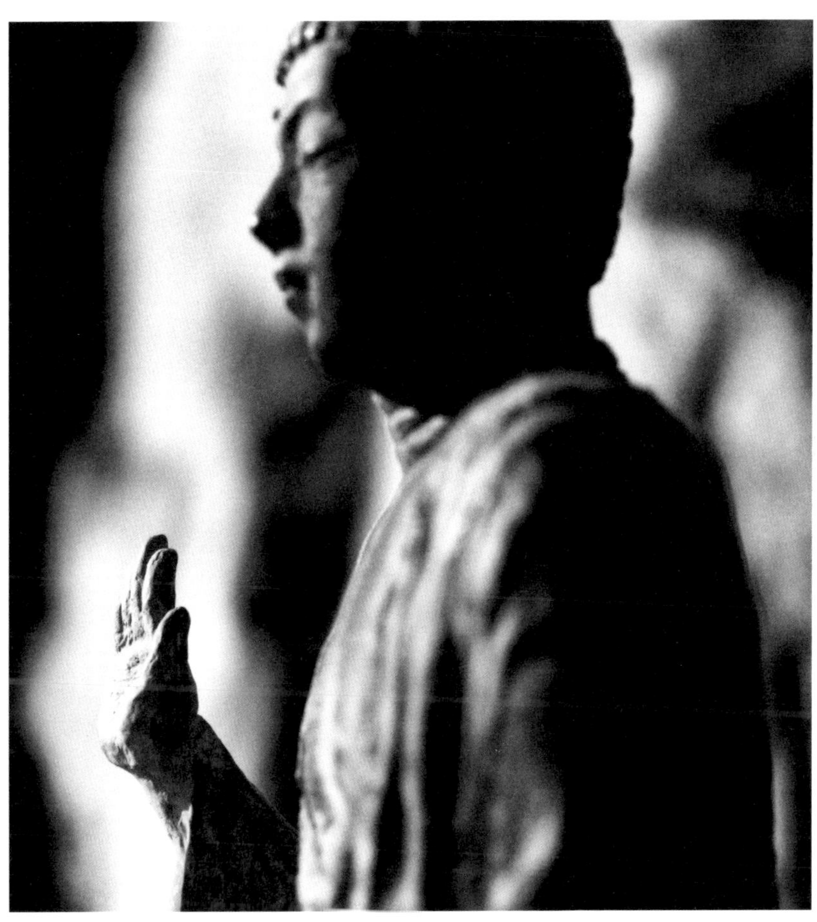

Fog-Shrouded Temple, Shosanji,
Tokushima, Shikoku, 2010

Hand of Buddha, Yakuri Temple,
Shikoku, 2002

JAPAN

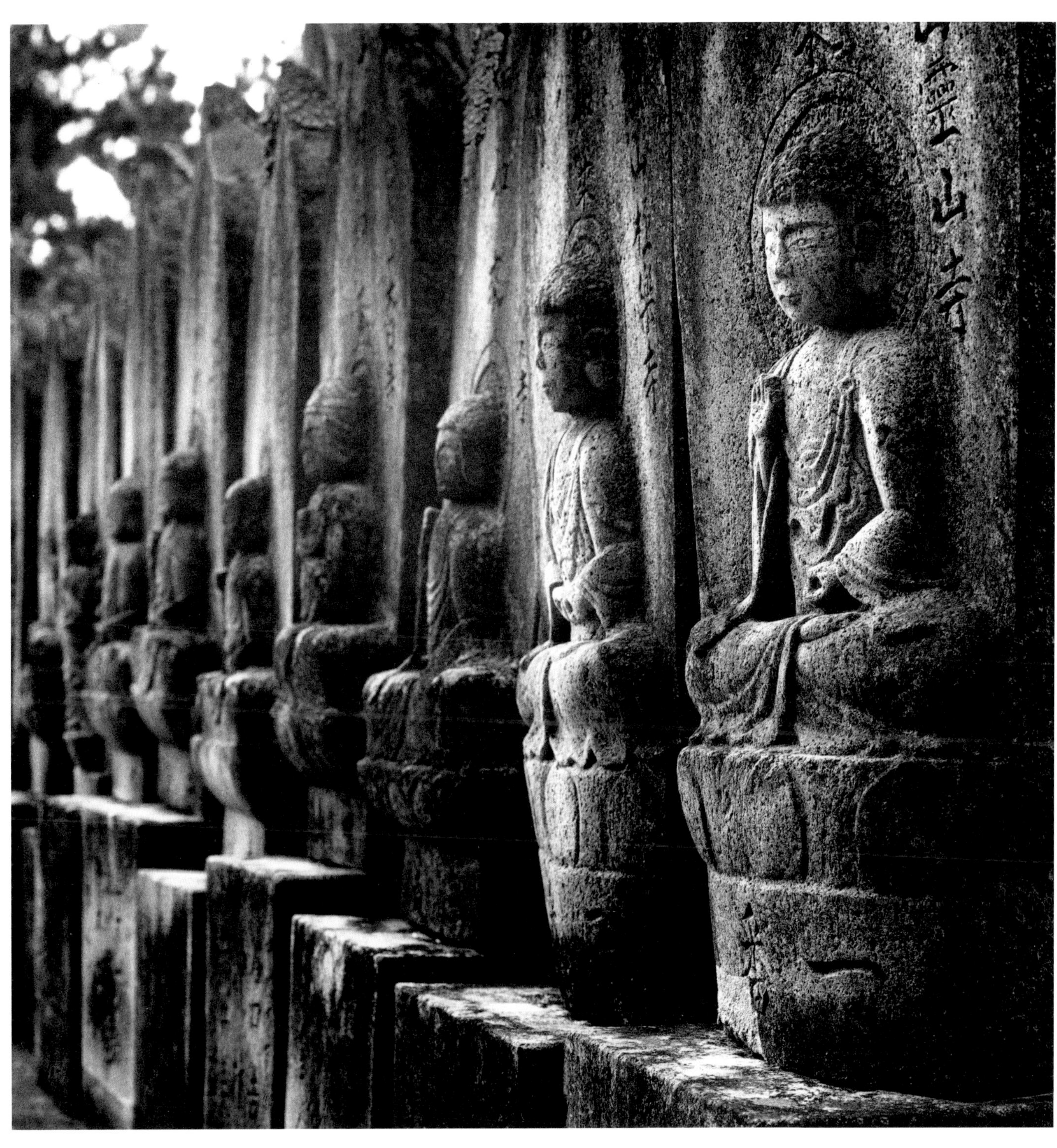

Manju Island, Toya Lake,
Hokkaido, 2002

Line of Buddhas, Kongofukuji,
Shikoku, 2003

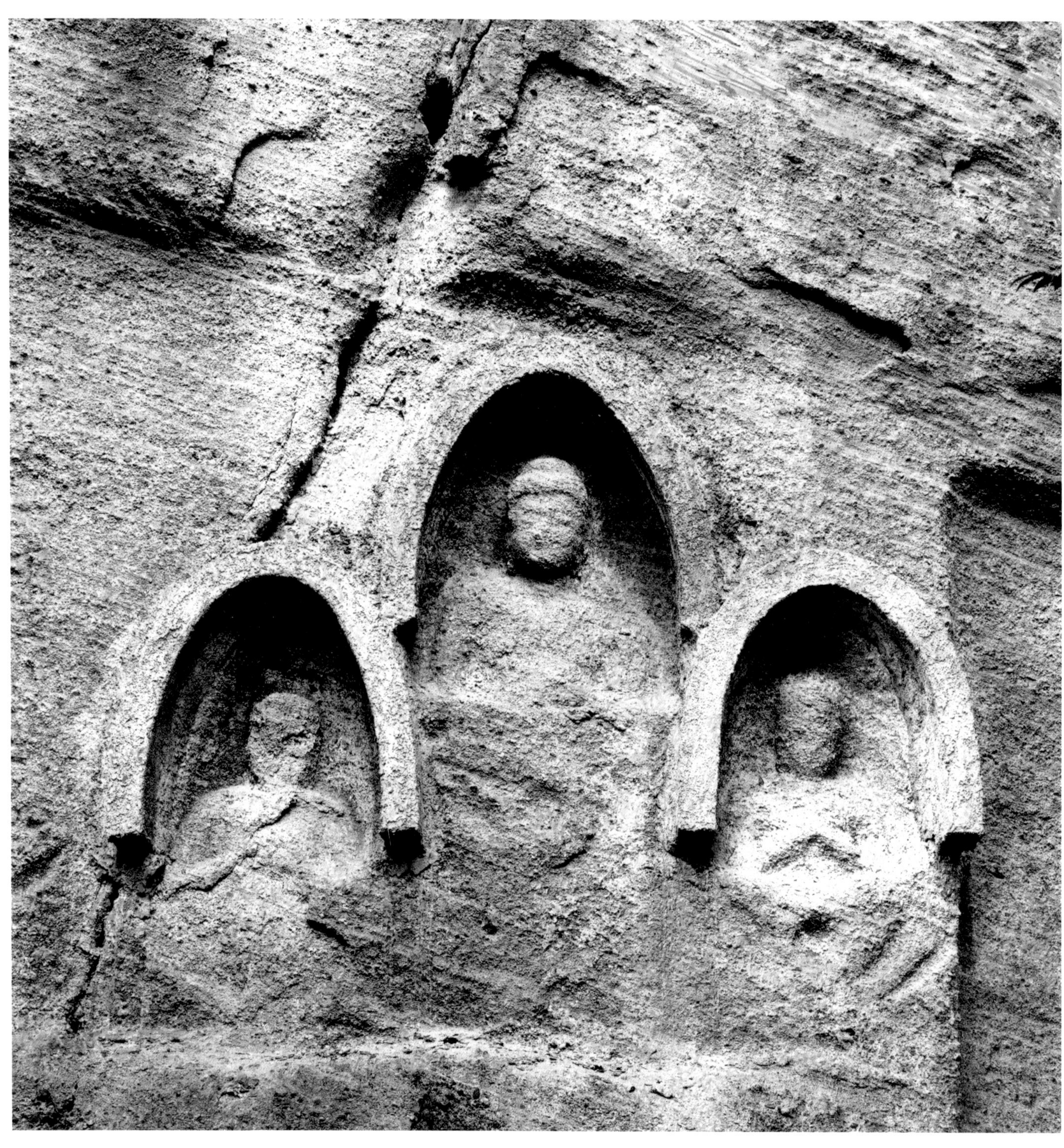

Buddha Wall Carvings,
Iyadaniji, Shikoku, 2003

Dusk View, Bentendake,
Koyasan, Honshu, 2007

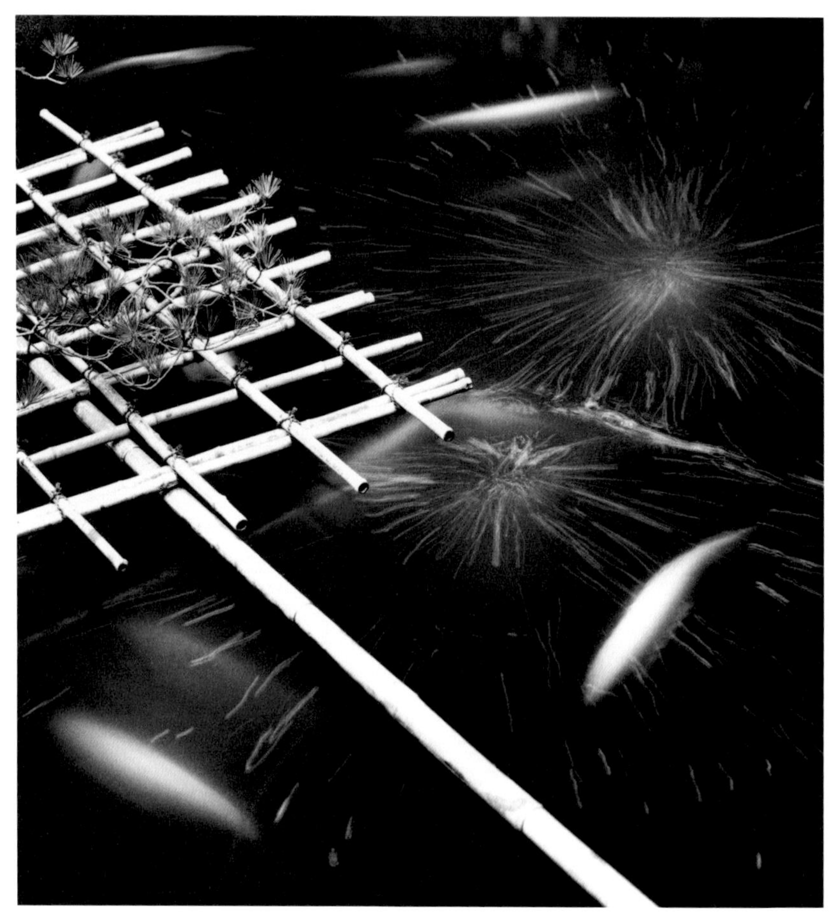

JAPAN

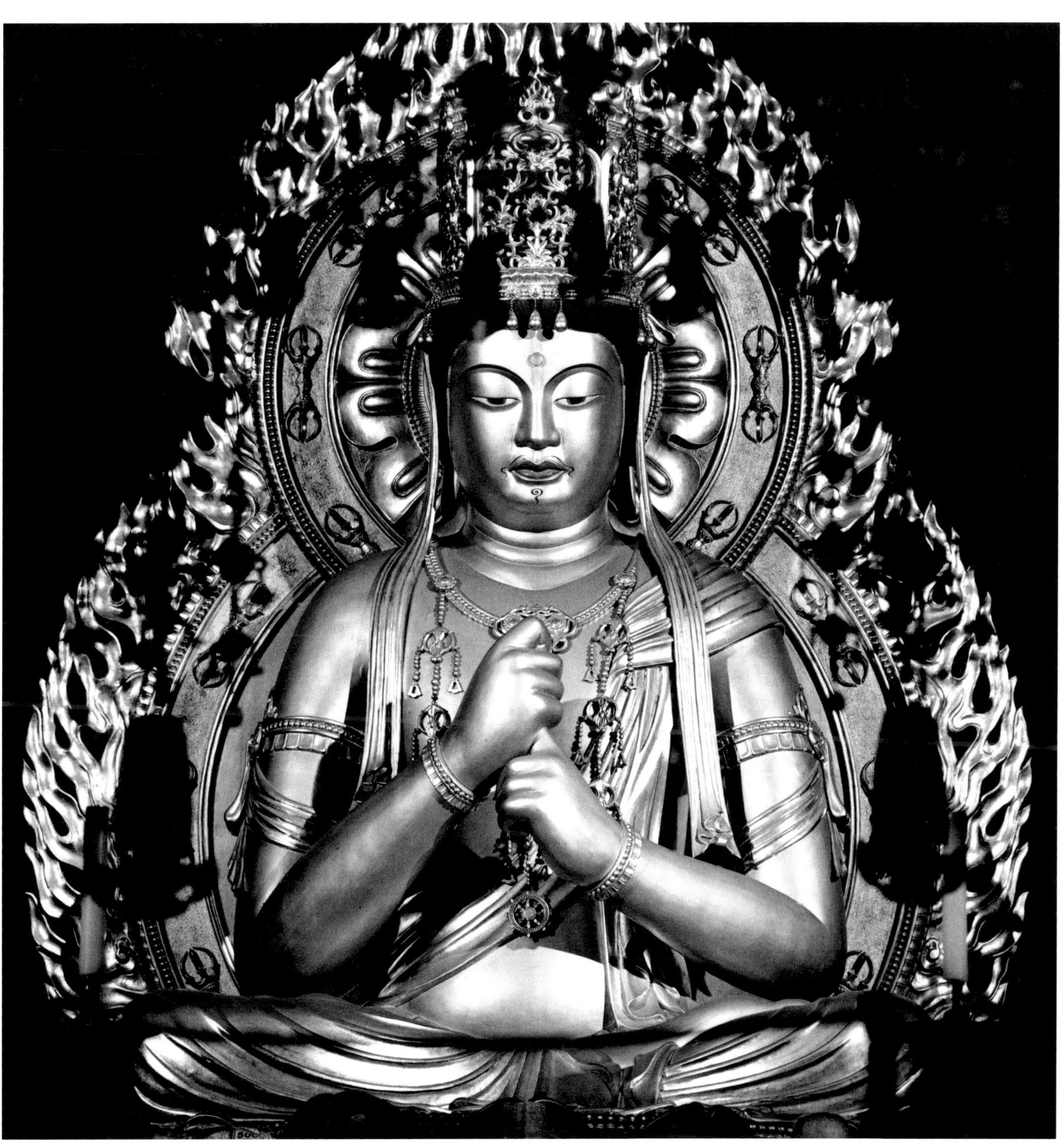

Temple Pond, Sanboh-in,
Koyasan, Honshu, 2006

Dainichi Nyorai, Koonji,
Shikoku, 2003

Stone Jizos, Okunoin,
Koyasan, Honshu, 2006

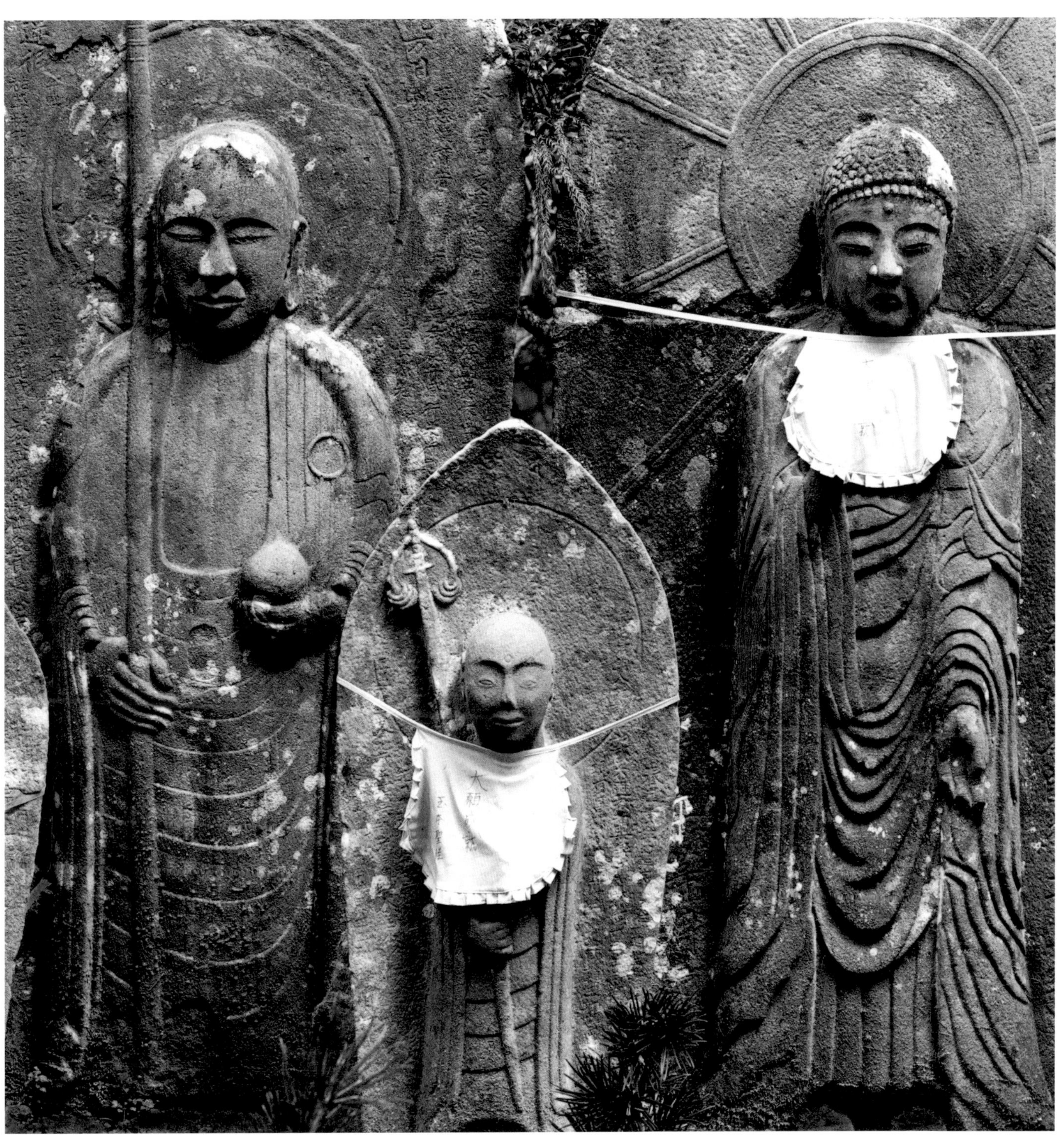

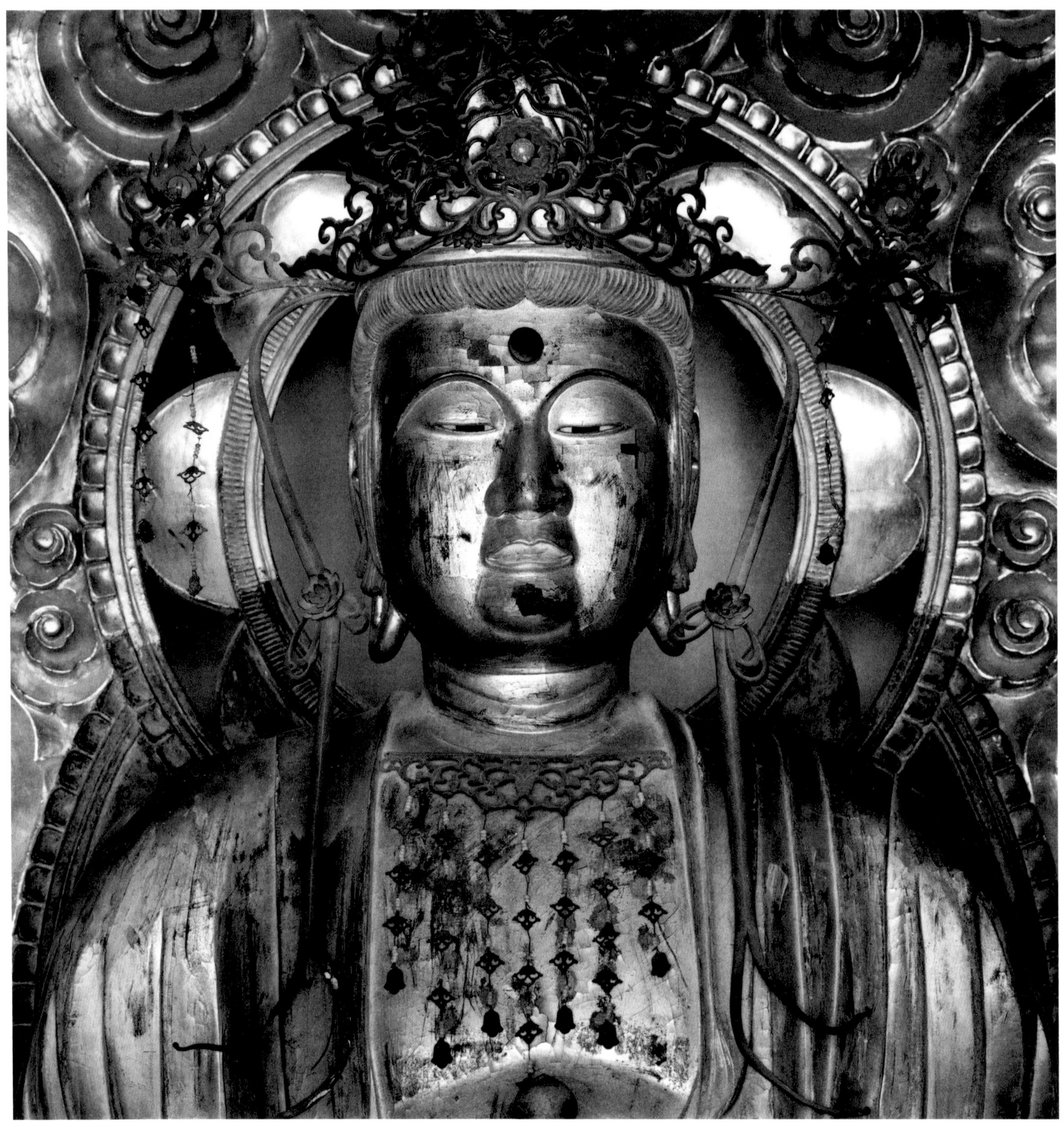

JAPAN

Head of Buddha, Jizo Temple,
Shikoku, 2002

Spider and Sacred Text, Study 2,
Gokurakuji, Shikoku, 2001

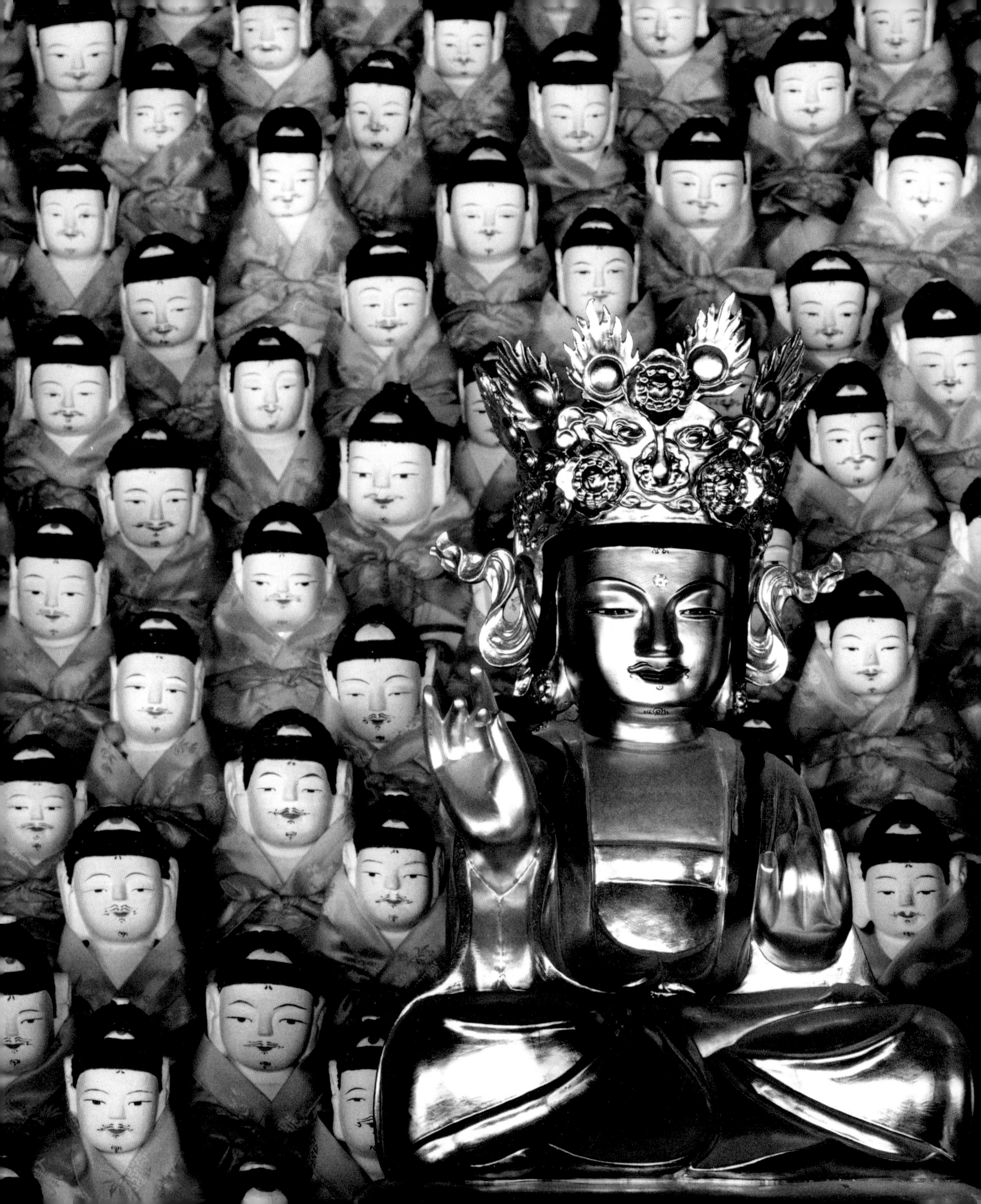

Korea

Seated Buddha, Geonbongsa Temple,
Goseong, Gangwon-do, 2013

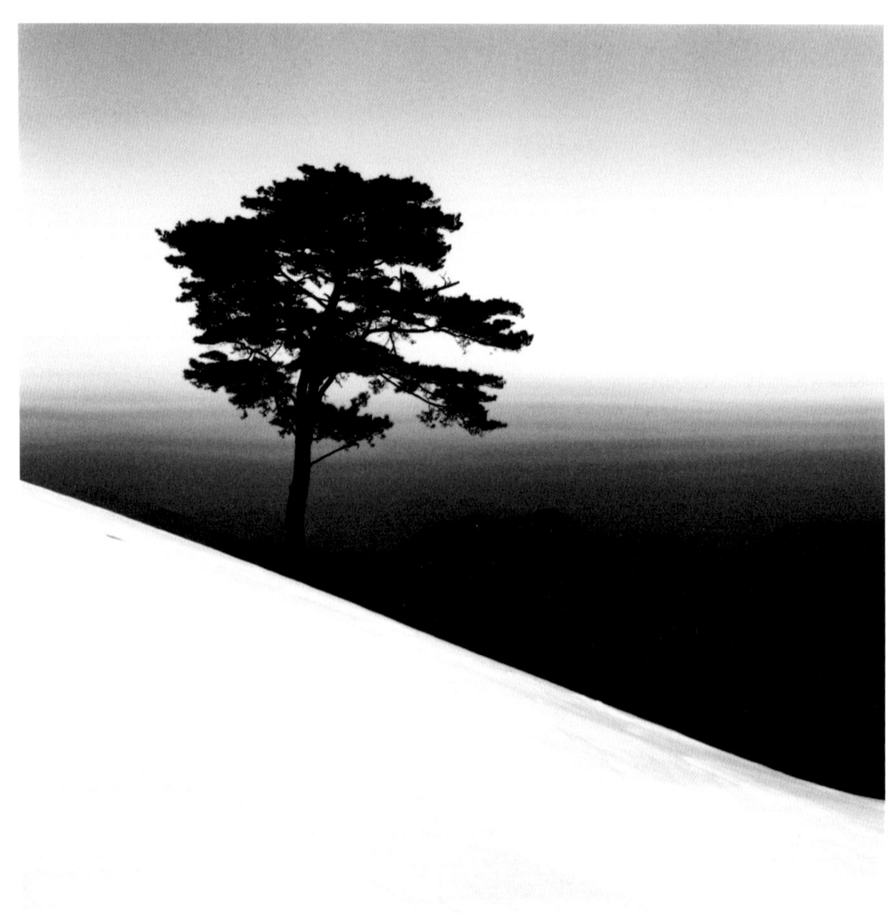

Mountain Tree, Danyang,
Chungcheongbukdo, 2011

Golden Maitreya Buddha,
Beopjusa Temple, Boeun,
Chungcheongbuk-do, 2007

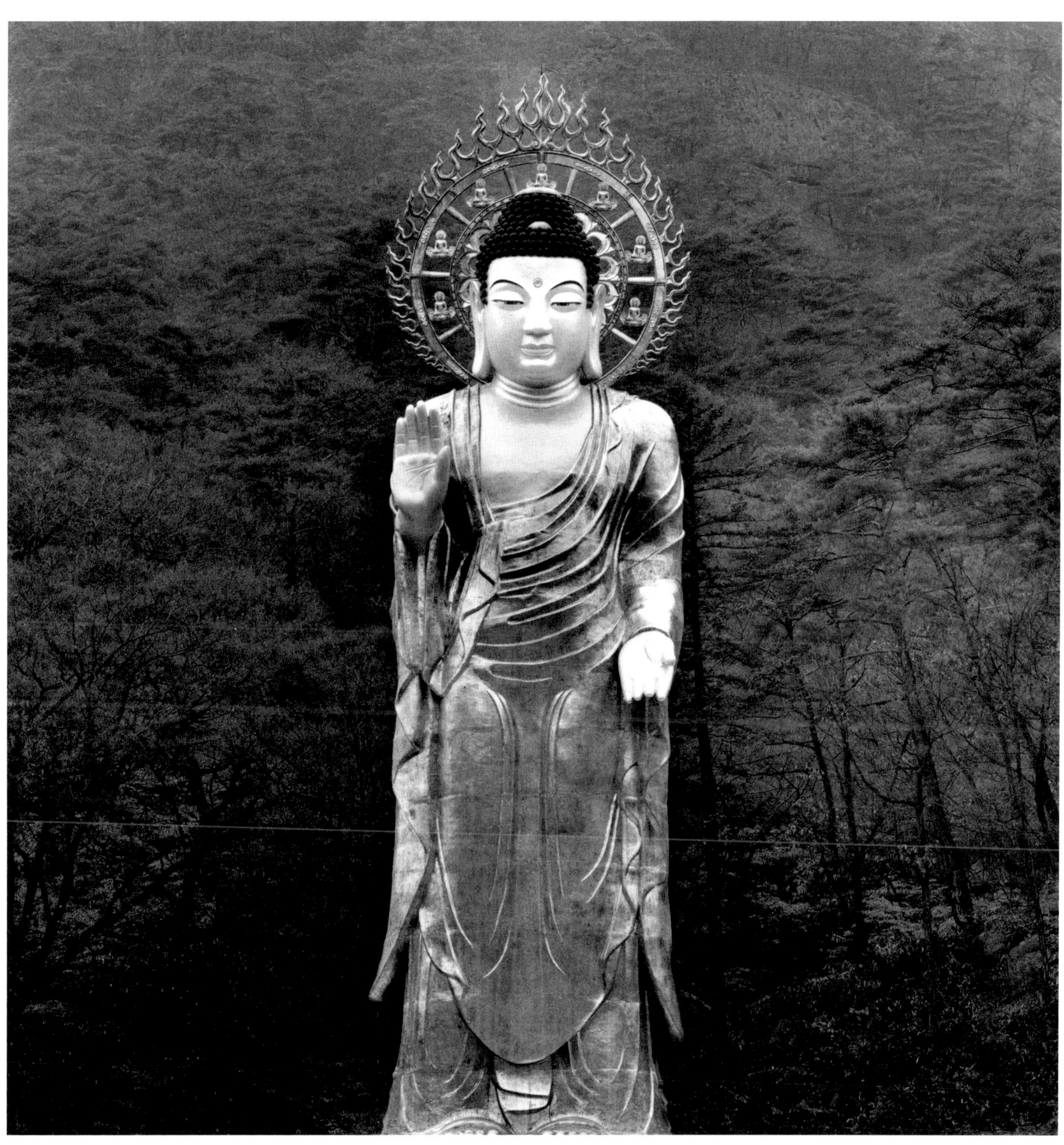

Rock-Carved Buddha,
Daeheungsa Temple Buddha,
Haenam, Jeollanam-do, 2018

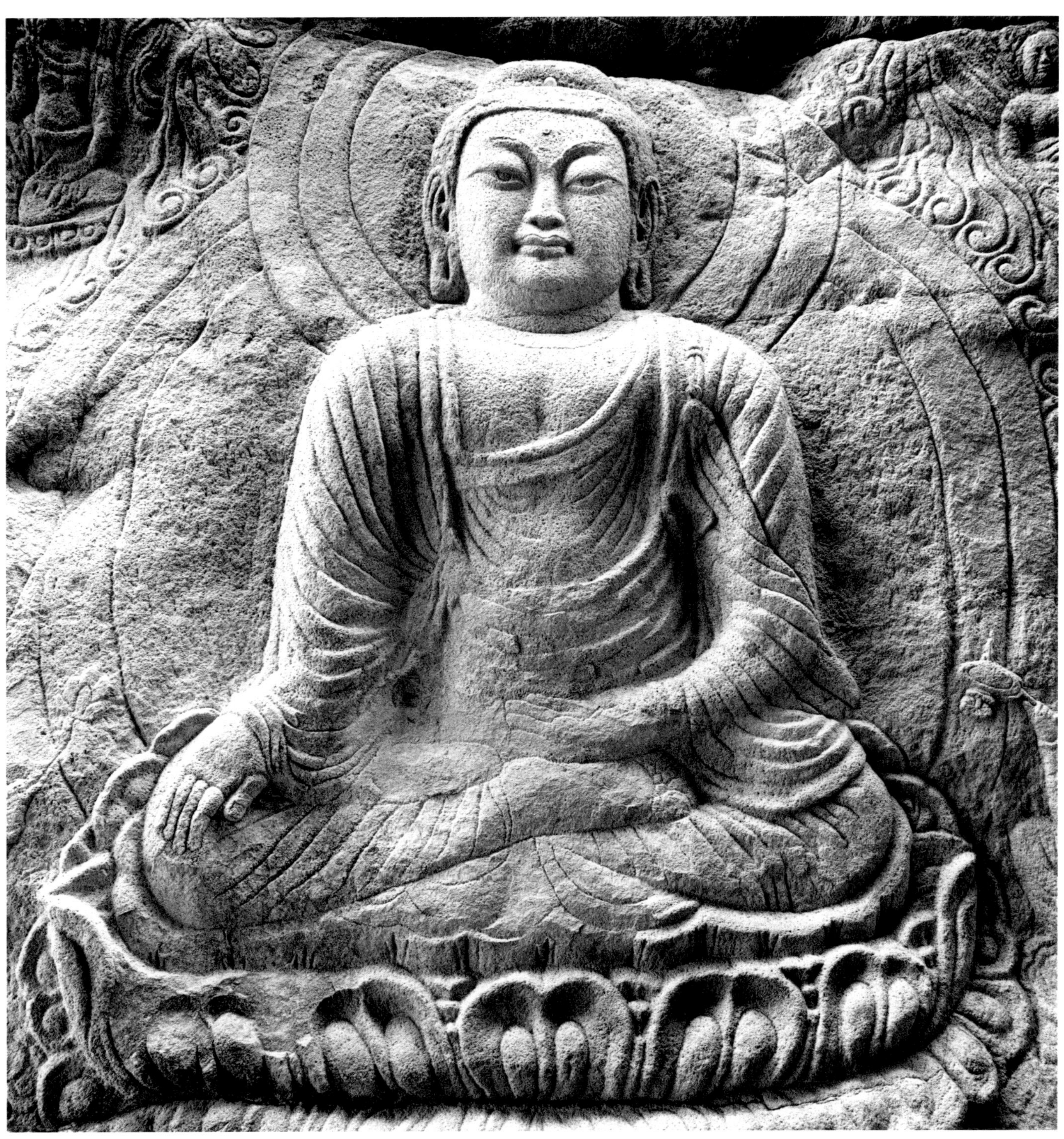

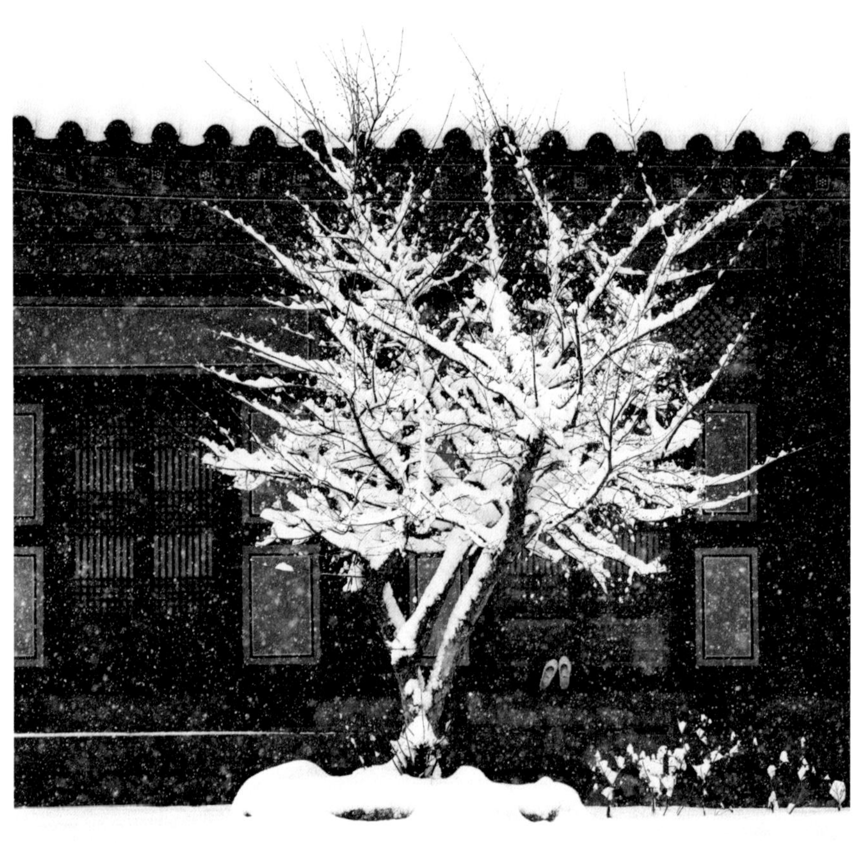

Tree and Slippers, Woljeongsa Temple, Gangwondo, 2005

Taean Dongmunri Maaesamjonbulipsang, Taean, Chungcheongnam-do, 2018

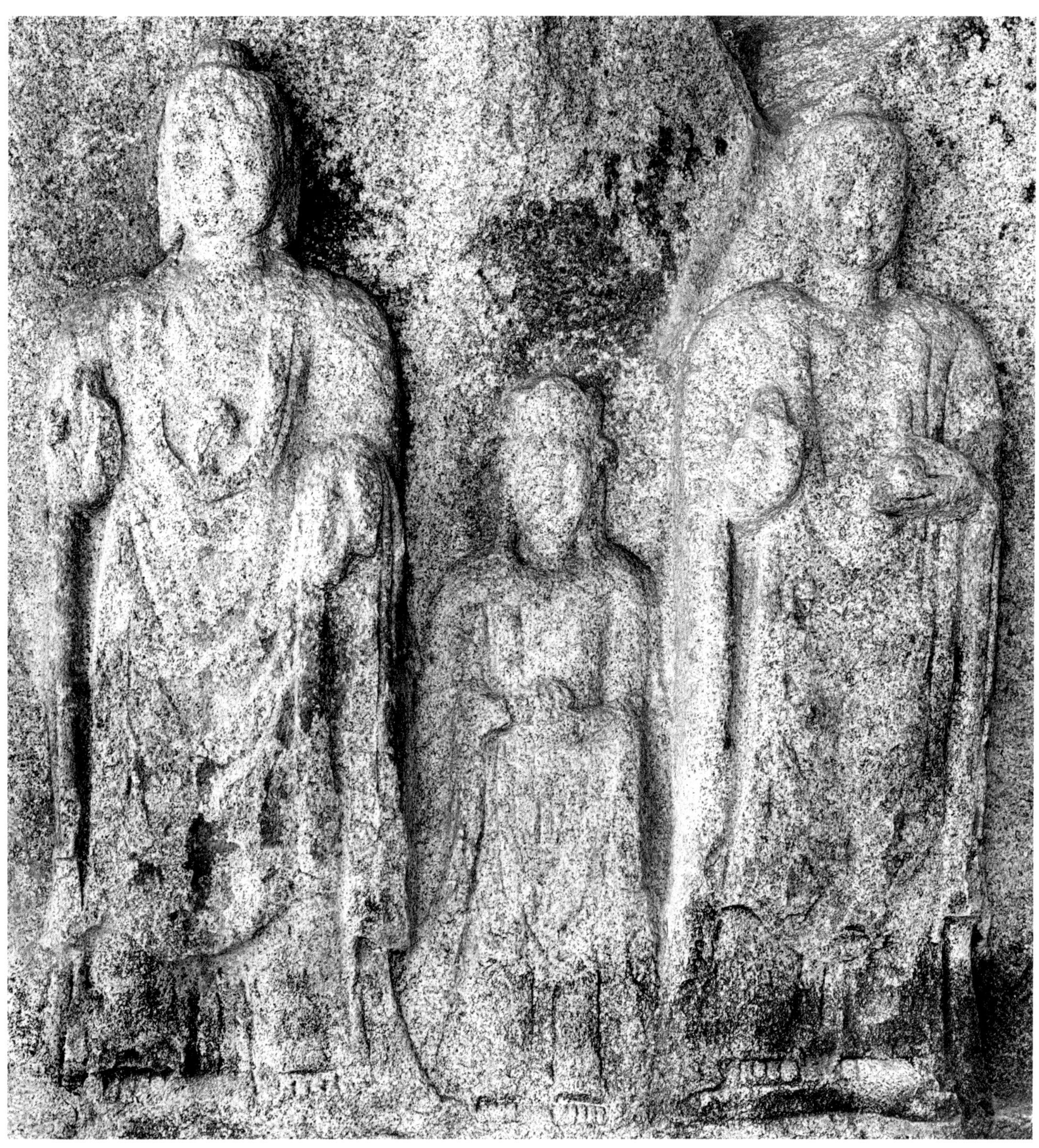

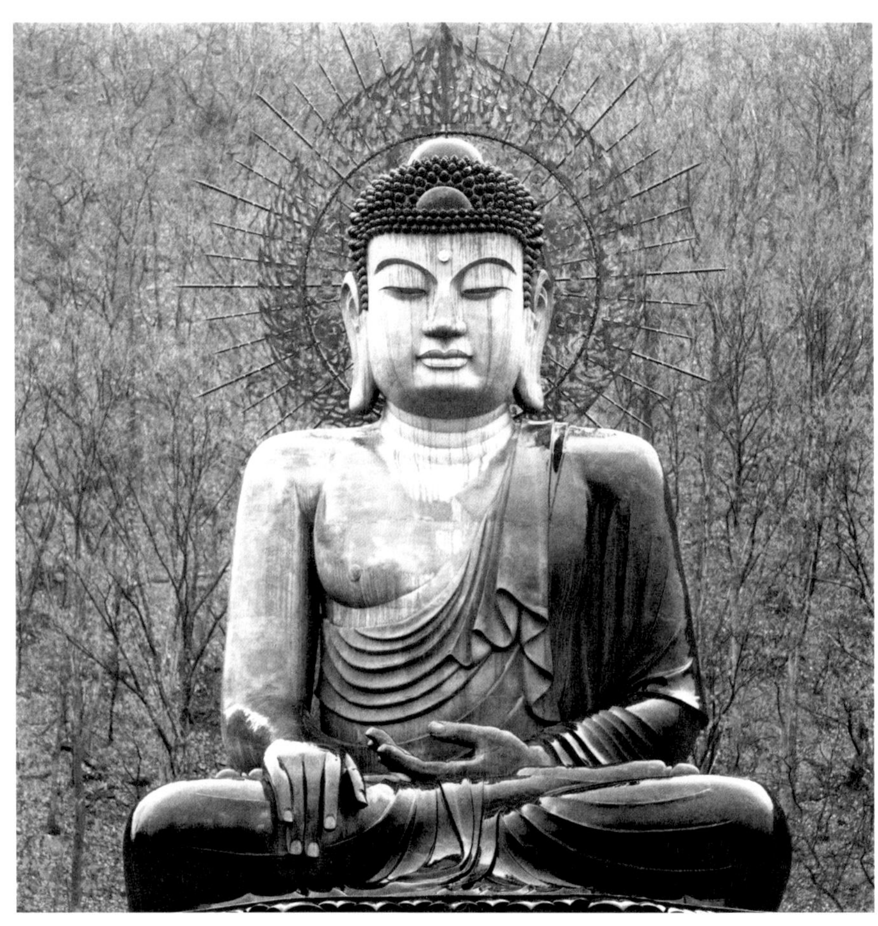

Seated Buddha Statue, Shin-Heung Temple, Gangwondo, 2005

Buddha near Demilitarized Zone, Cheorwon, Gangwon-do, 2007

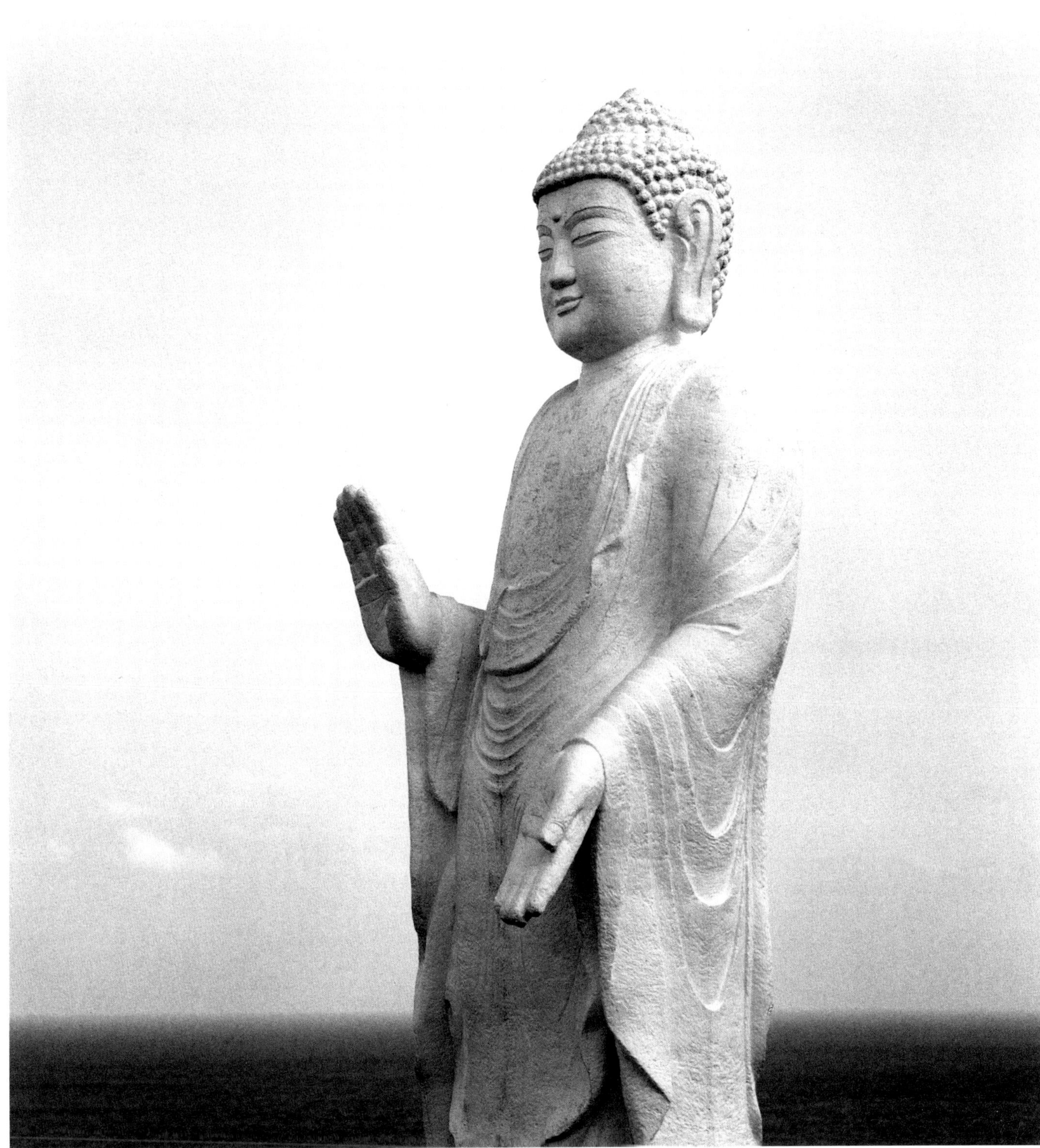

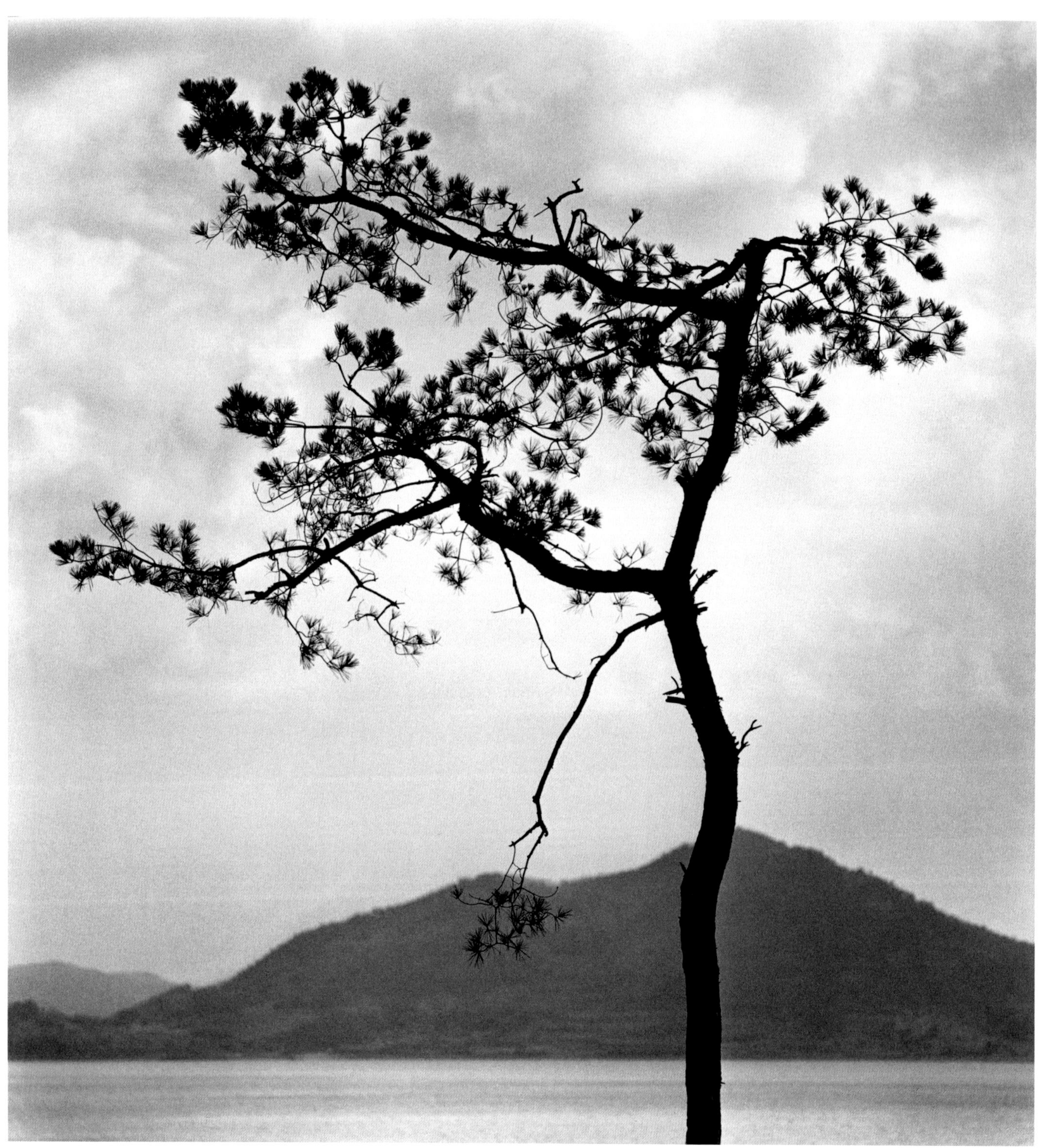

KOREA

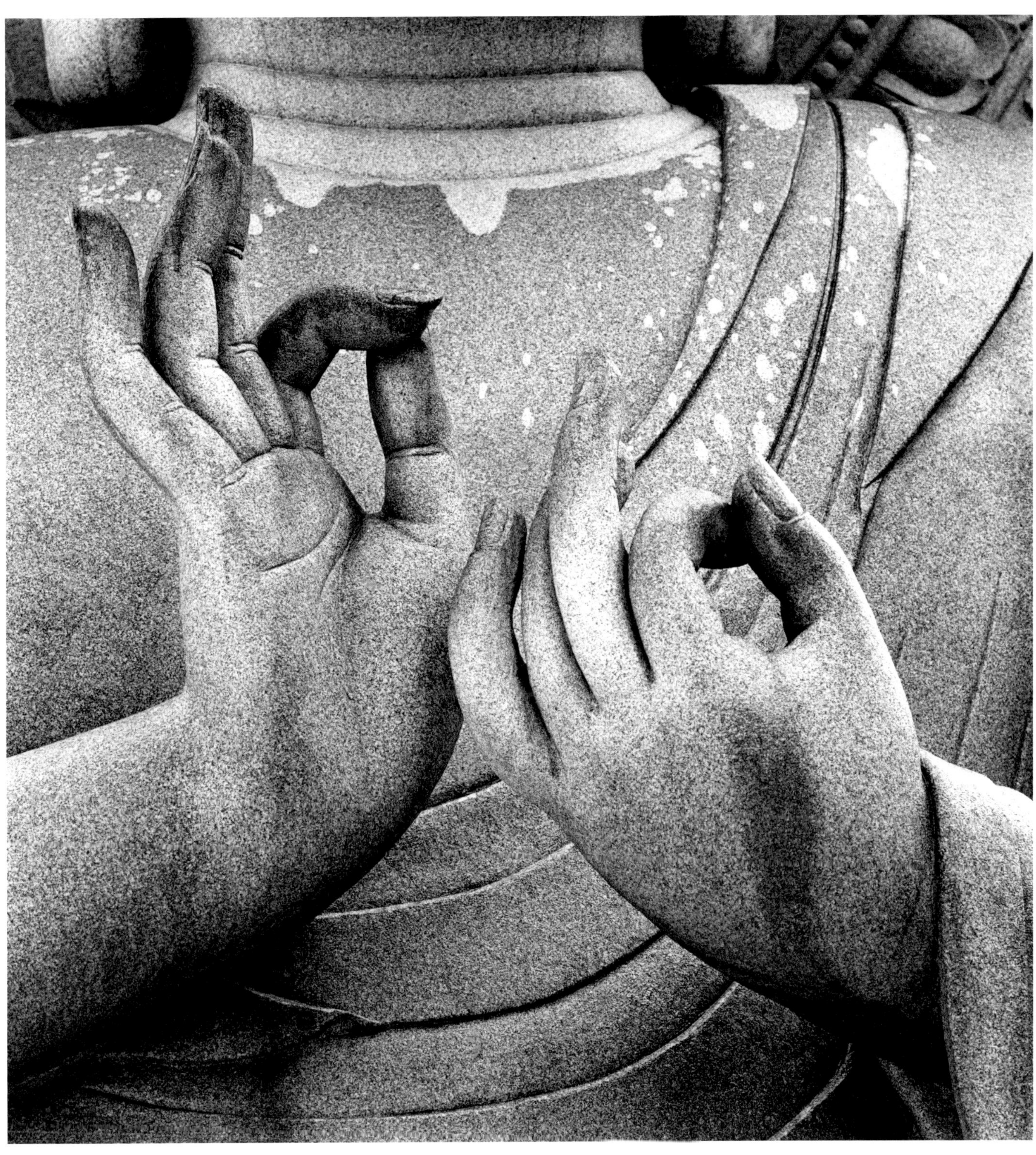

Particular Pine, Jeonil-ri,
Jeollanam-do, 2018

Mudrā of Teaching,
Gwaneumsa Temple, Jeju Island, 2012

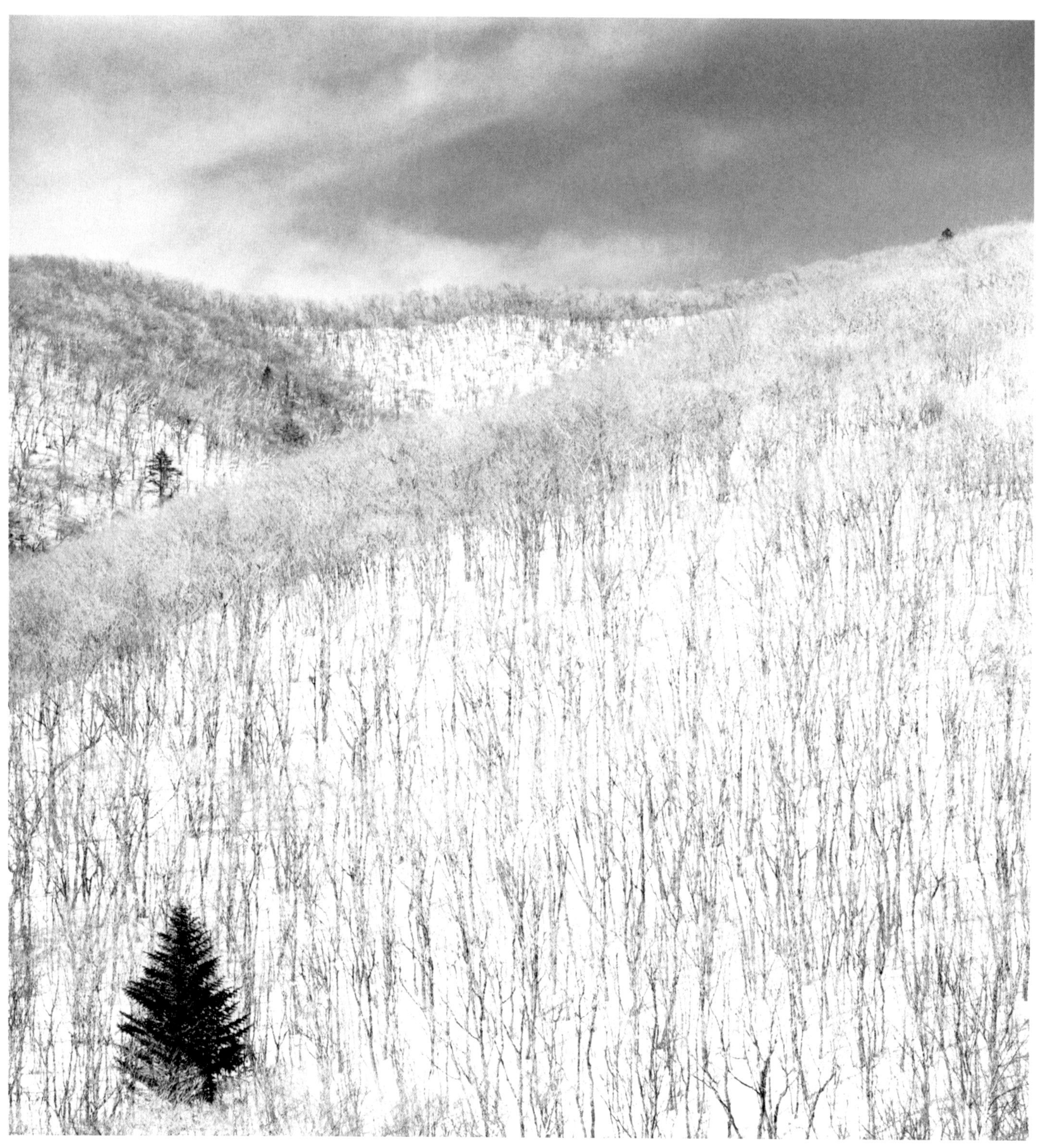

KOREA

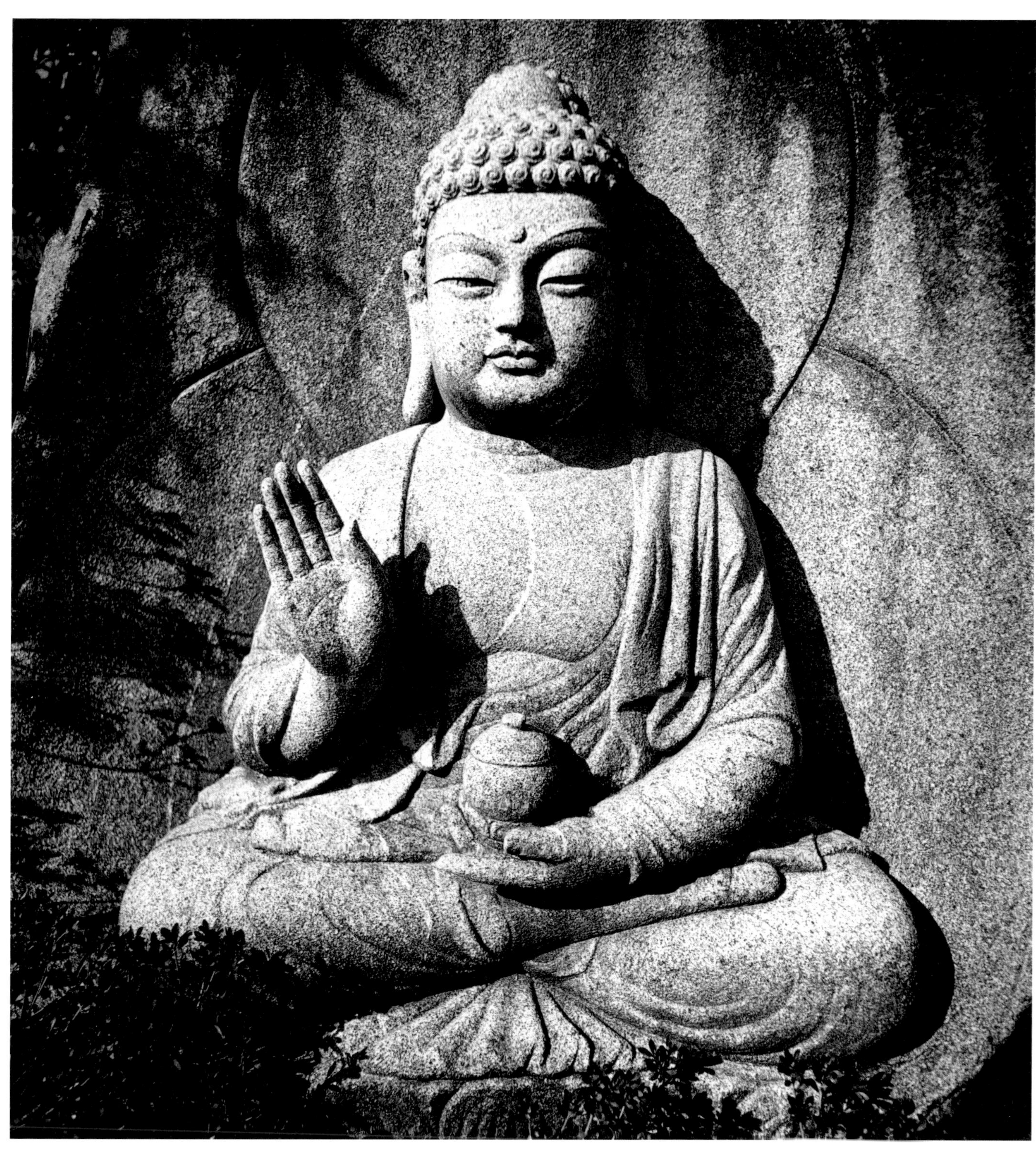

Snow-Covered Hillside,
Pyongchang, 2012

Medicine Buddha, Nammireuksa,
Gangjin, Jeollanam-do, 2018

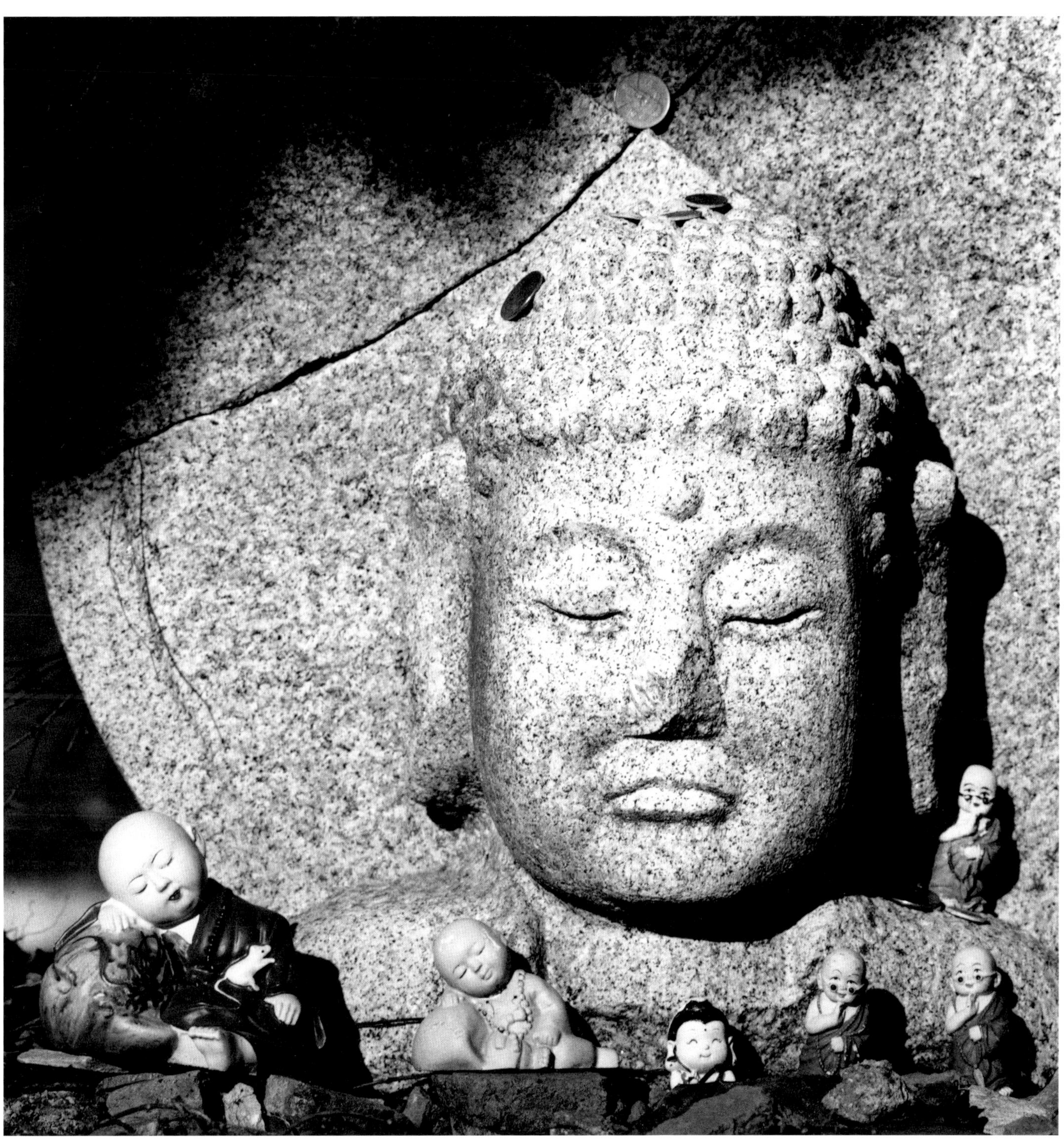

Buddha and Monks, Geonbongsa Temple, Goseong, Gangwon-do, 2013

Lamp and Temple, Jonjaanji,
Jeju Island, 2012

Standing Buddha,
Manbulsa Temple, Yeongcheon,
Gyeongsangbuk-do, 2018

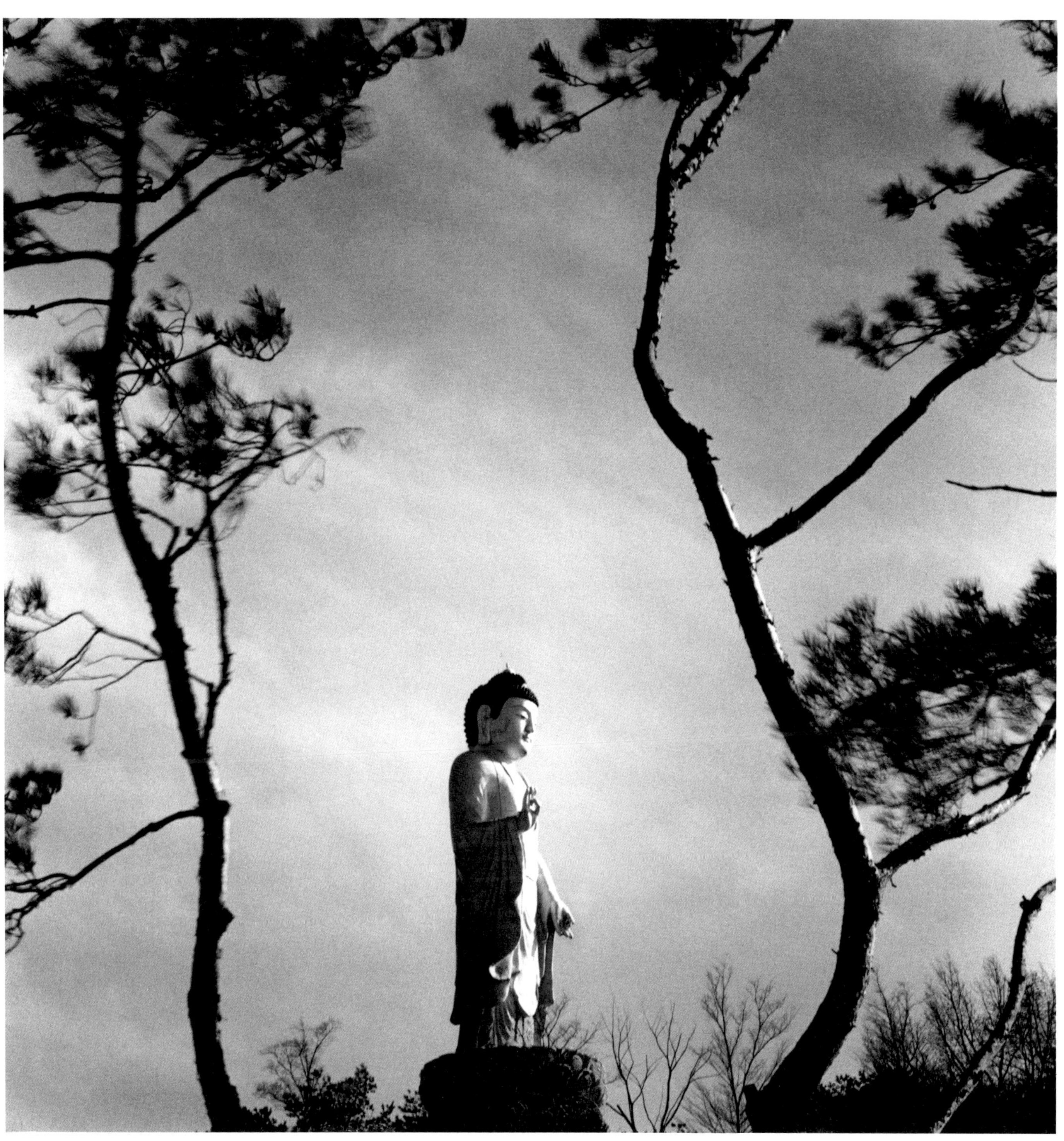

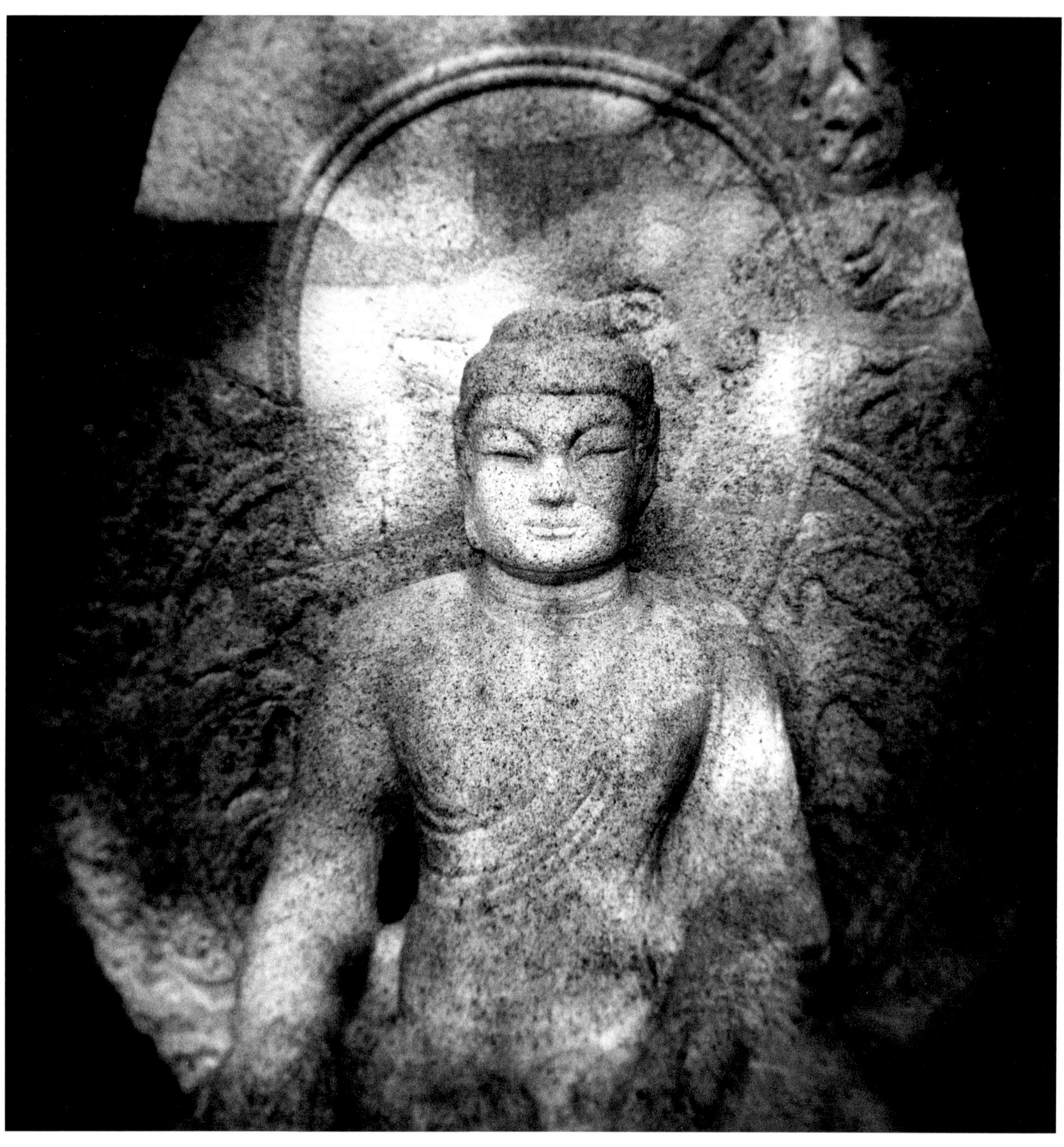

Seated Stone Buddha, Gyeongju,
Gyeongsangbuk-do, 2010

Buddha, Bird and Oranges,
Jogyesa Temple, Seoul, 2018

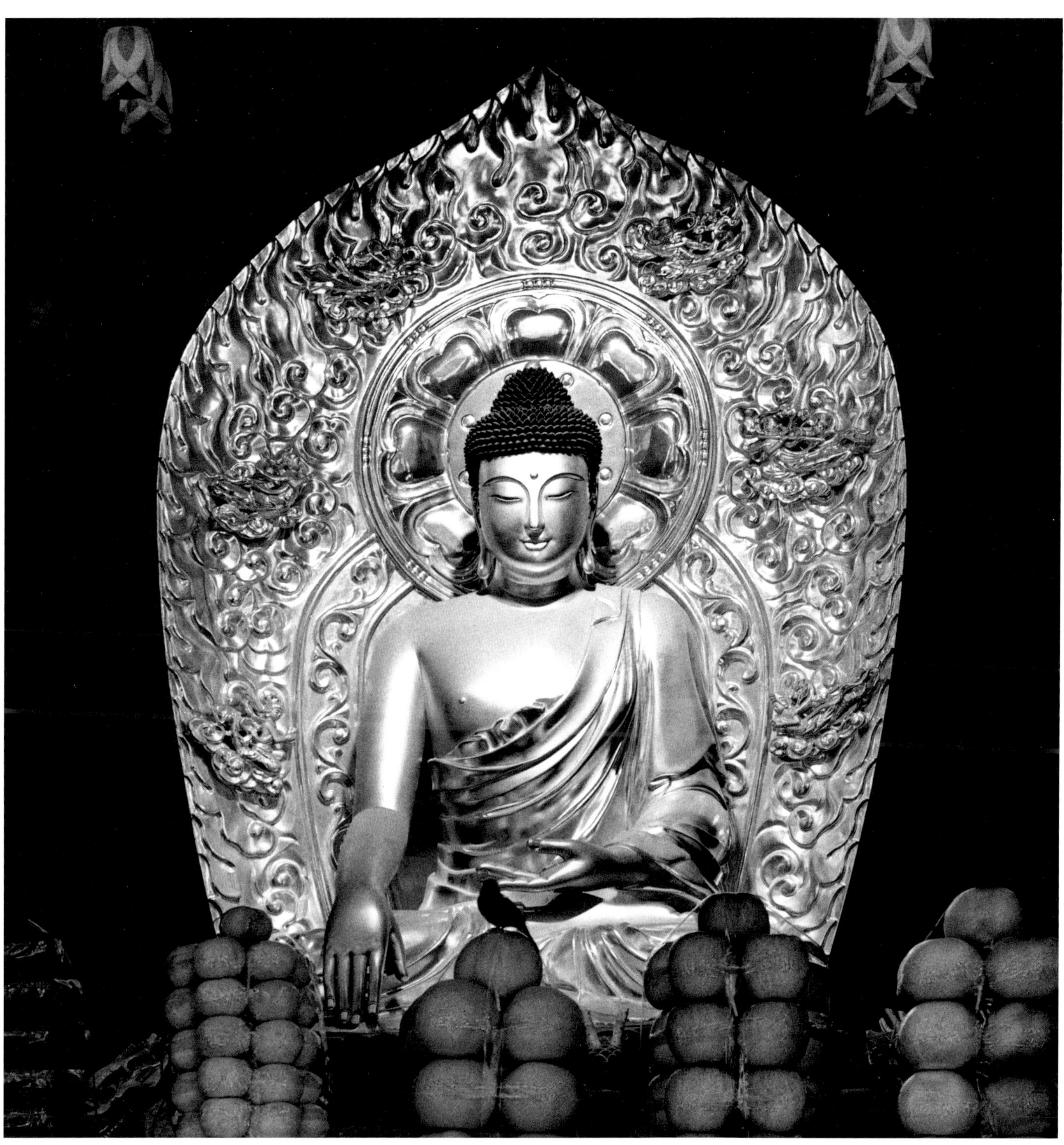

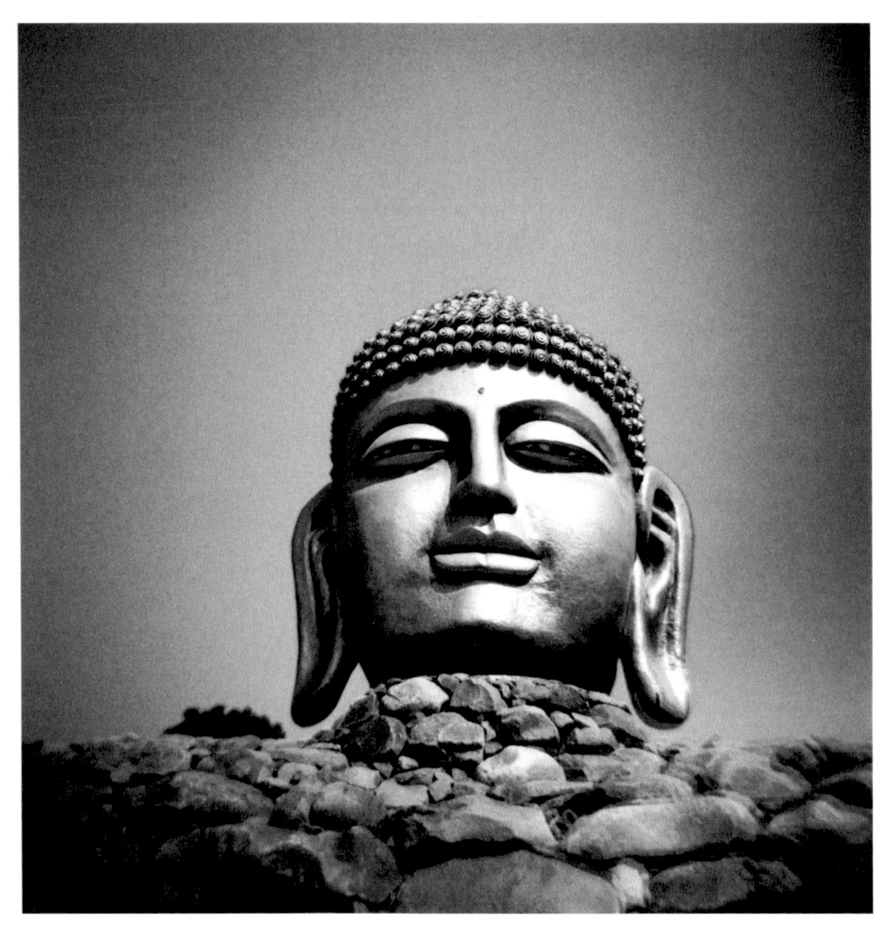

KOREA

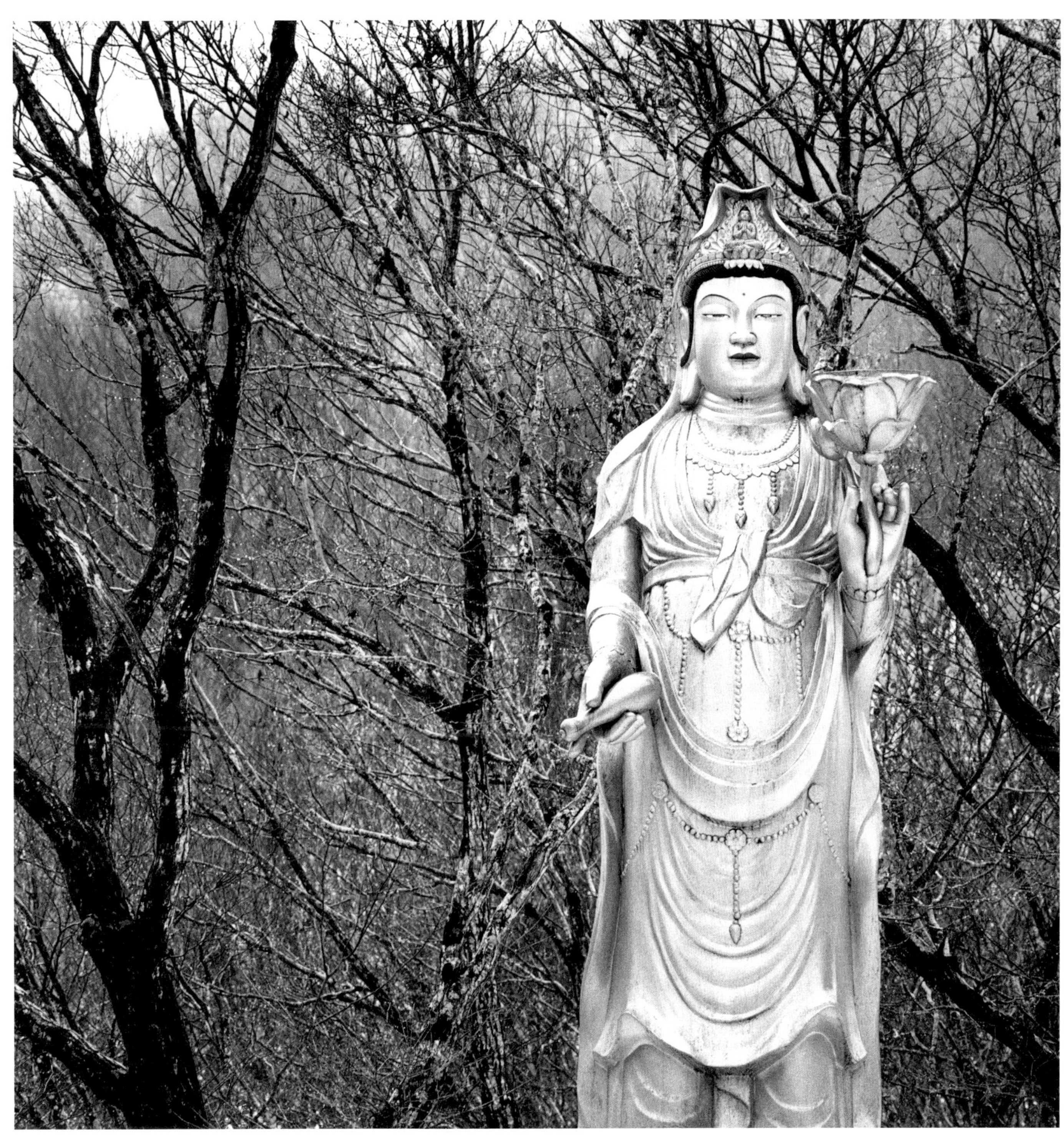

Buddha Head, Waujeong Temple,
Yongin, Gyeonggi-do, 2010

Bodhisattva Guanyin, Cheonwangsa
Temple, Jeju Island, 2012

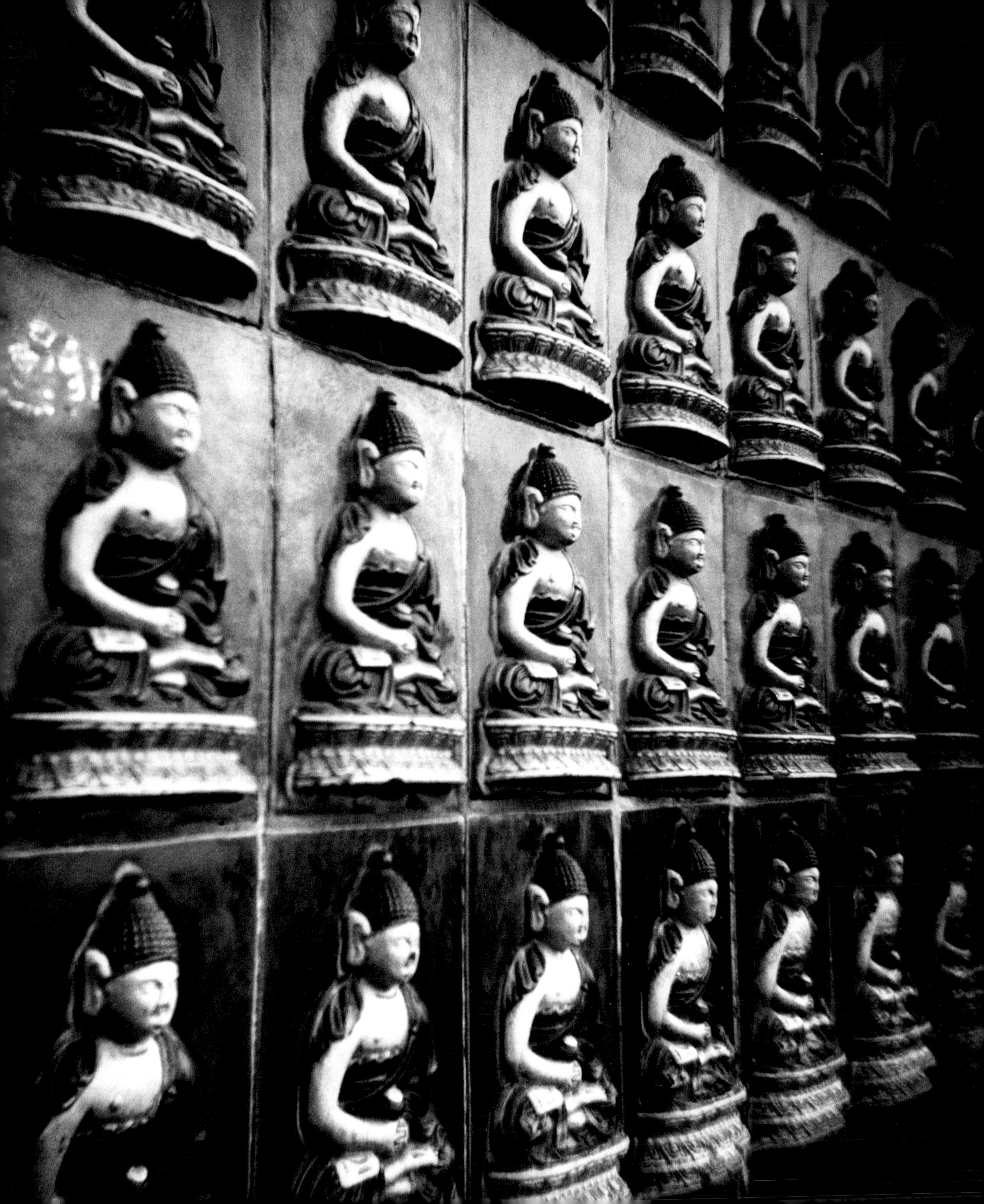

China

Wall of Buddhas, Summer Palace,
Beijing, 2007

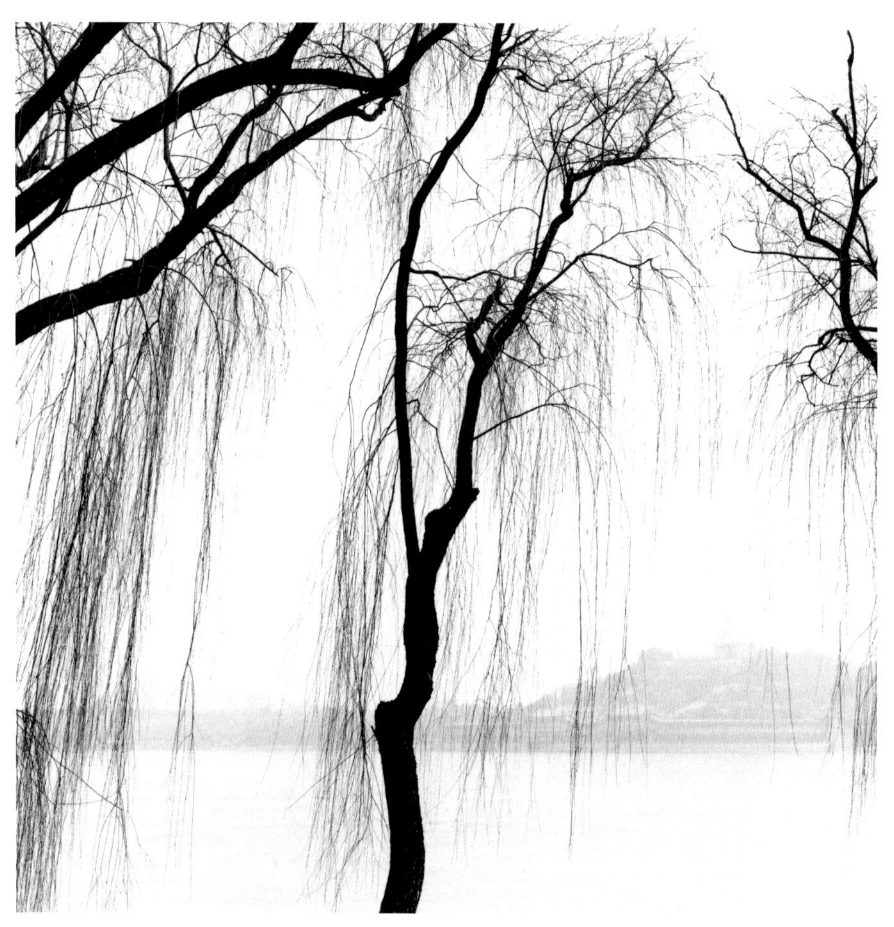

CHINA

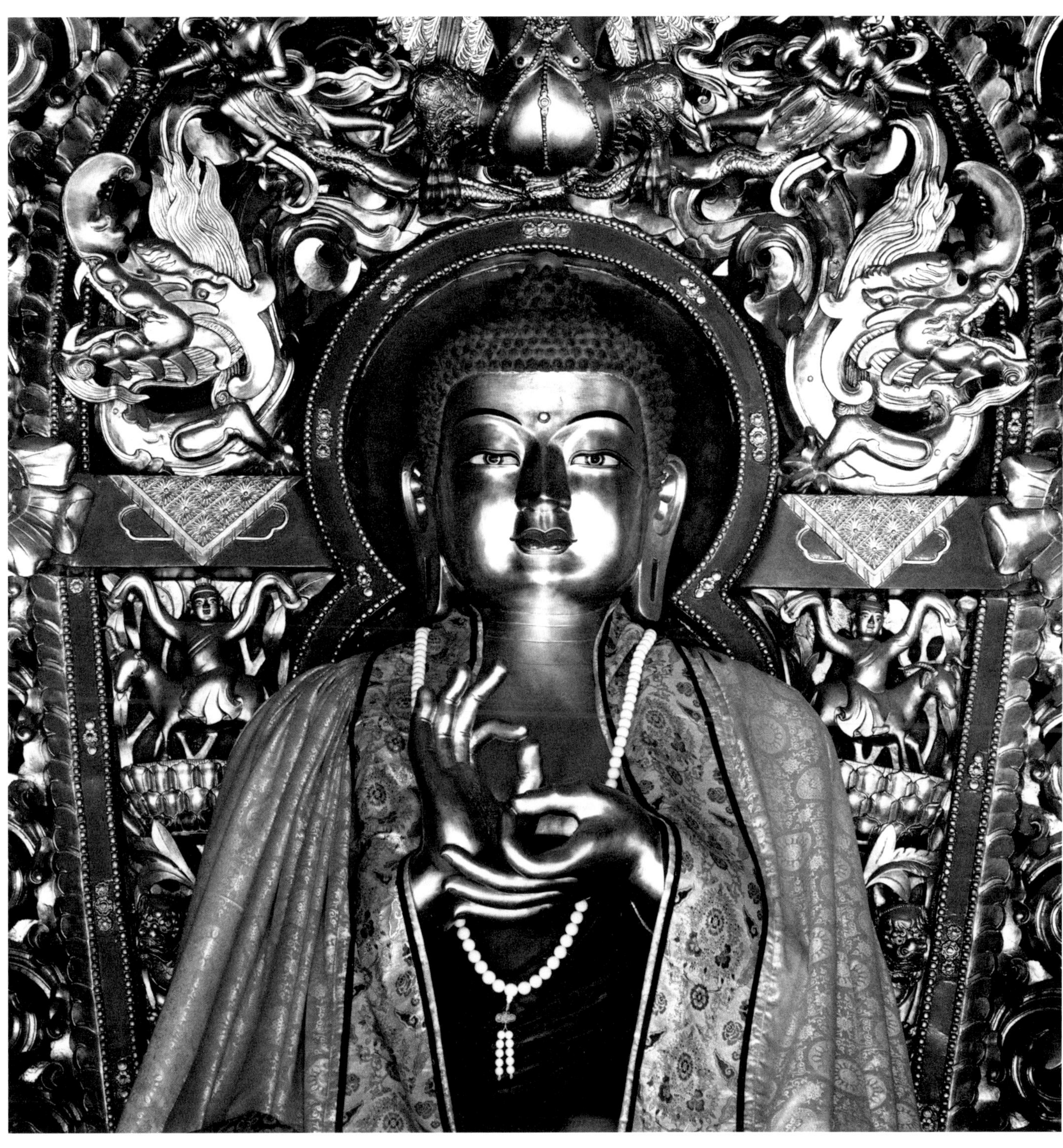

White Stūpa, Beihai Park,
Beijing, 2007

Yonghegong, Lama Temple,
Beijing, 2016

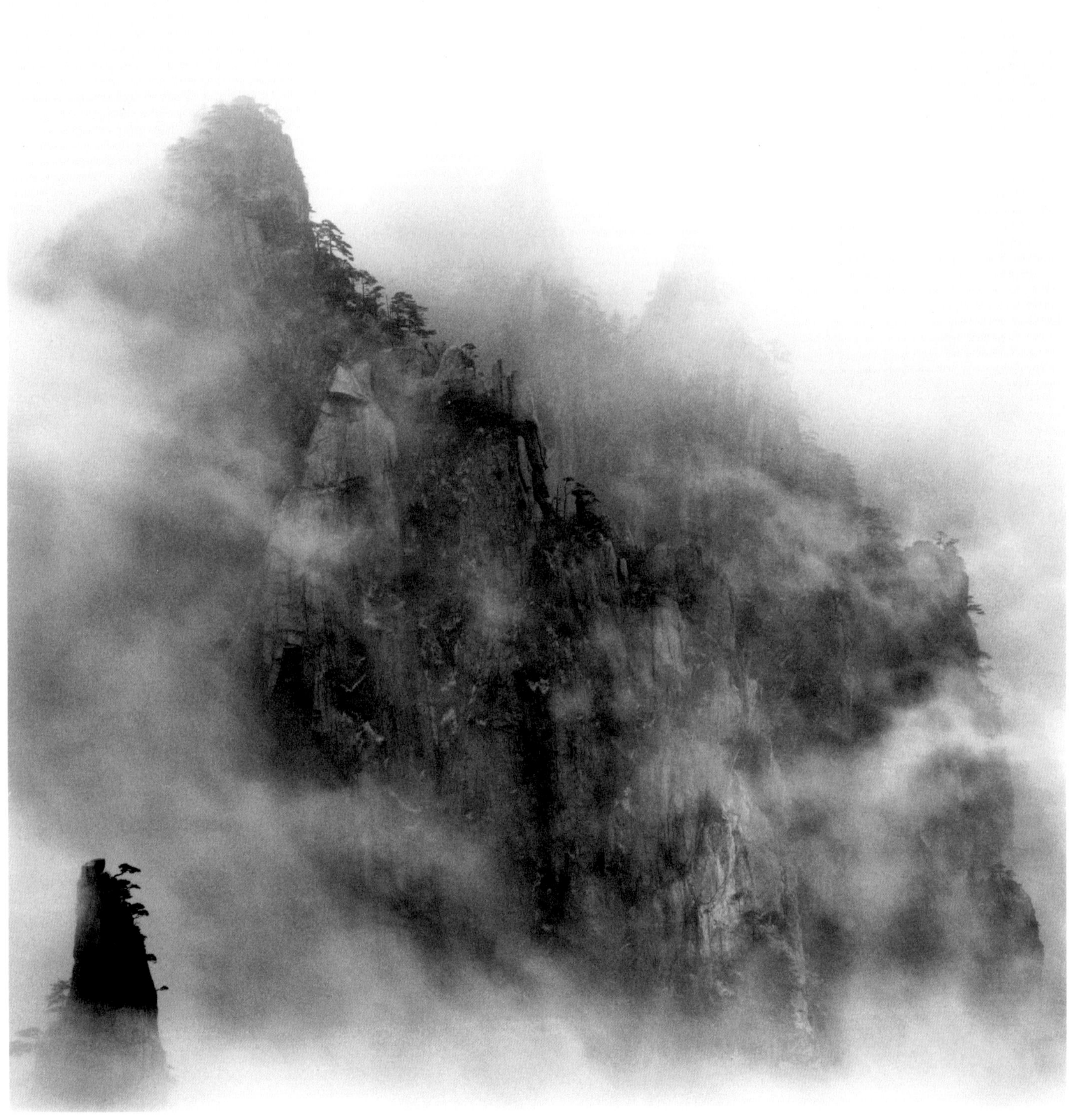

CHINA

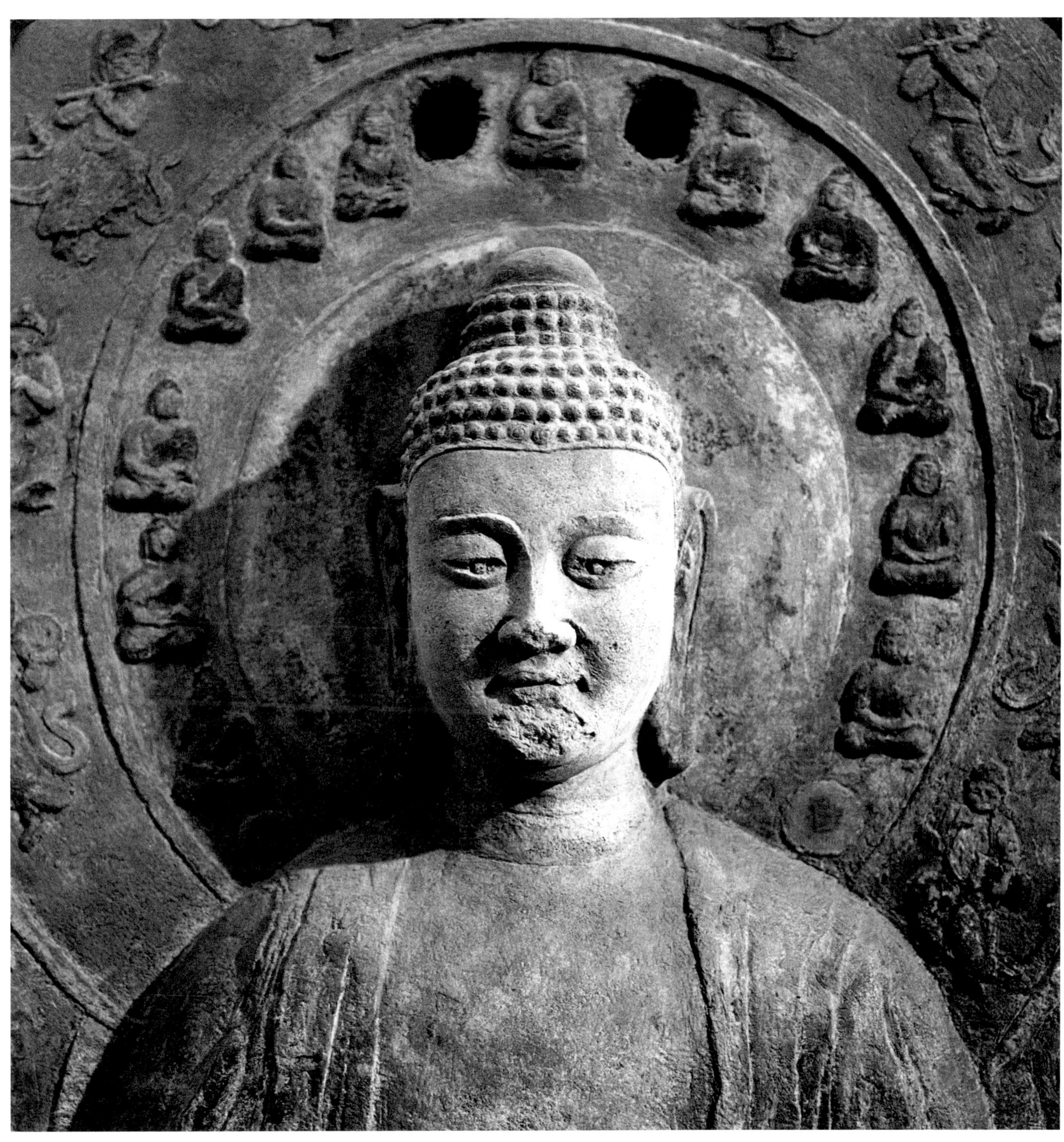

Huangshan Mountains, Study 1,
Anhui, 2008

Stone Carving, Study 1,
Zhenjue Temple, Beijing, 2016

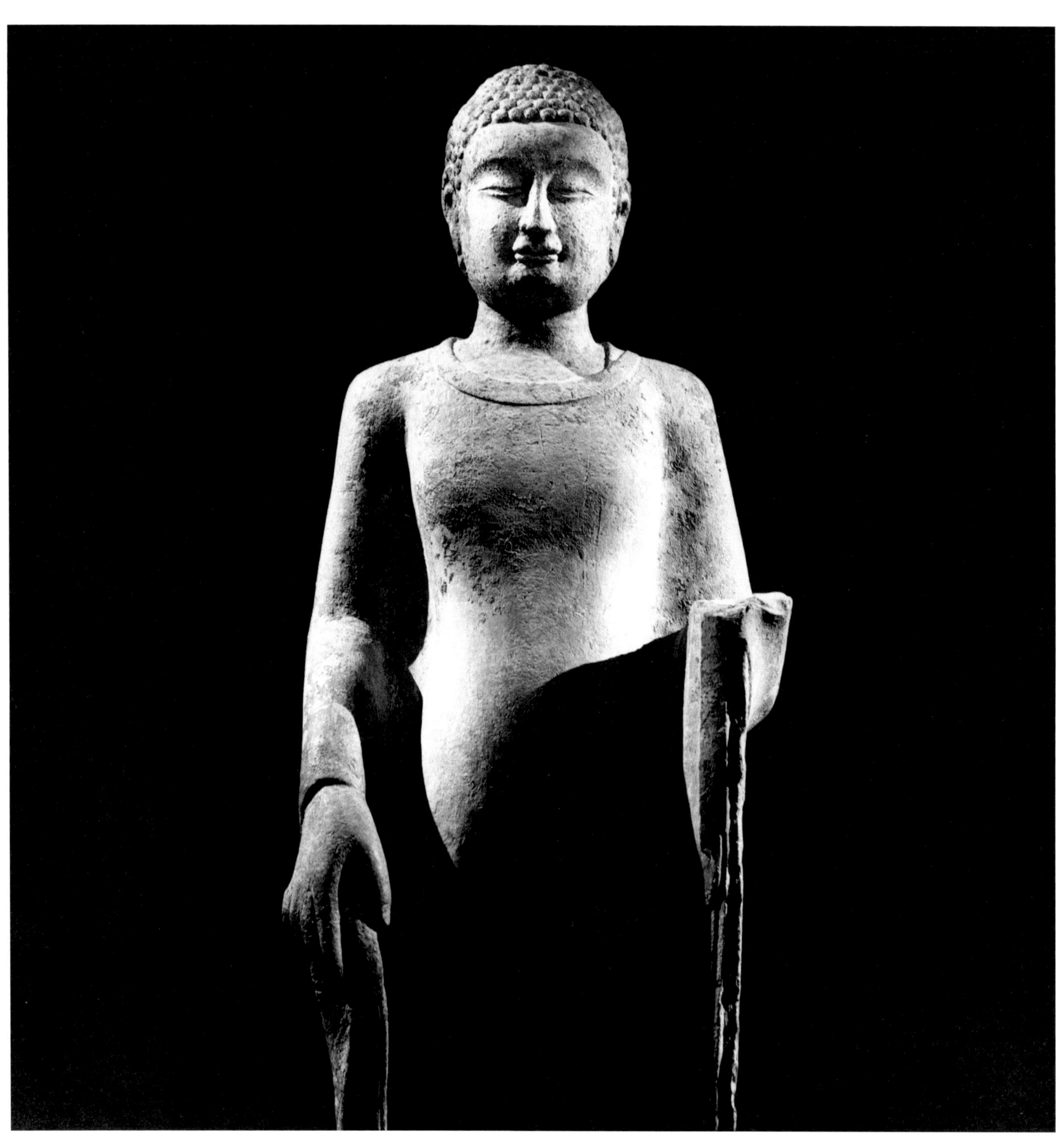

Vairocana, Shandong, at the Musée Guimet, Paris, 2018

Forbidden City Tree, Study 2, Beijing, 2011

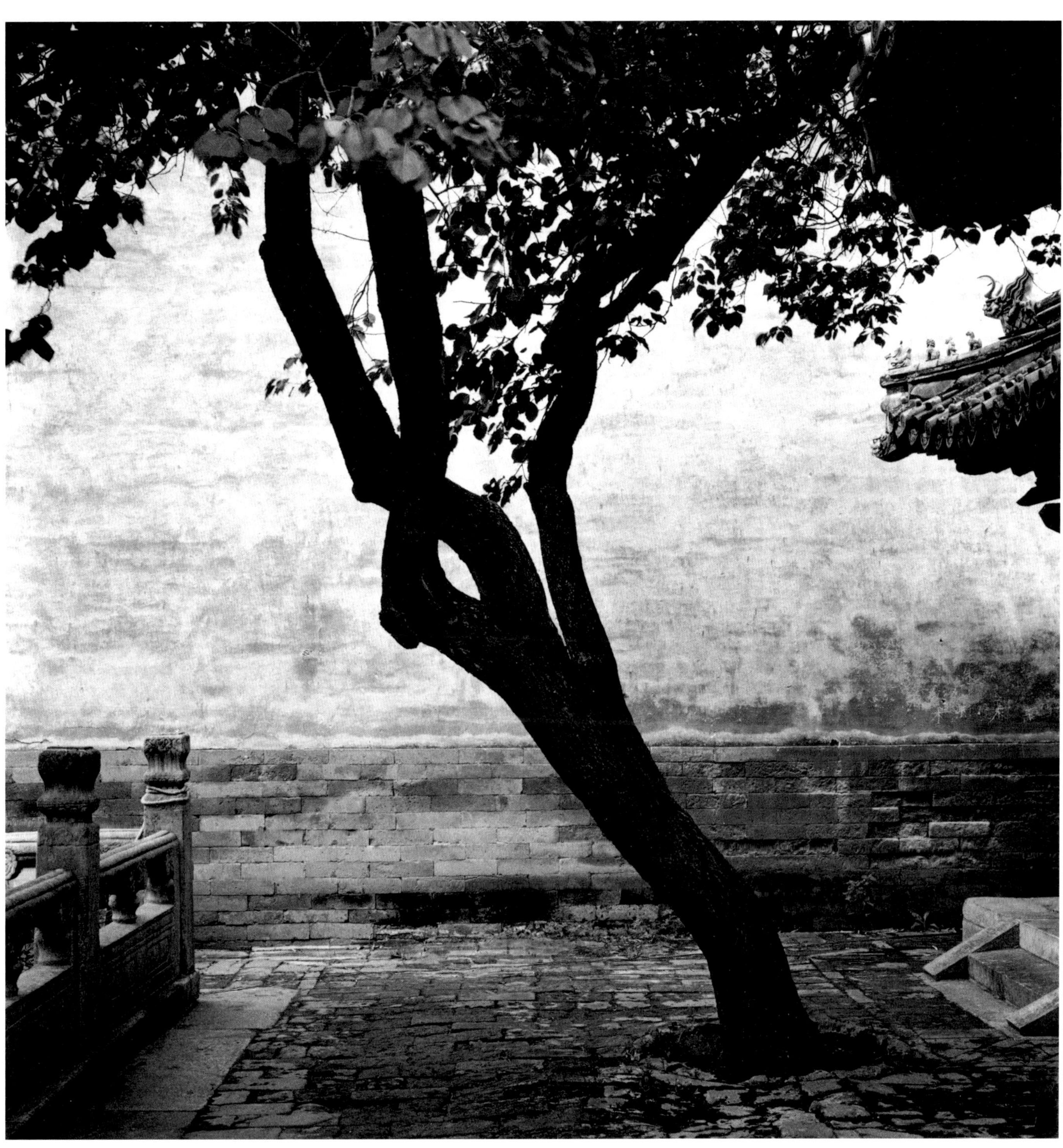

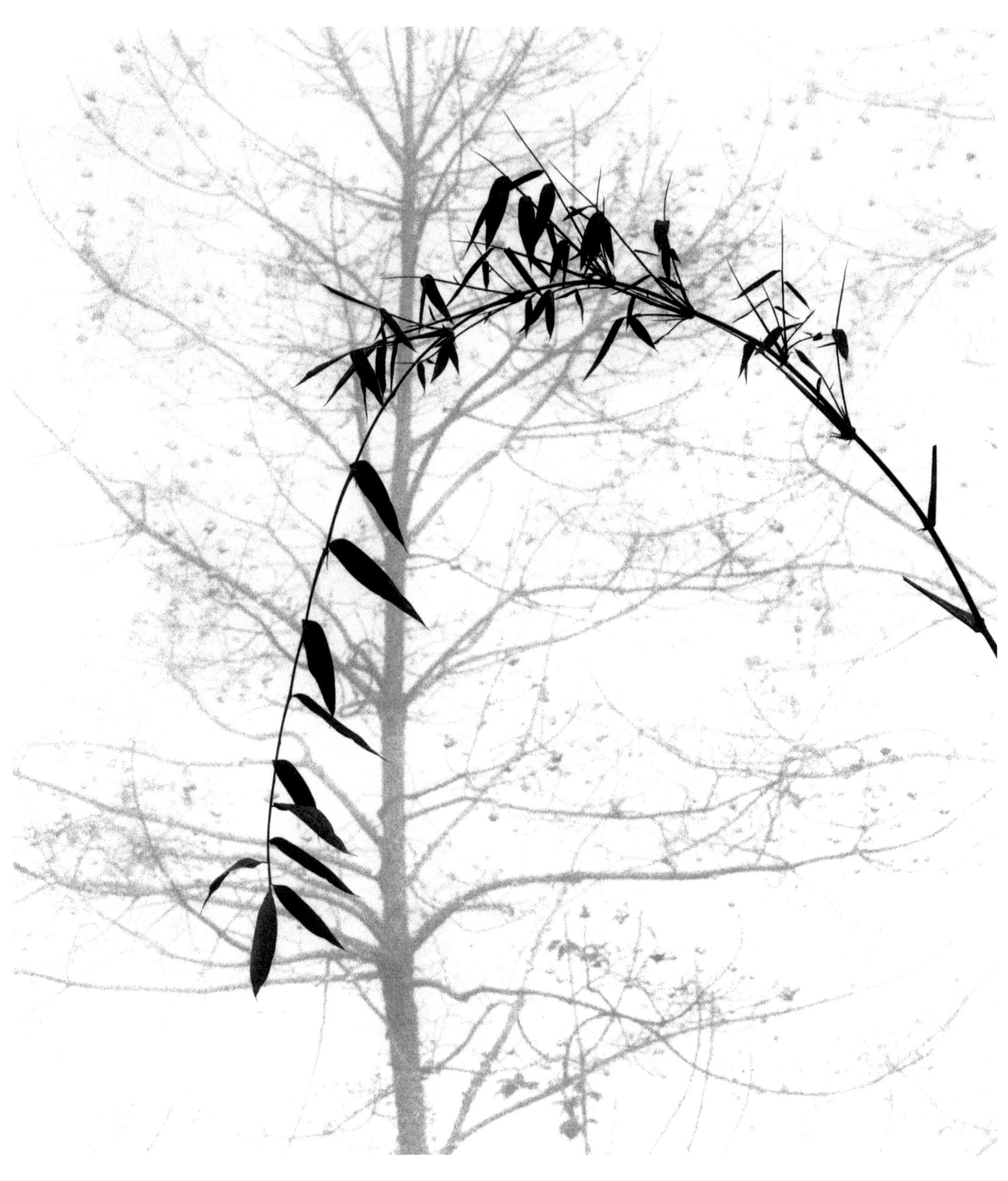

Bamboo and Tree,
Qingkou Village, Yunnan, 2013

Seated Buddha at the
Musée Guimet, Paris, 2018

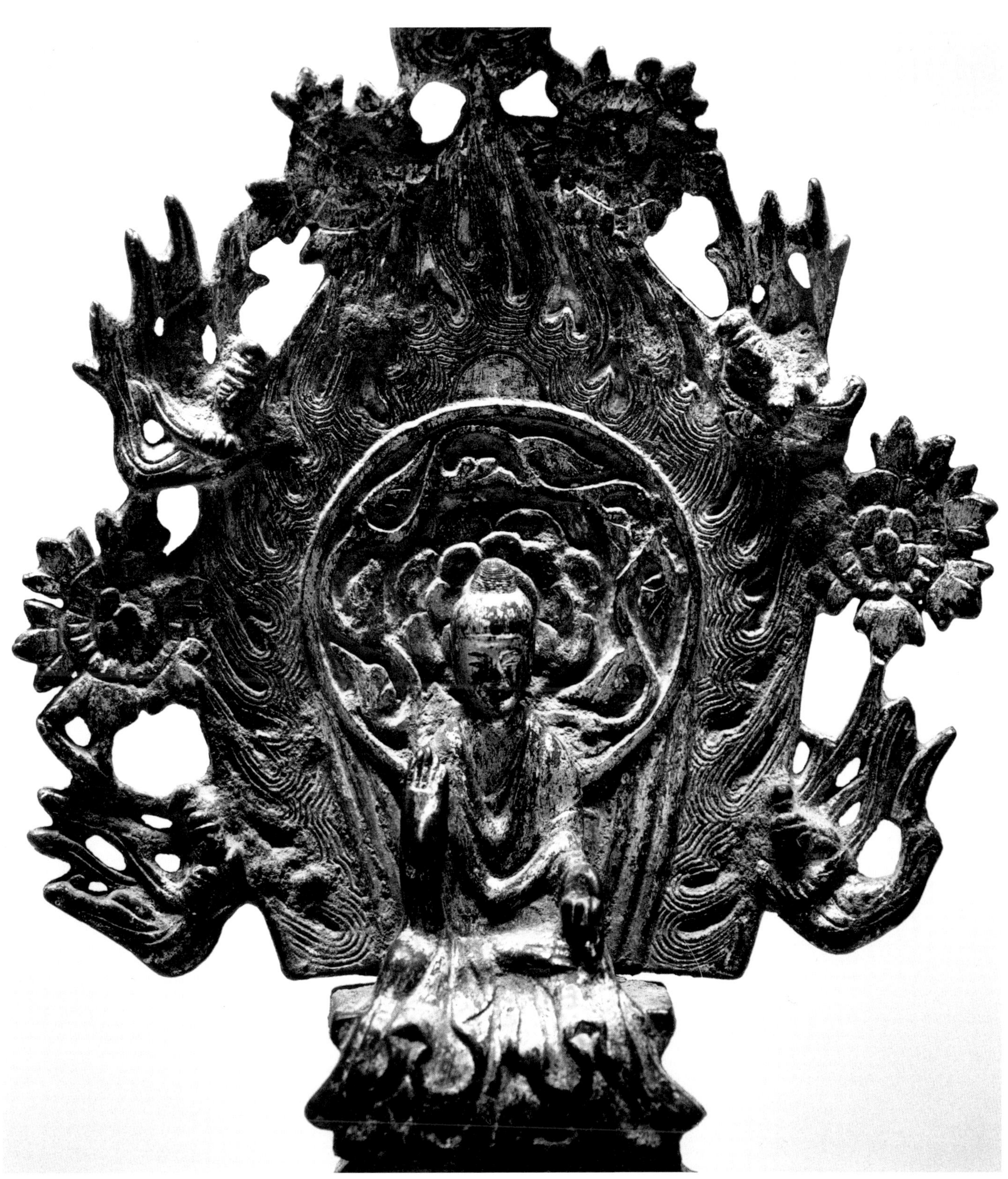

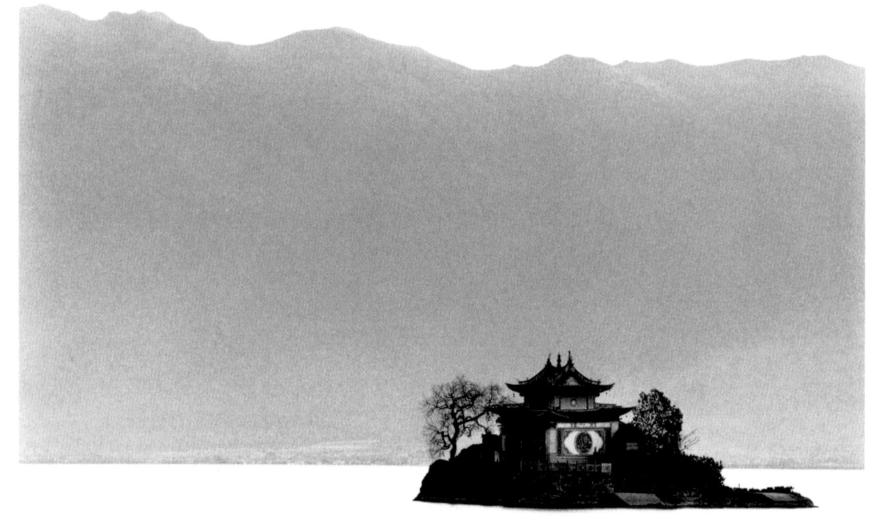

Xiao Putuo Island,
Erhai Lake, Yunnan, 2013

Seated Buddha from Xinjiang, at the
Musée Guimet, Paris, 2018

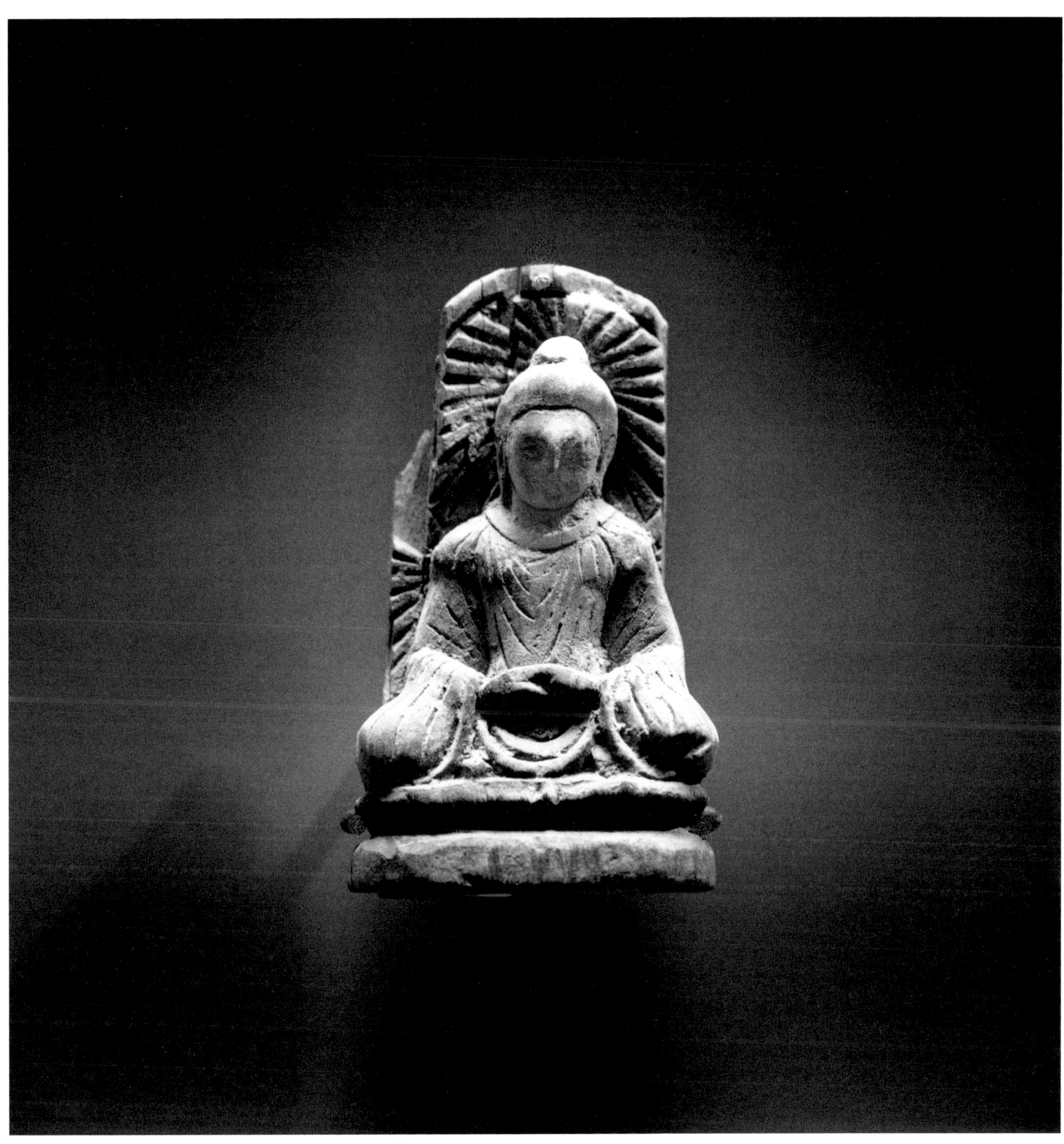

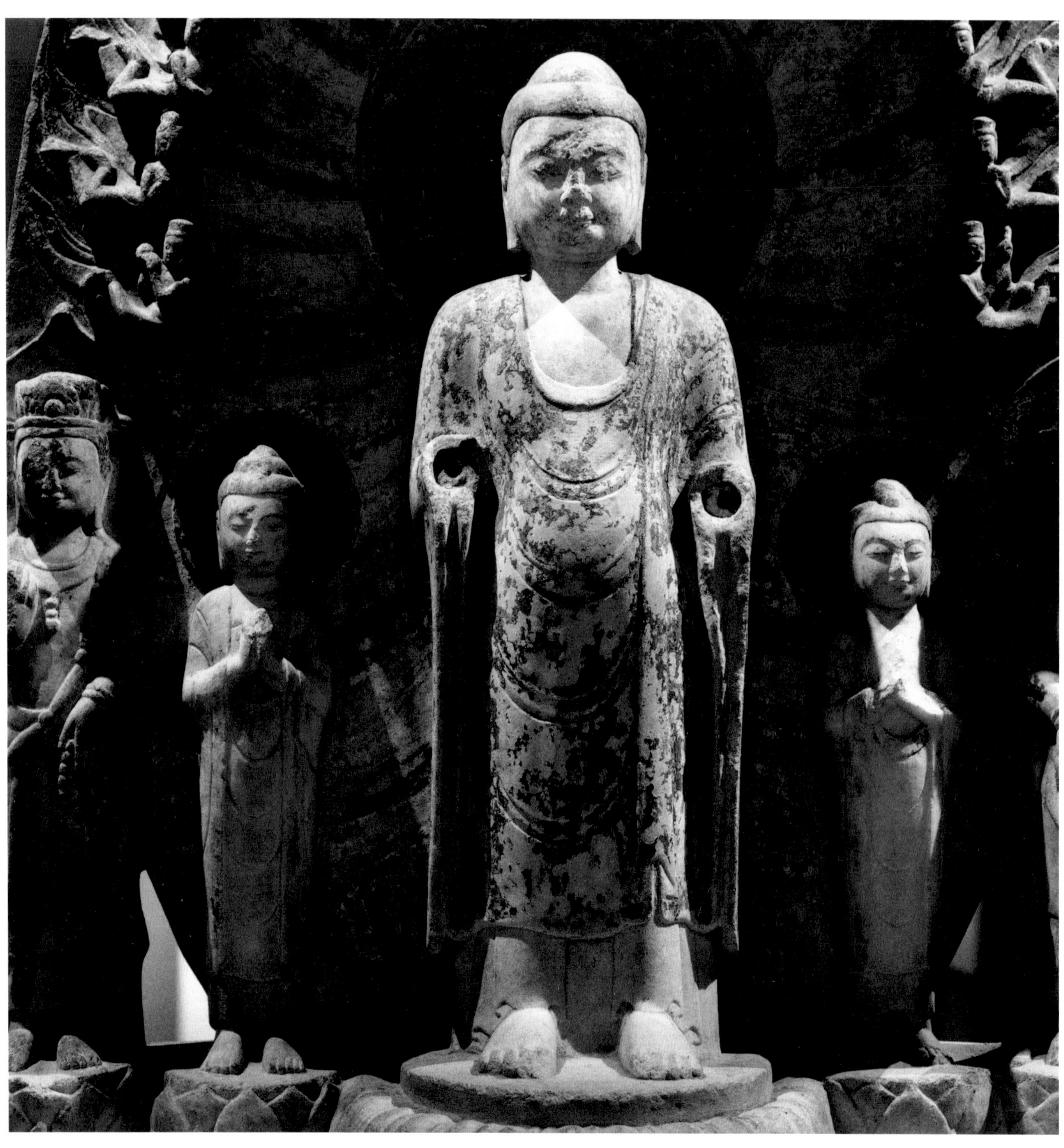

Standing Buddha at the Musée Guimet, Paris, 2018

Xinjiang Garden and Zhi Yun Pagoda, Nantong, Jiangsu, 2015

CHINA

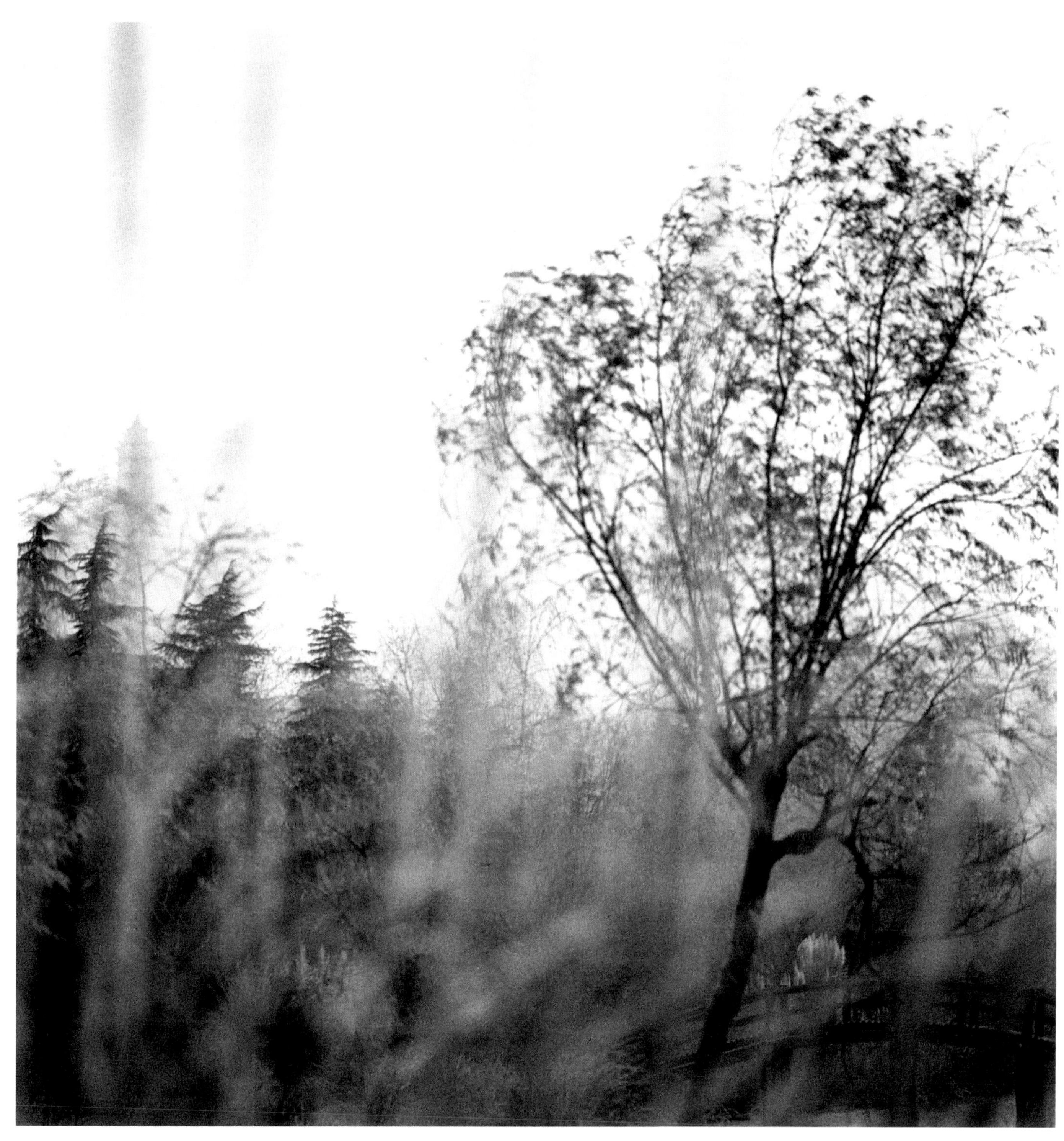

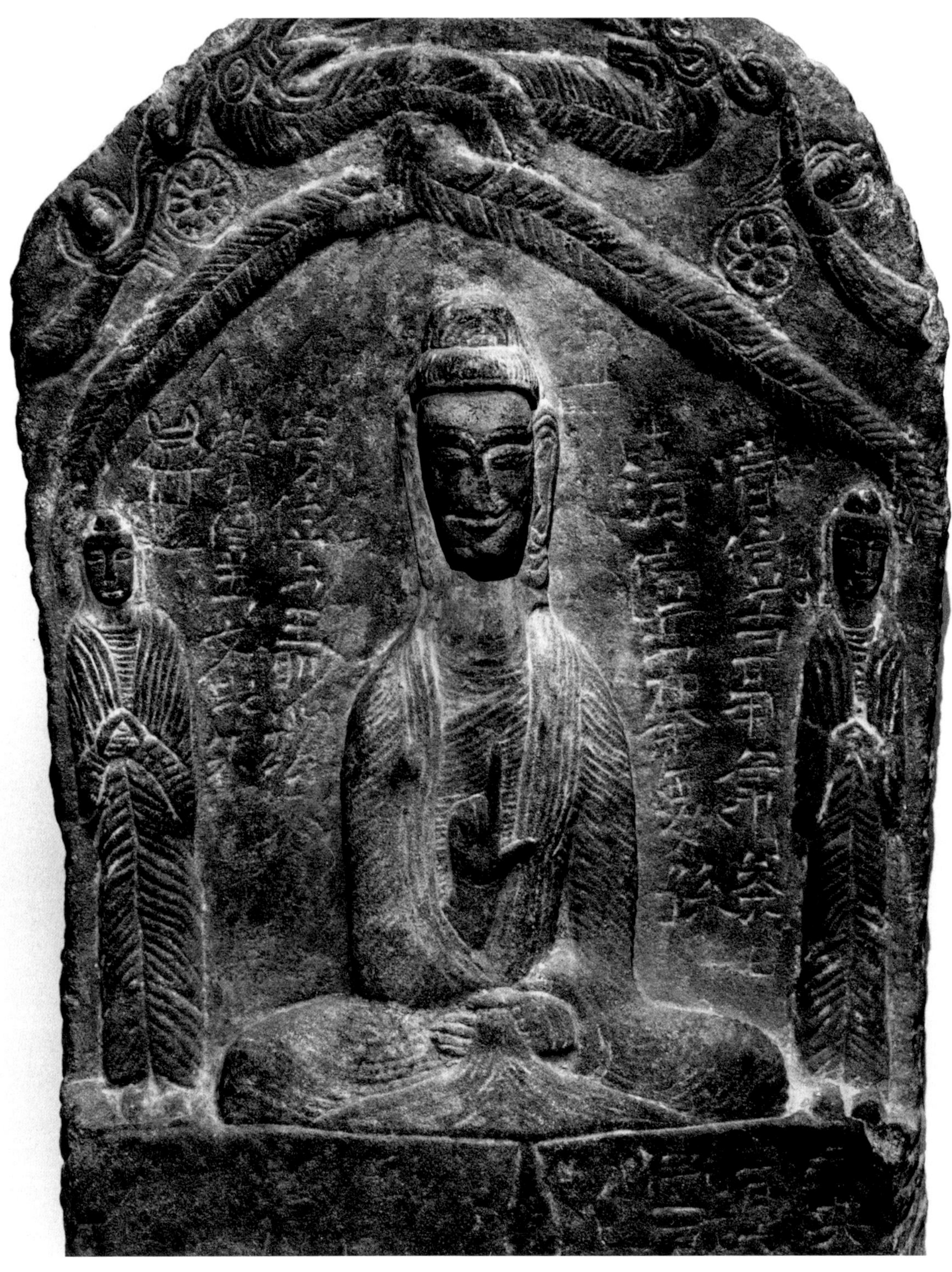

CHINA

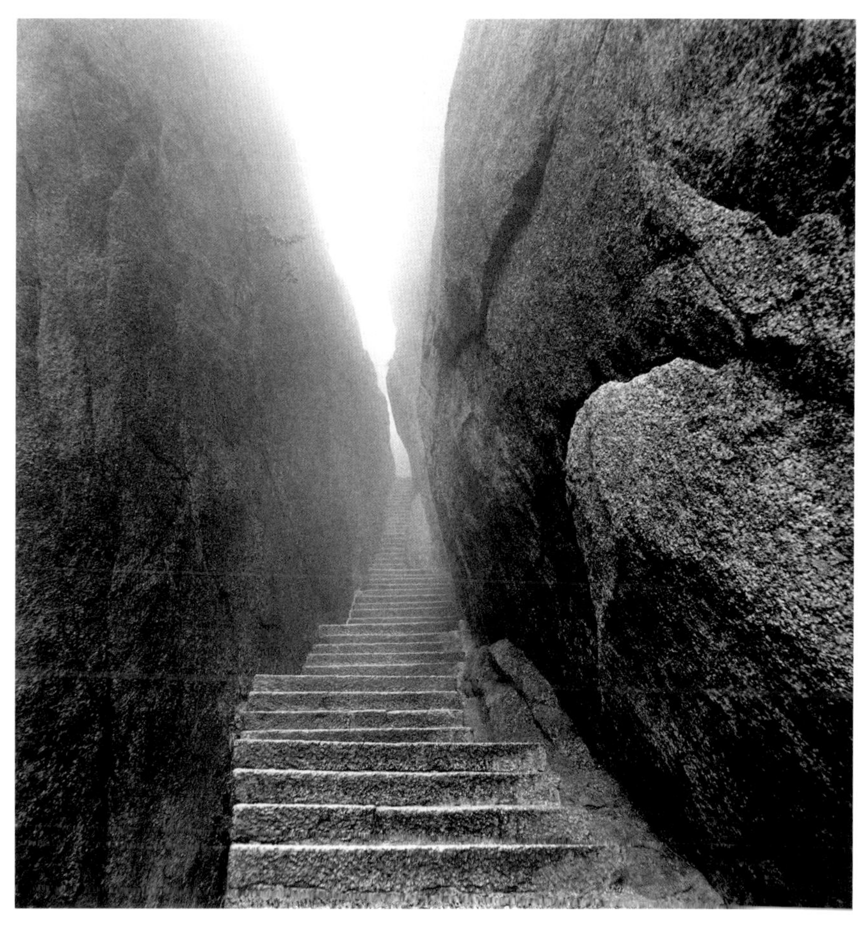

Taoist Triad at the Musée Guimet,
Paris, 2018

Huangshan Mountains, Study 32,
Anhui, 2009

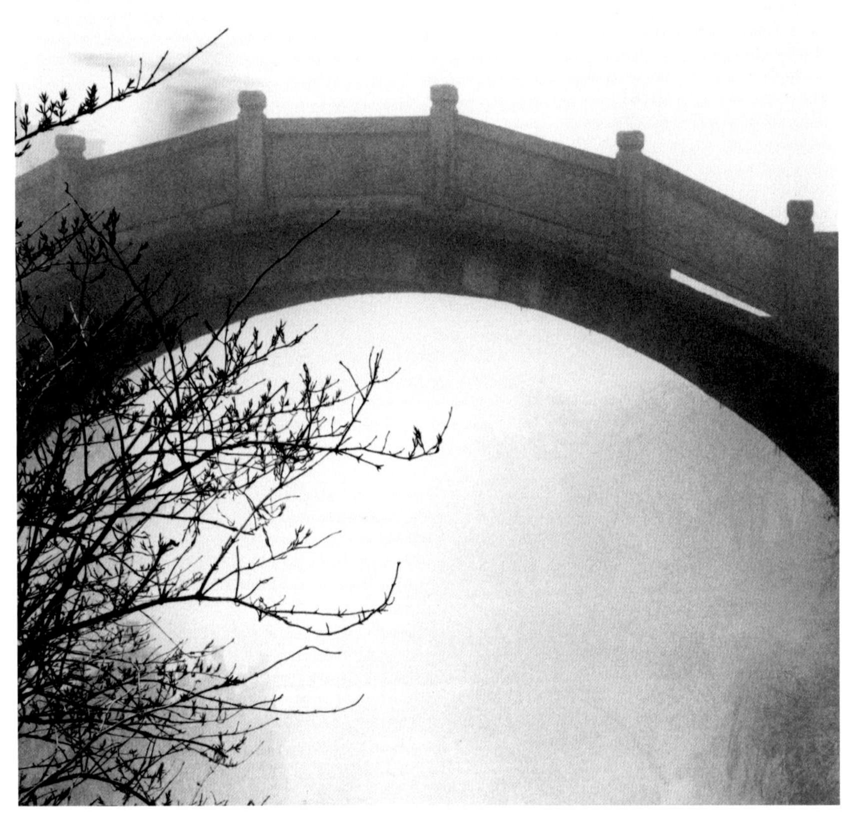

Huangshan Mountains,
Study 36, Anhui, 2008

Buddha Śākyamuni from Dunhuang,
at the Musée Guimet, Paris, 2018

CHINA

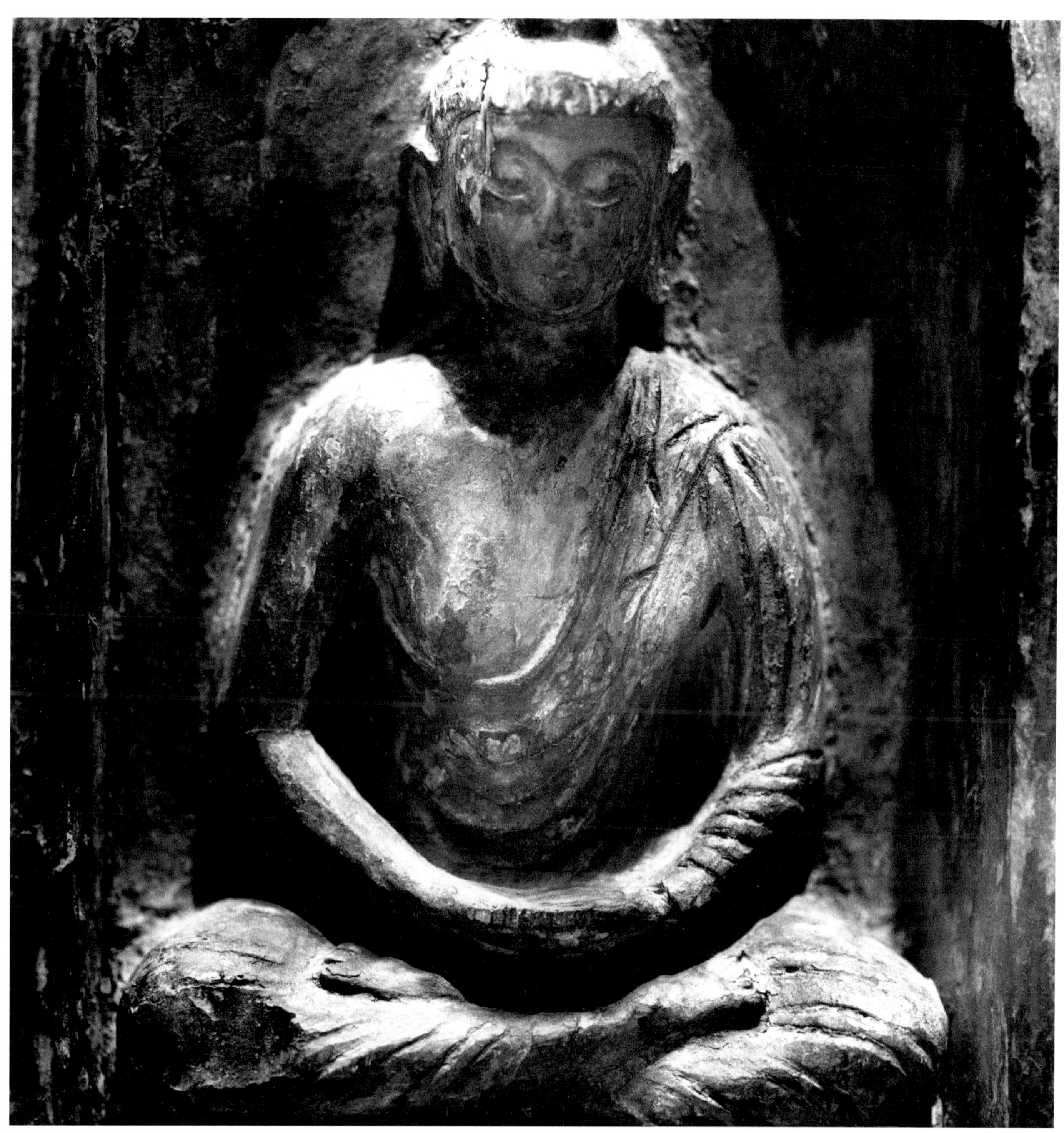

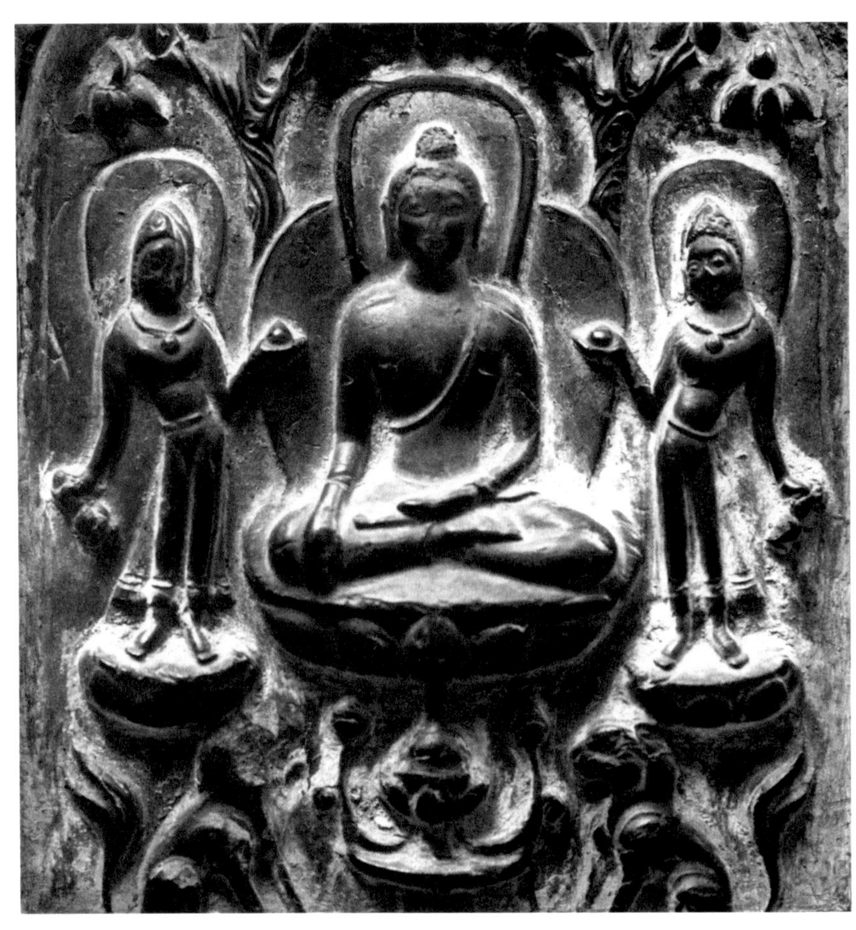

Amitābha Triad at the
Musée Guimet, Paris, 2018

Huangshan Mountains, Study 3,
Anhui, 2008

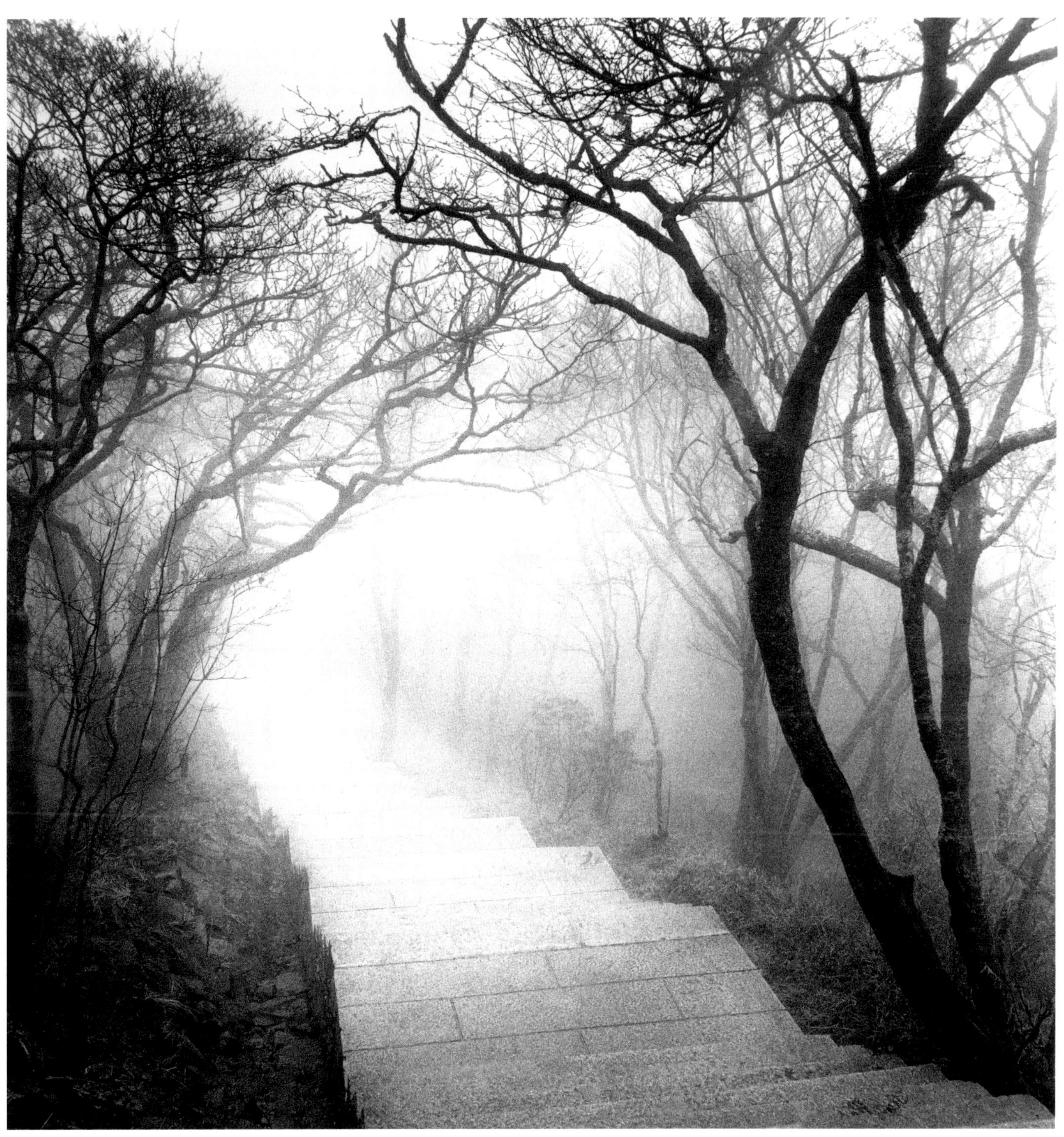

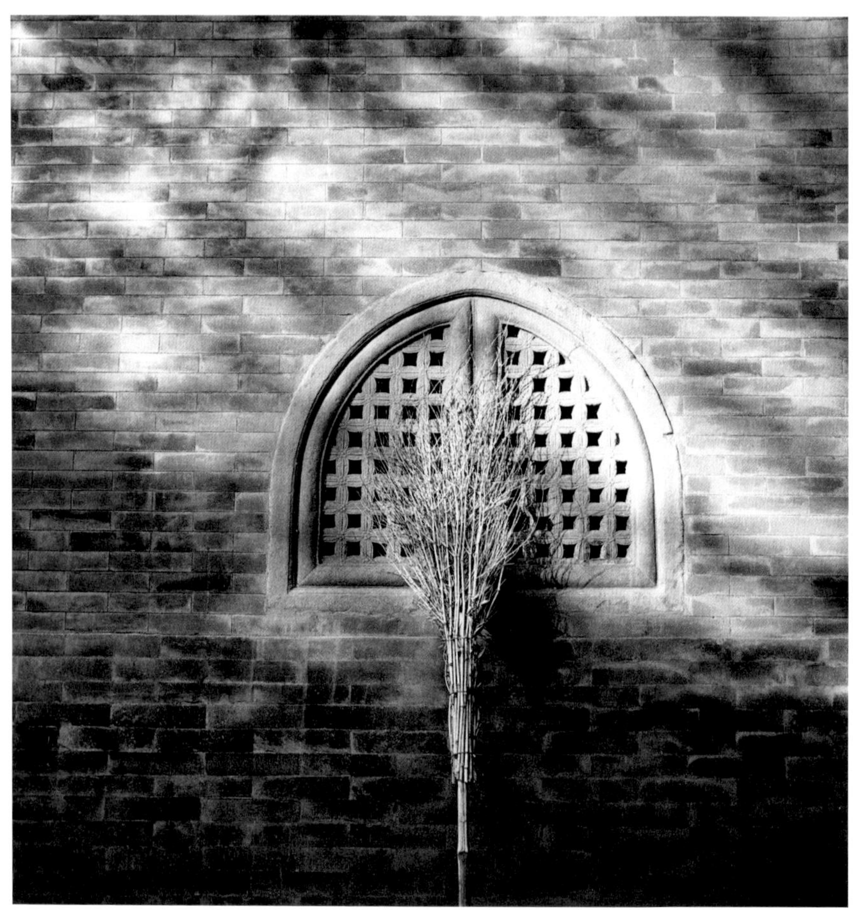

CHINA

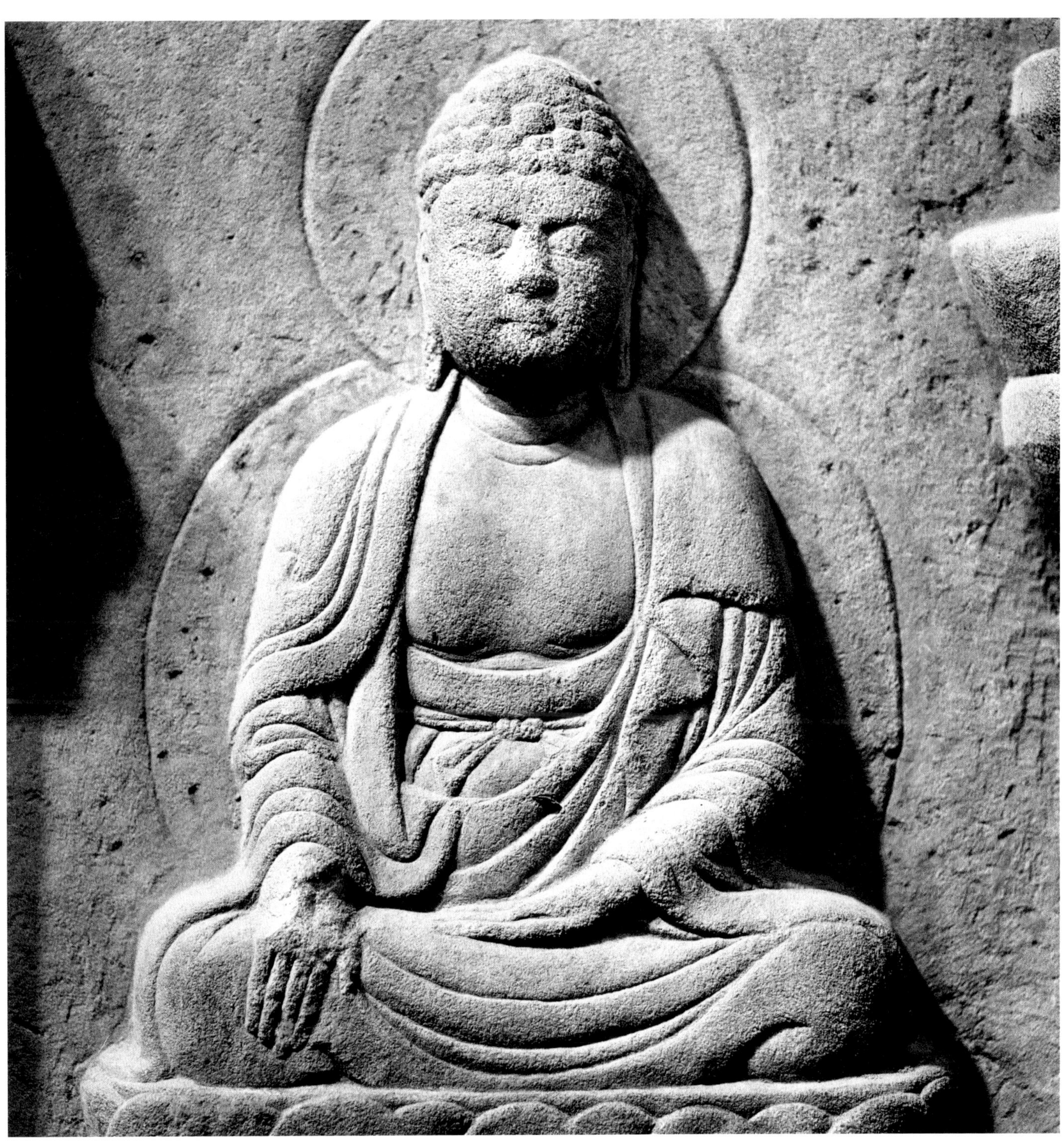

Gardener's Broom, Zhenjue Temple, Beijing, 2016

Stone Carving, Study 2, Zhenjue Temple, Beijing, 2016

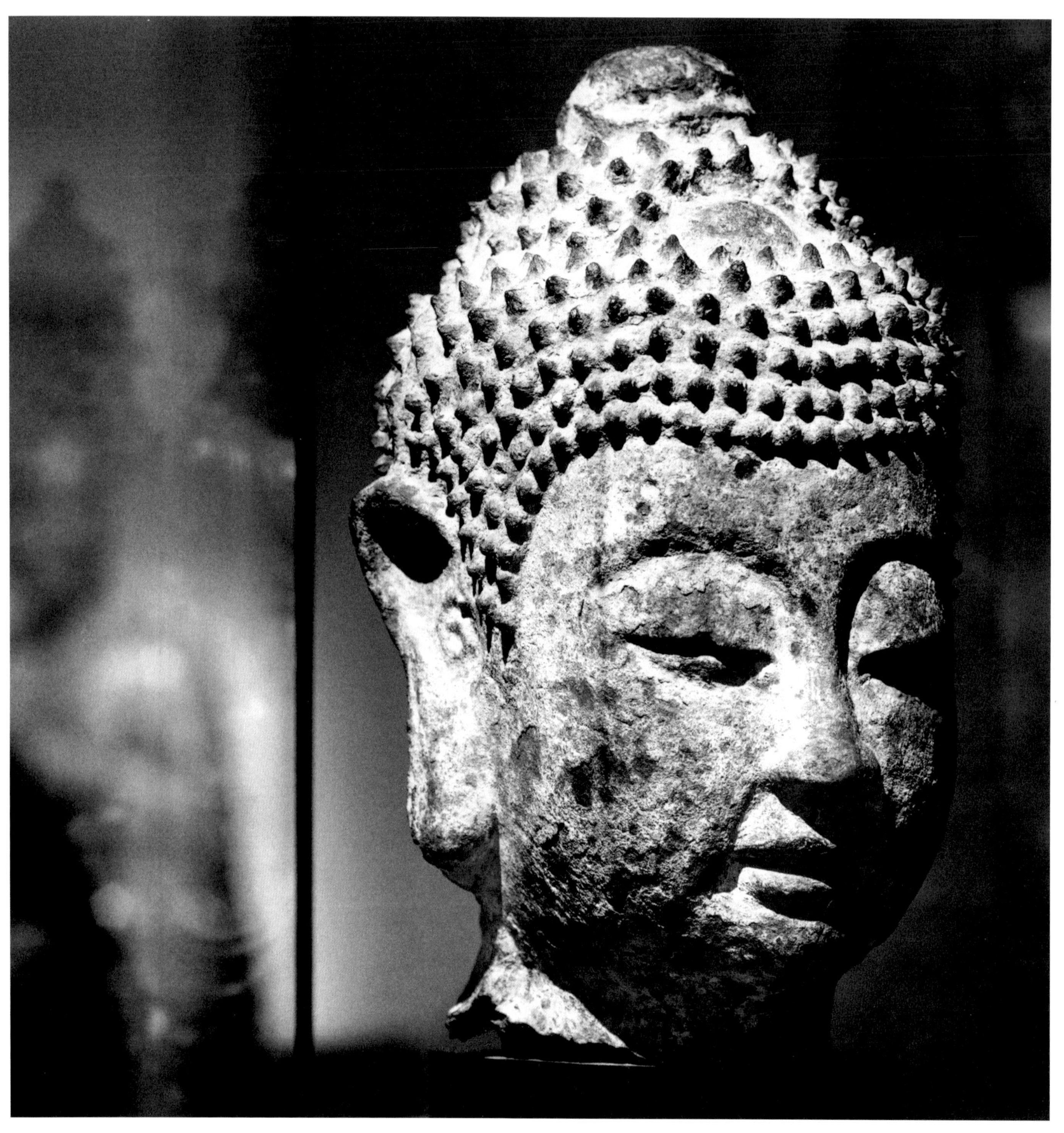

Buddha head at the
Musée Guimet,
Paris, 2018

Rooftop and Foliage,
Tanzhe Temple, Beijing, 2017

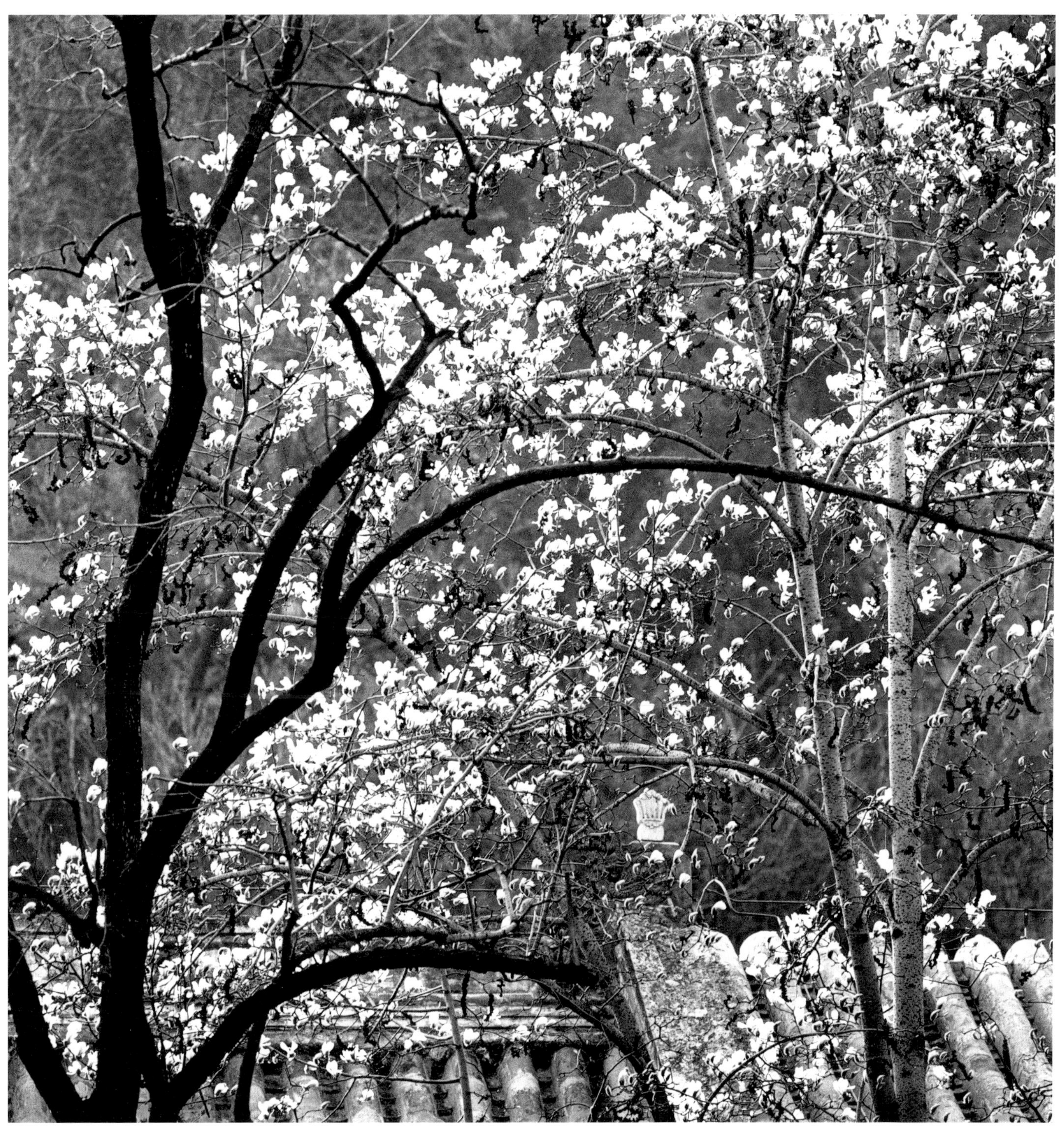

CHINA

Tian Tan Buddha,
Lantau Island, 2011

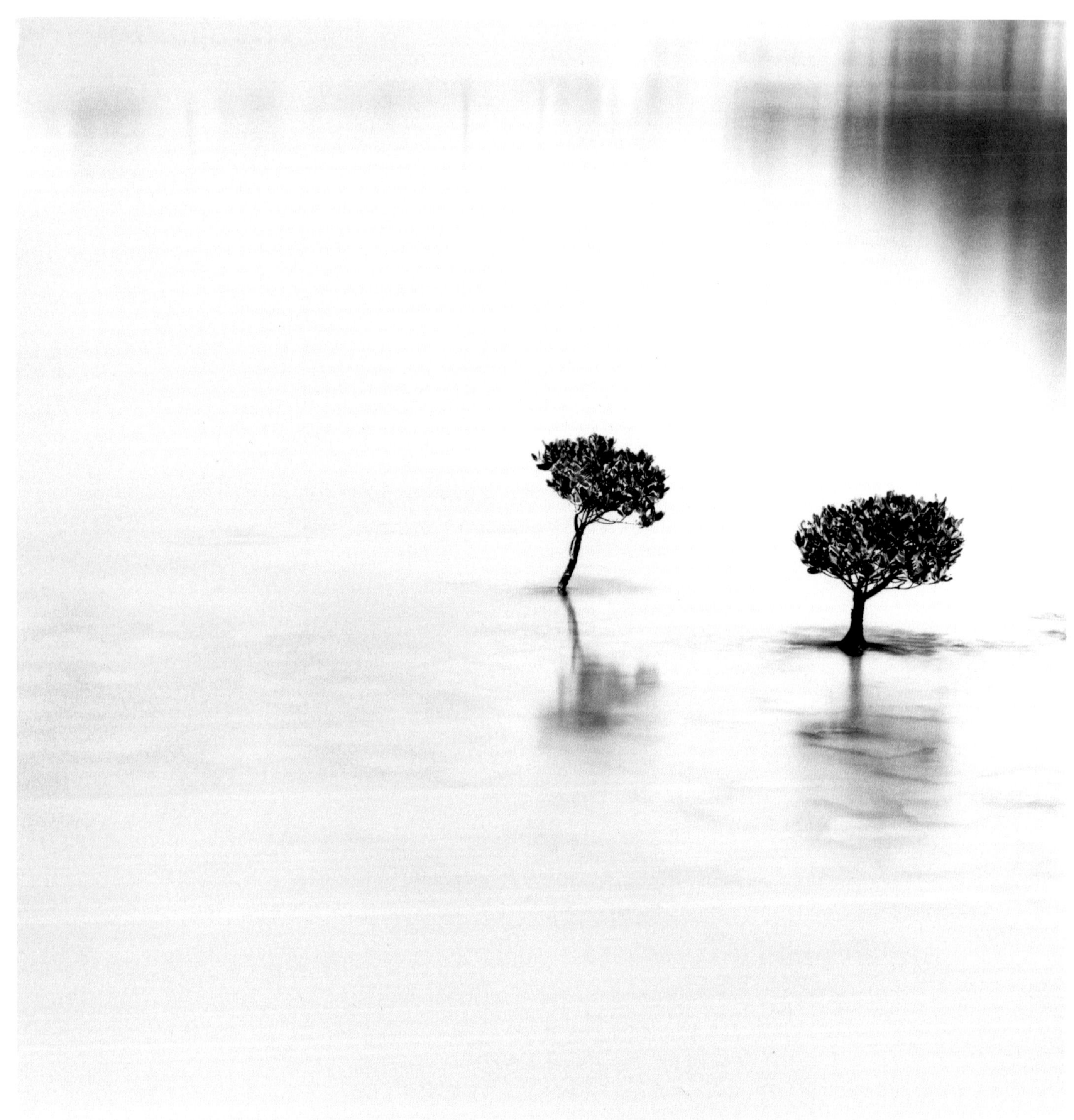

CHINA

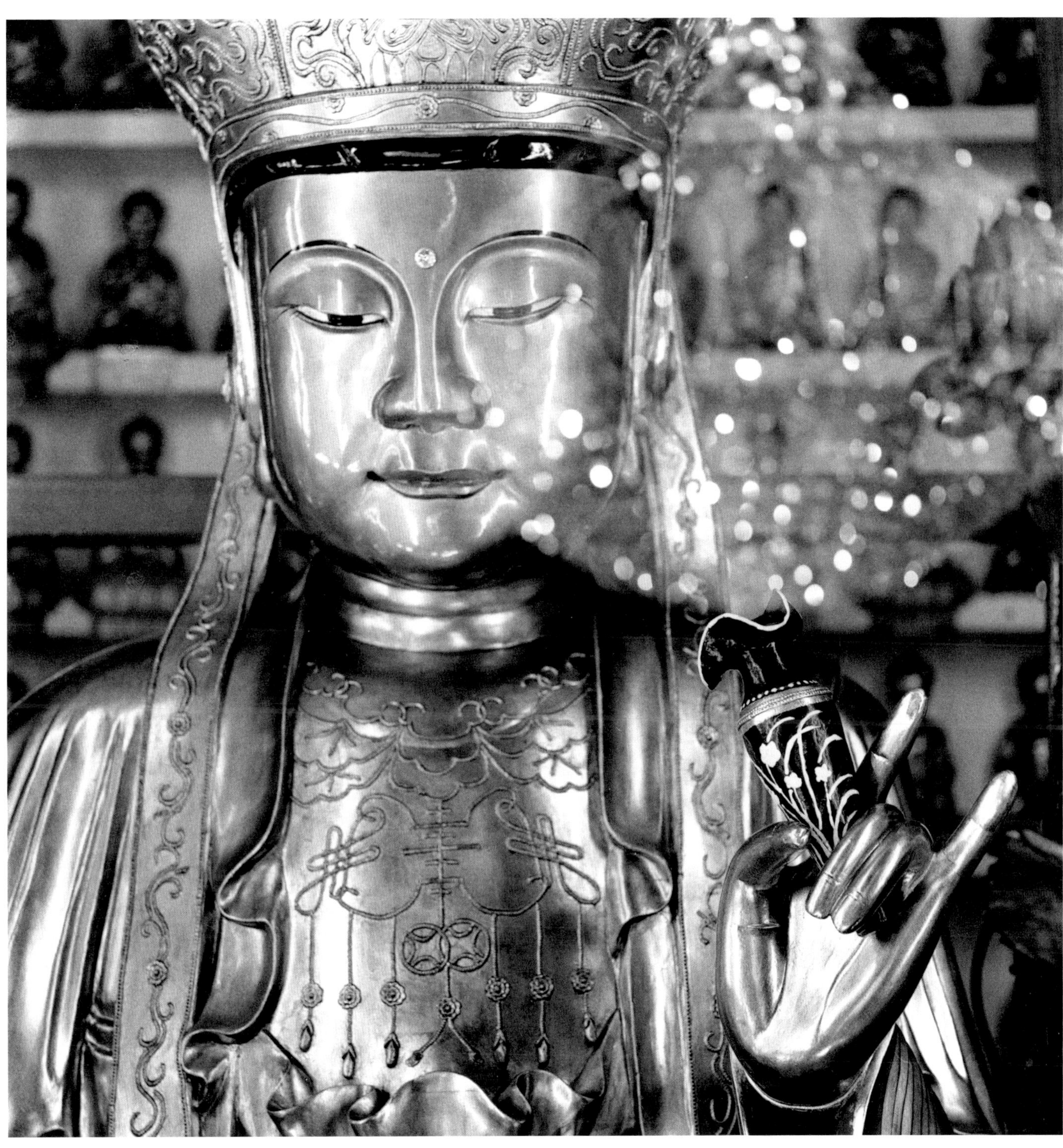

Two Mangrove Plants,
Lantau Island, 2007

Monastery Reflection,
Sha Tin, 2007

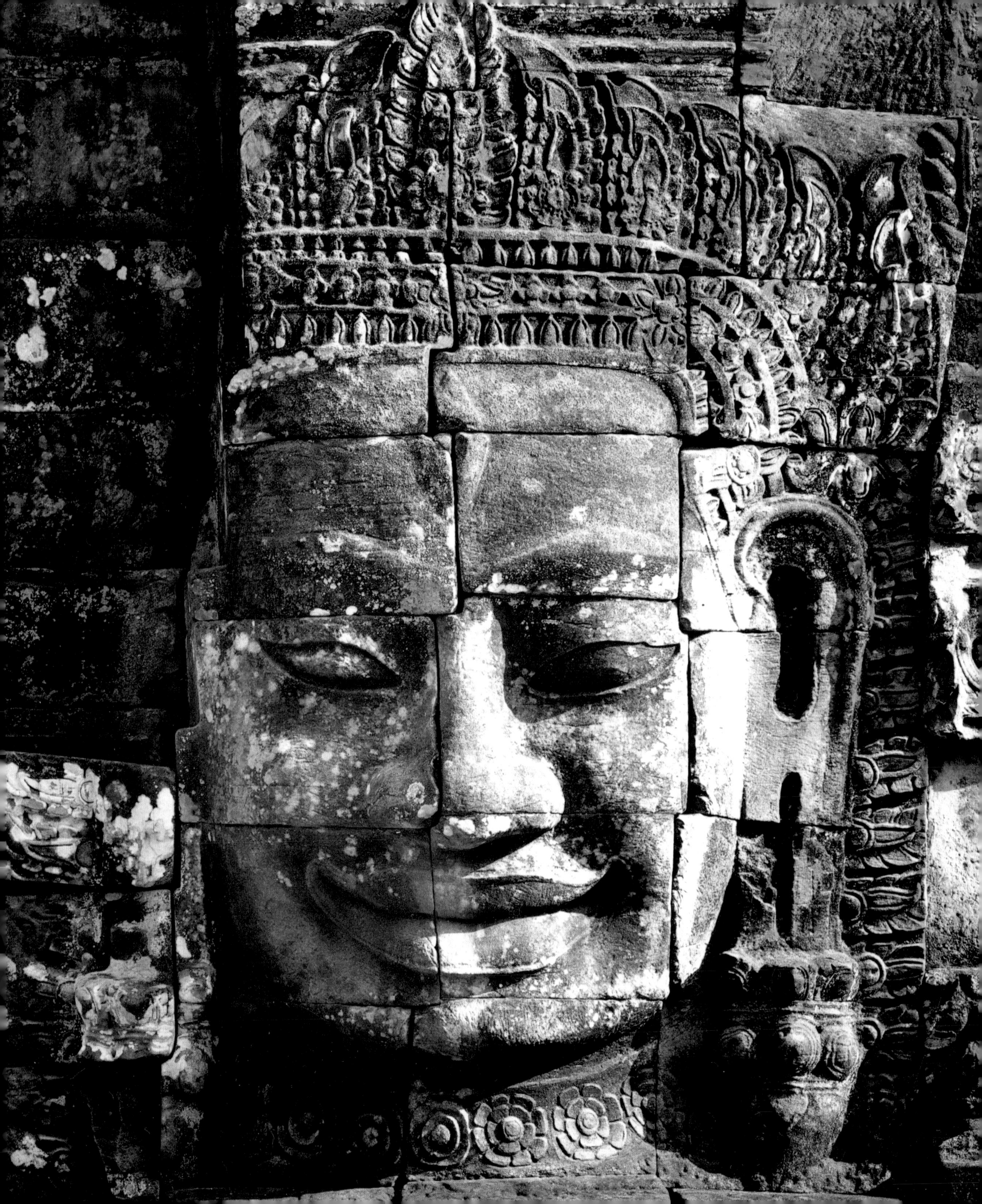

Cambodia

Bayon Temple Head, Angkor, 2018

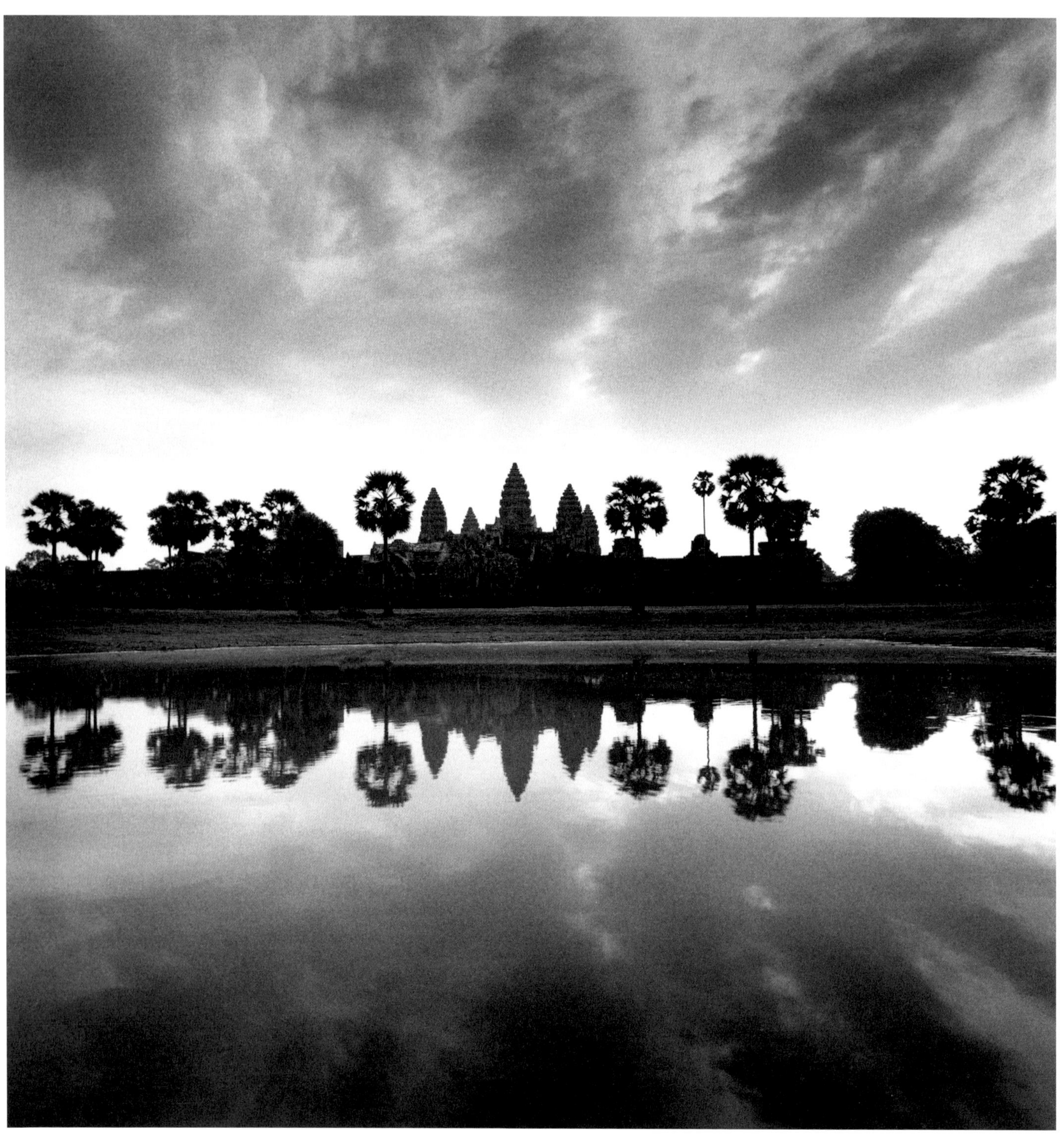

CAMBODIA

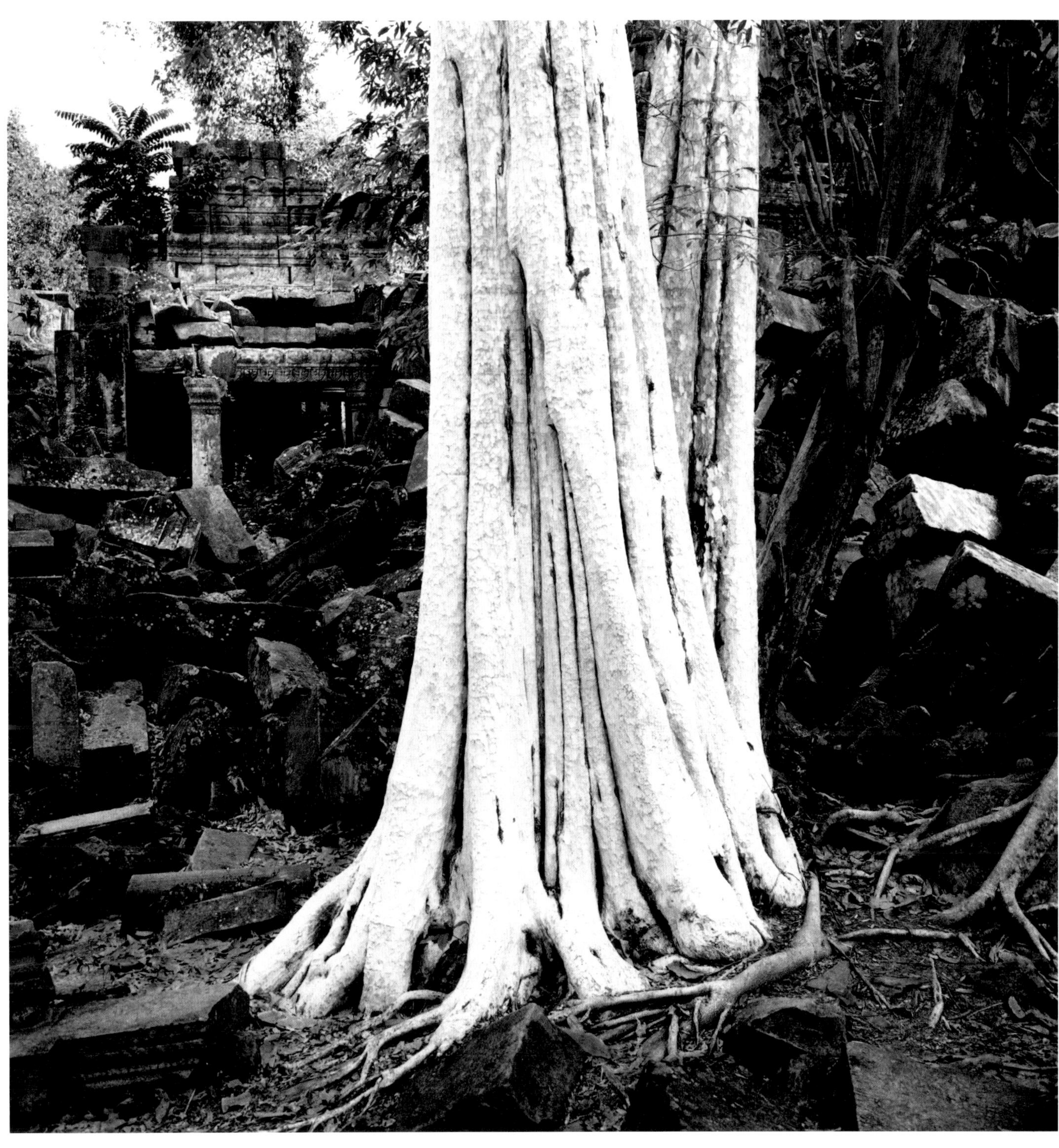

Daybreak Reflection,
Angkor Wat, 2018

Tree and Temple, Ta Prohm, 2018

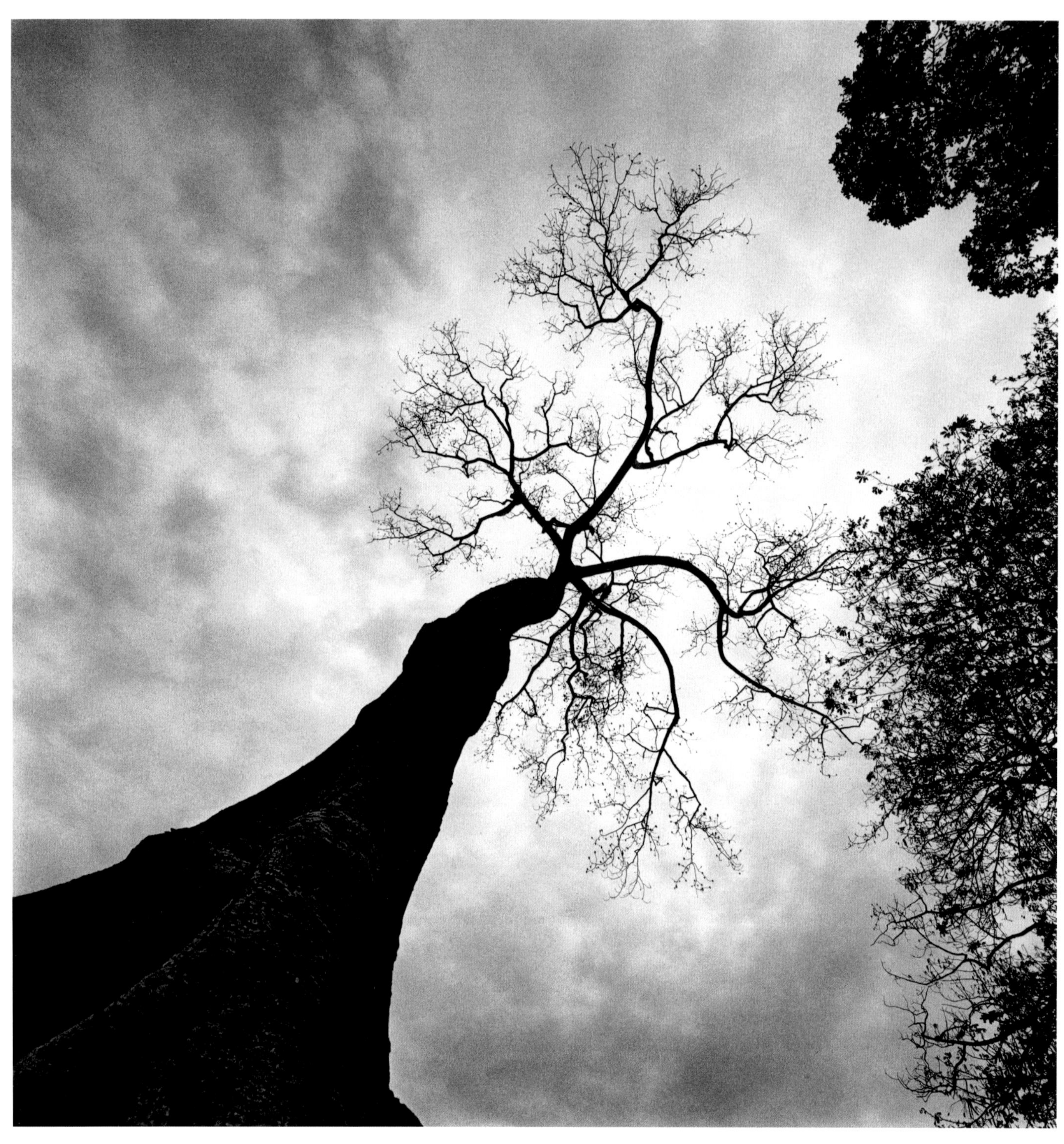

Ta Prohm Tree, Study 2,
Angkor, 2018

Ta Prohm Windows,
Angkor, 2018

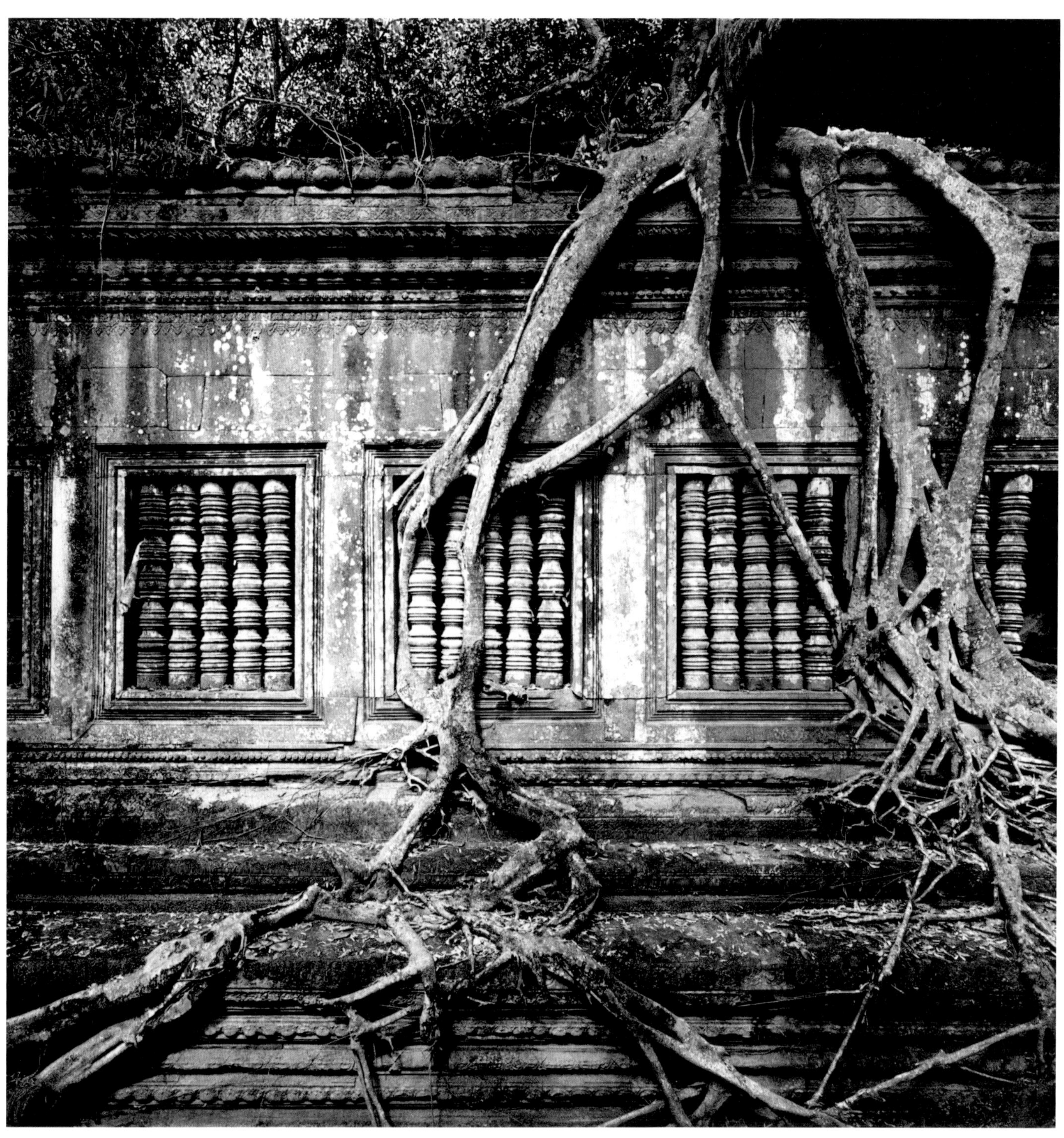

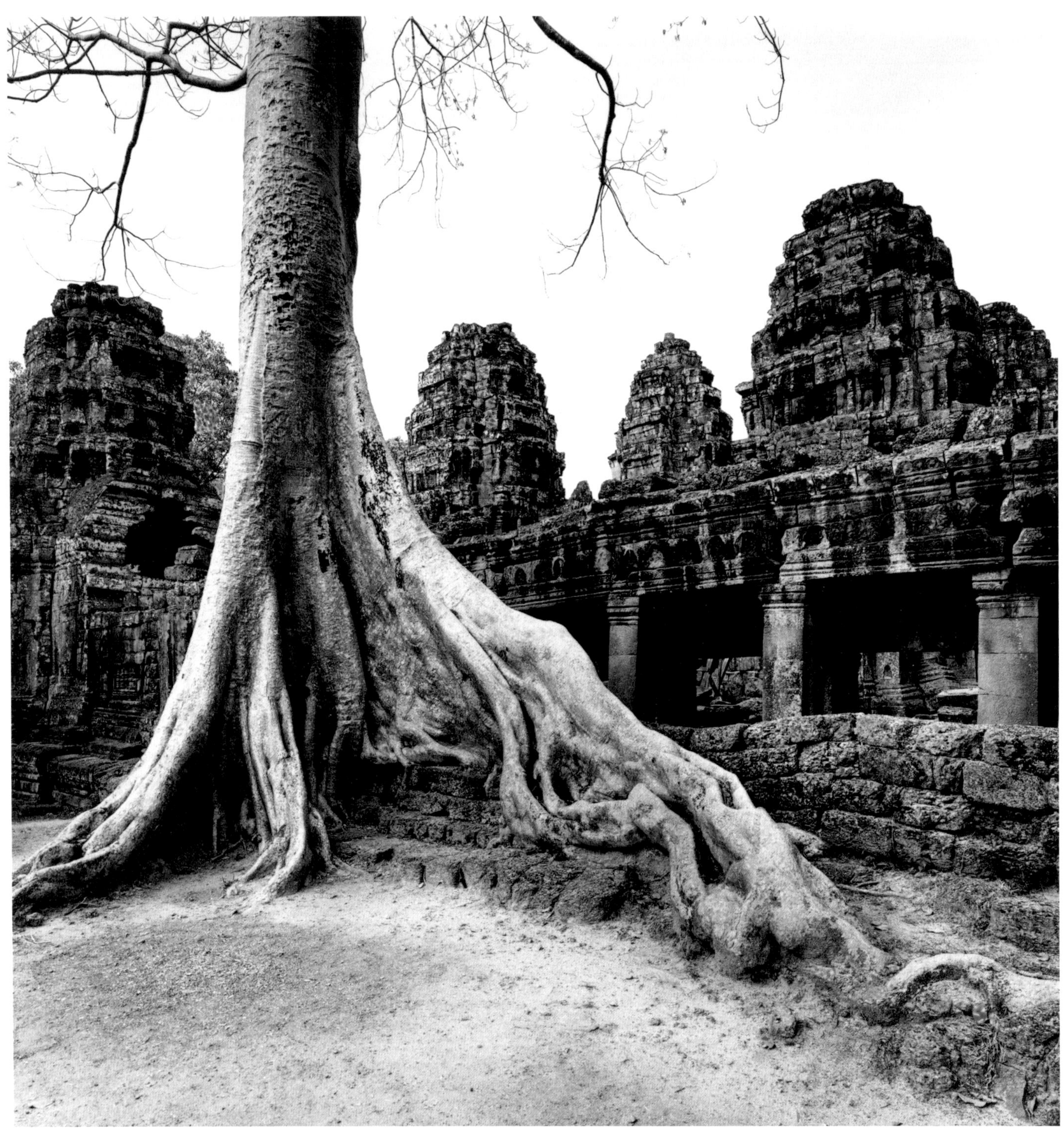

Fig Tree,
Angkor Thom, 2018

Bayon Temple Heads,
Angkor, 2018

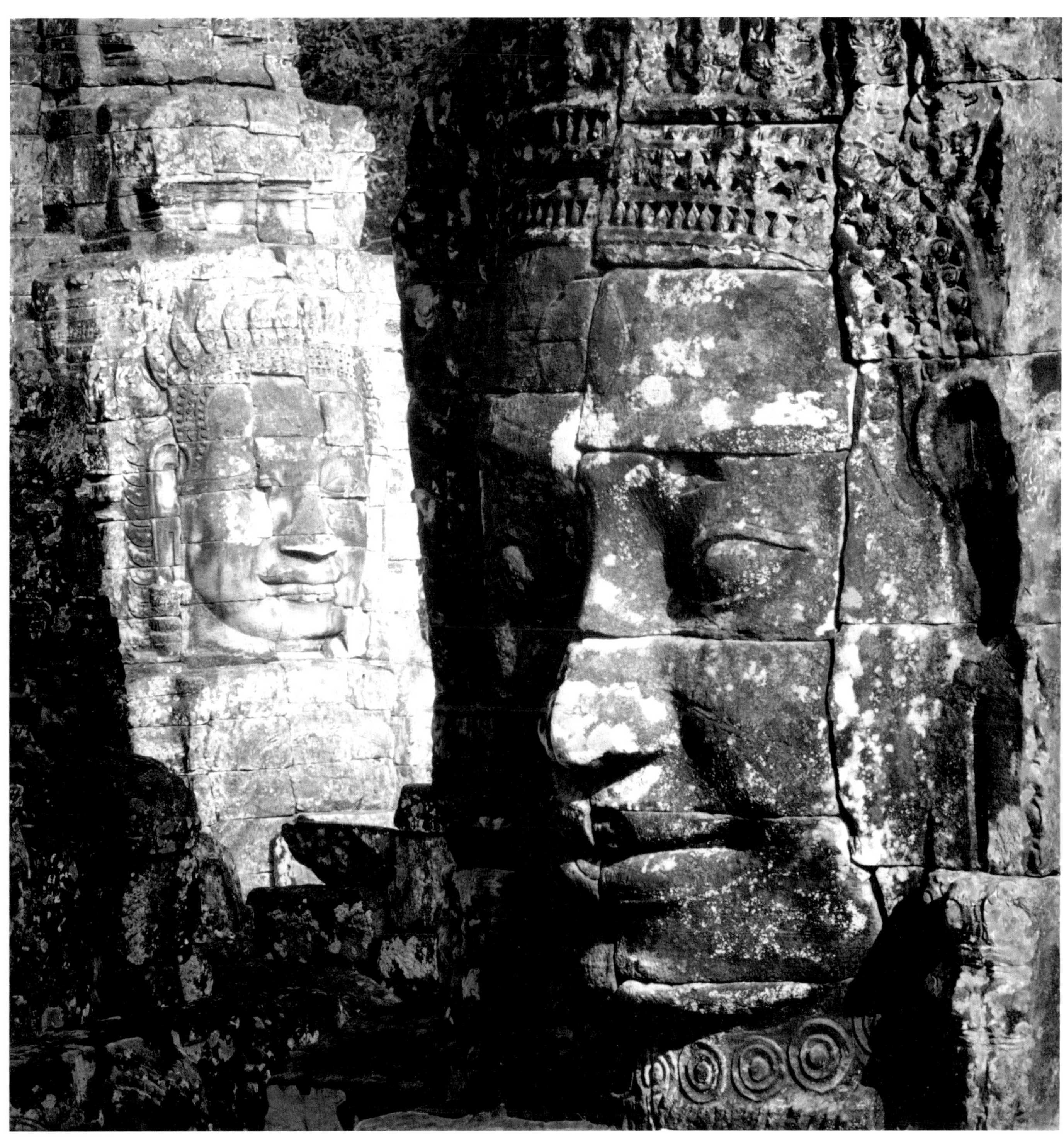

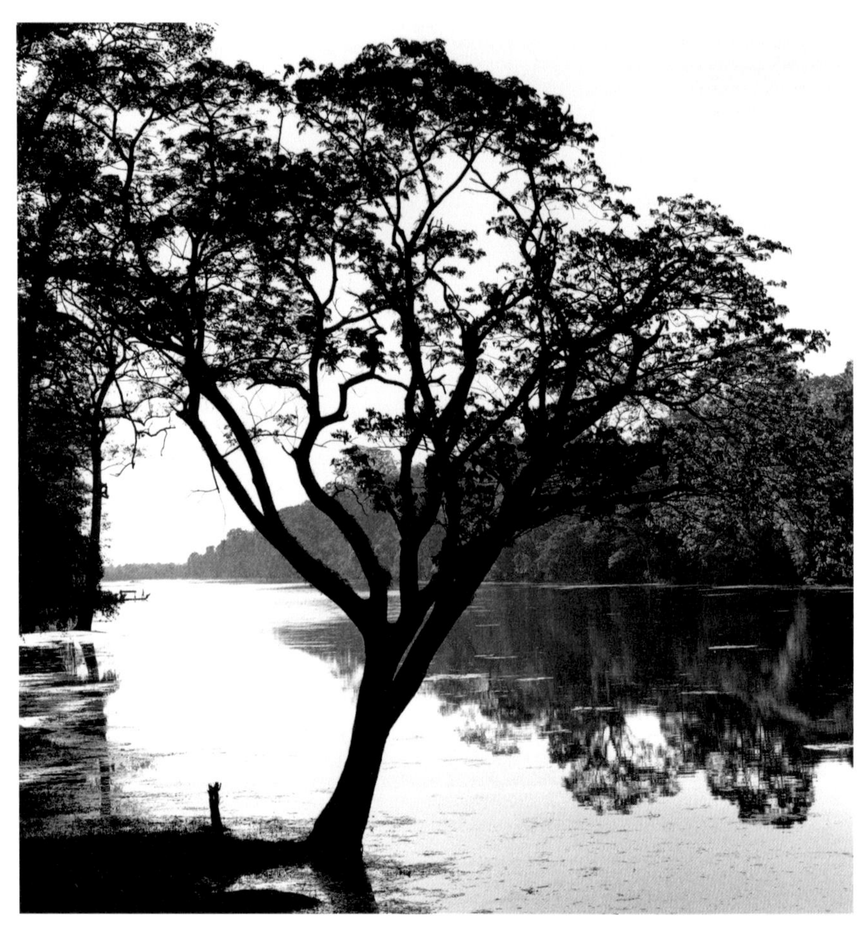

CAMBODIA

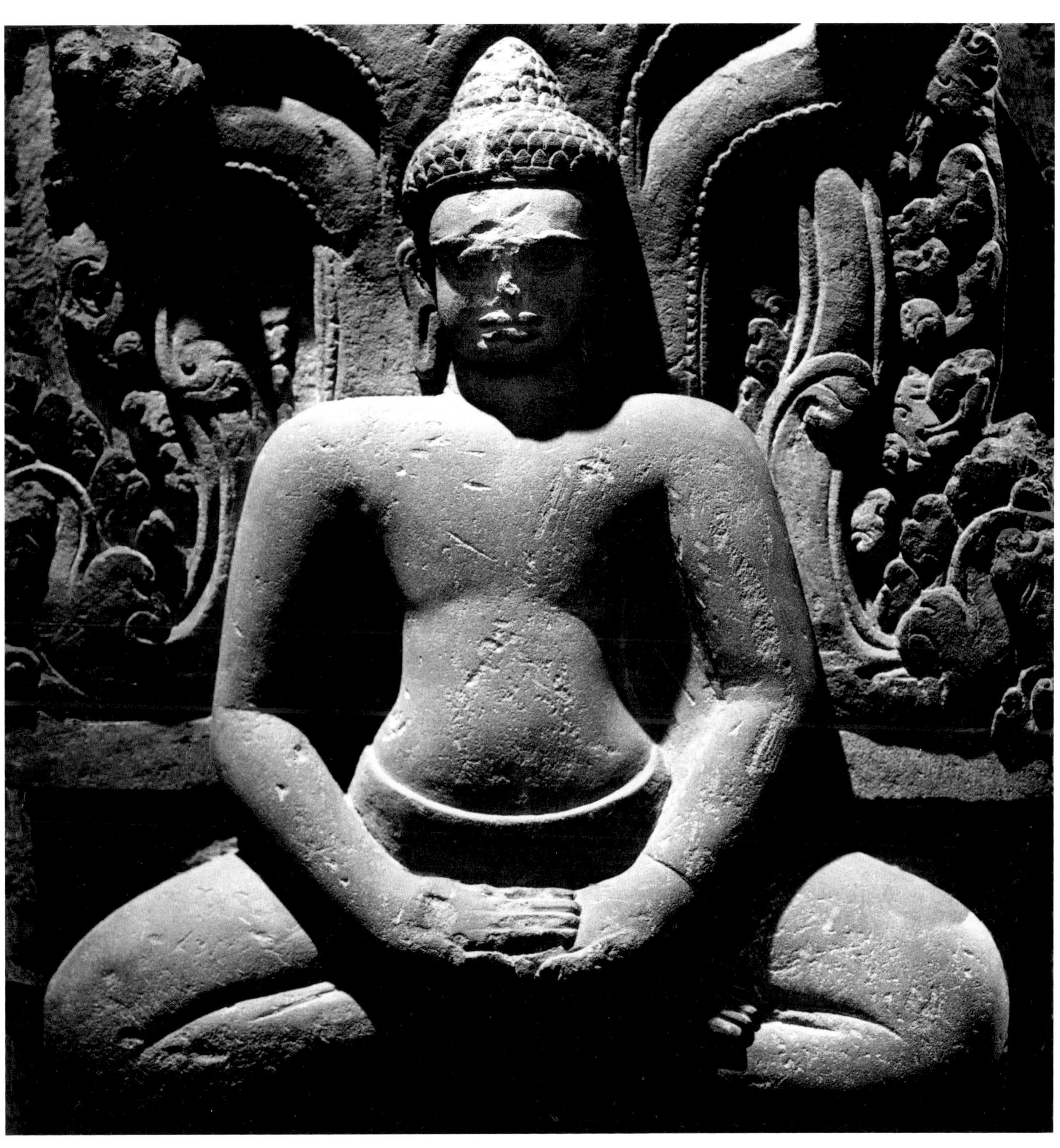

Near Angkor Thom,
Siem Reap, 2018

Buddhist monument (detail),
from the Phnom Srok district,
at the Musée Guimet, Paris, 2018

A moulding at the Bayon Temple, Angkor, at the Musée Guimet, Paris, 2018

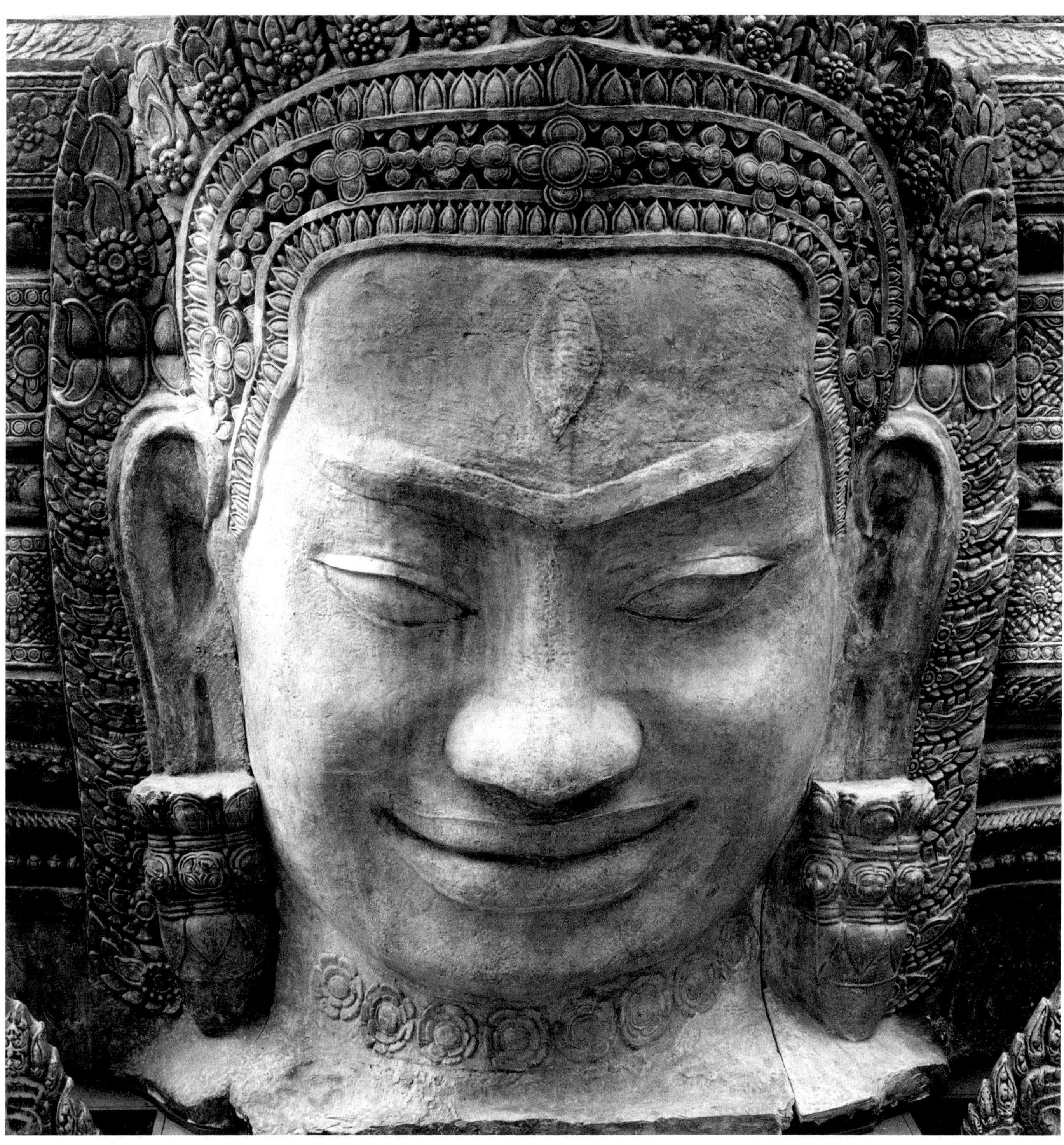

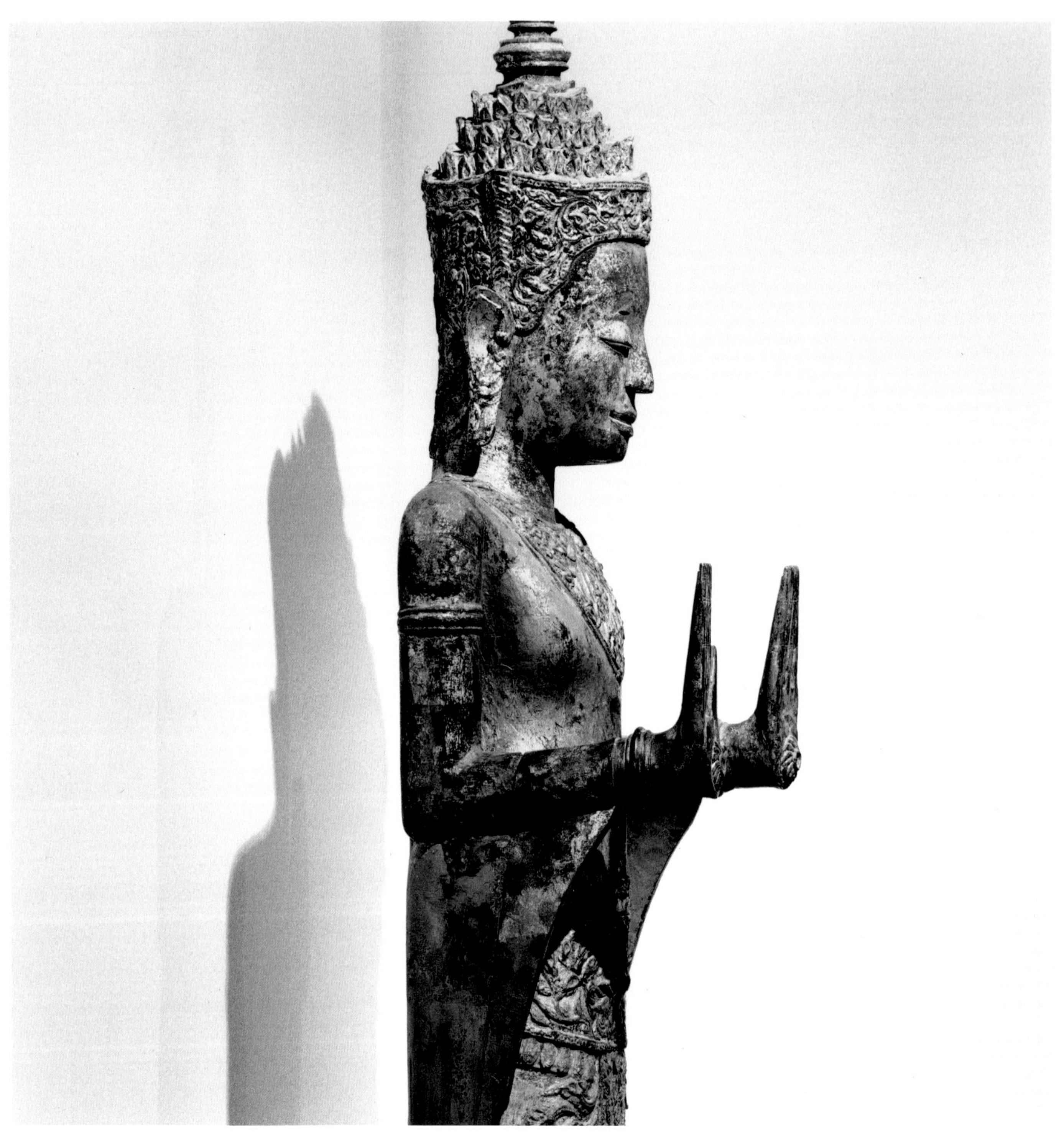

CAMBODIA

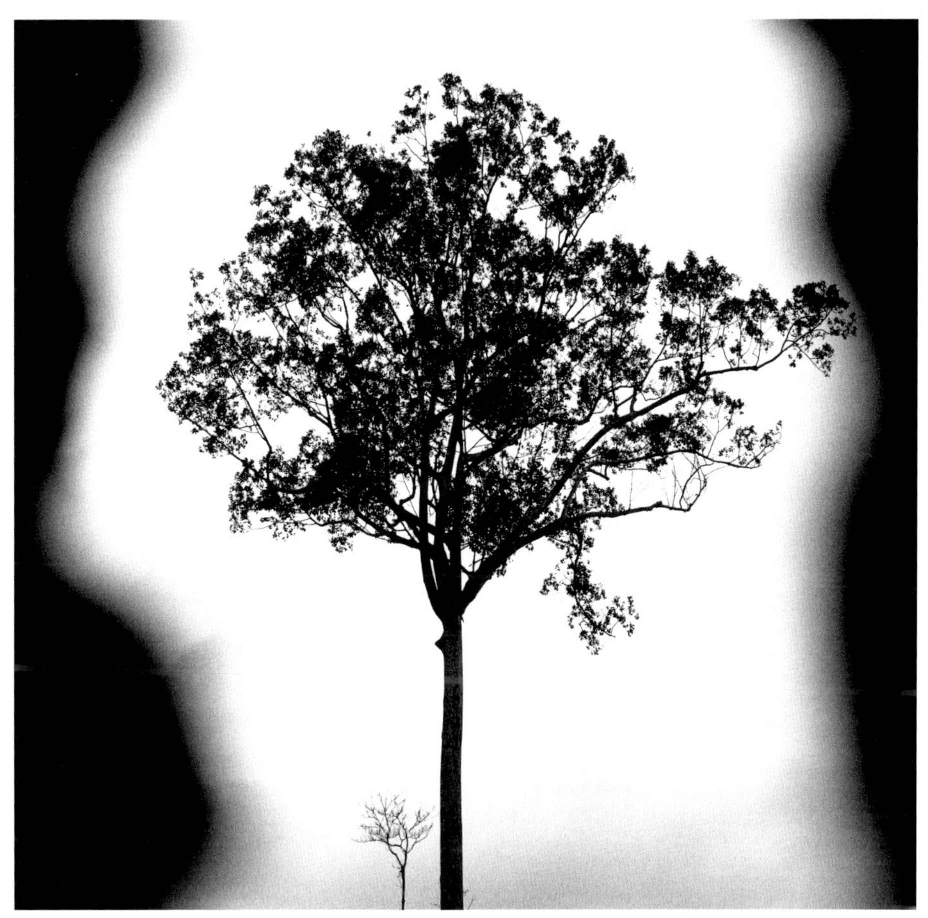

Adorned Buddha at the
Musée Guimet, Paris, 2018

Banteay Srei Trees,
Angkor, 2018

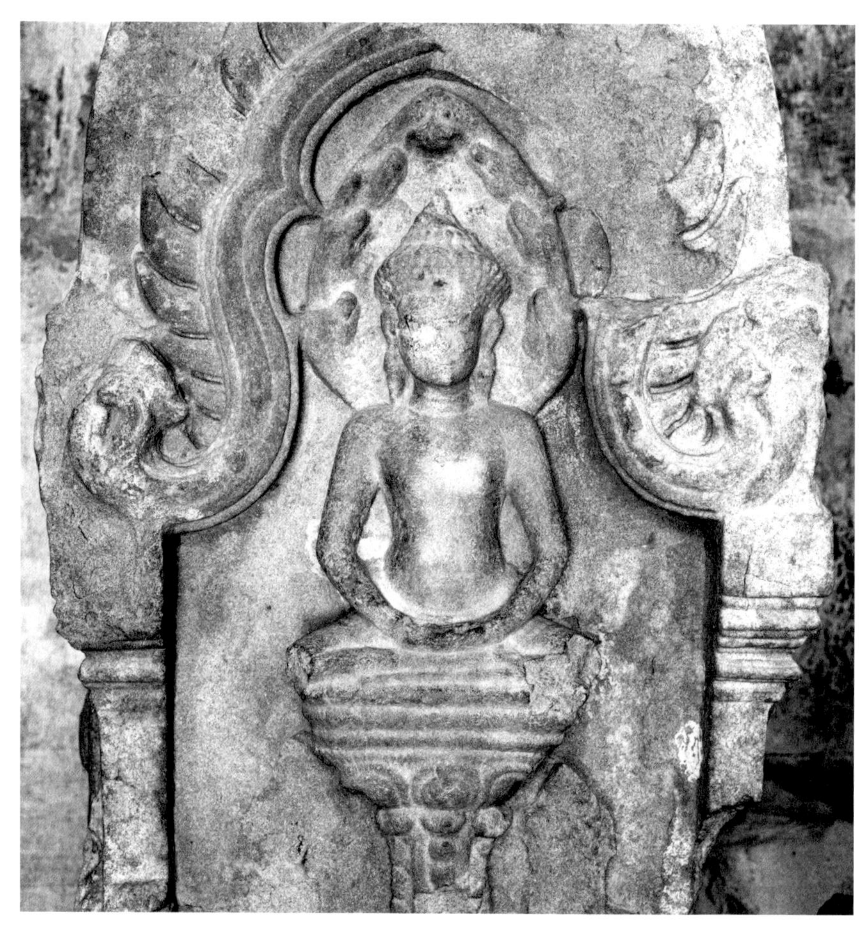

Buddha Relief,
Angkor Wat, 2018

Buddha and Flowers,
Angkor Wat, 2018

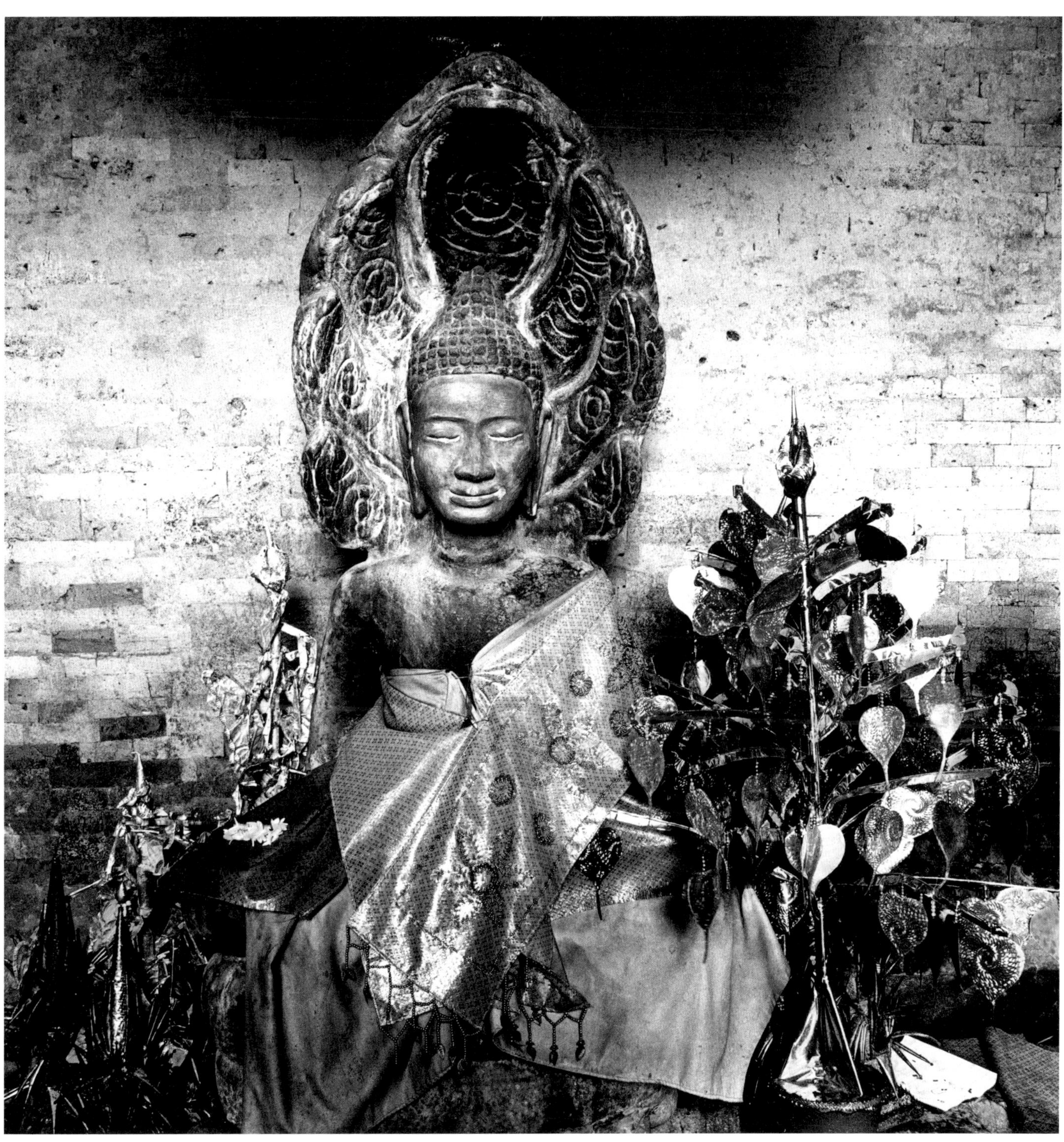

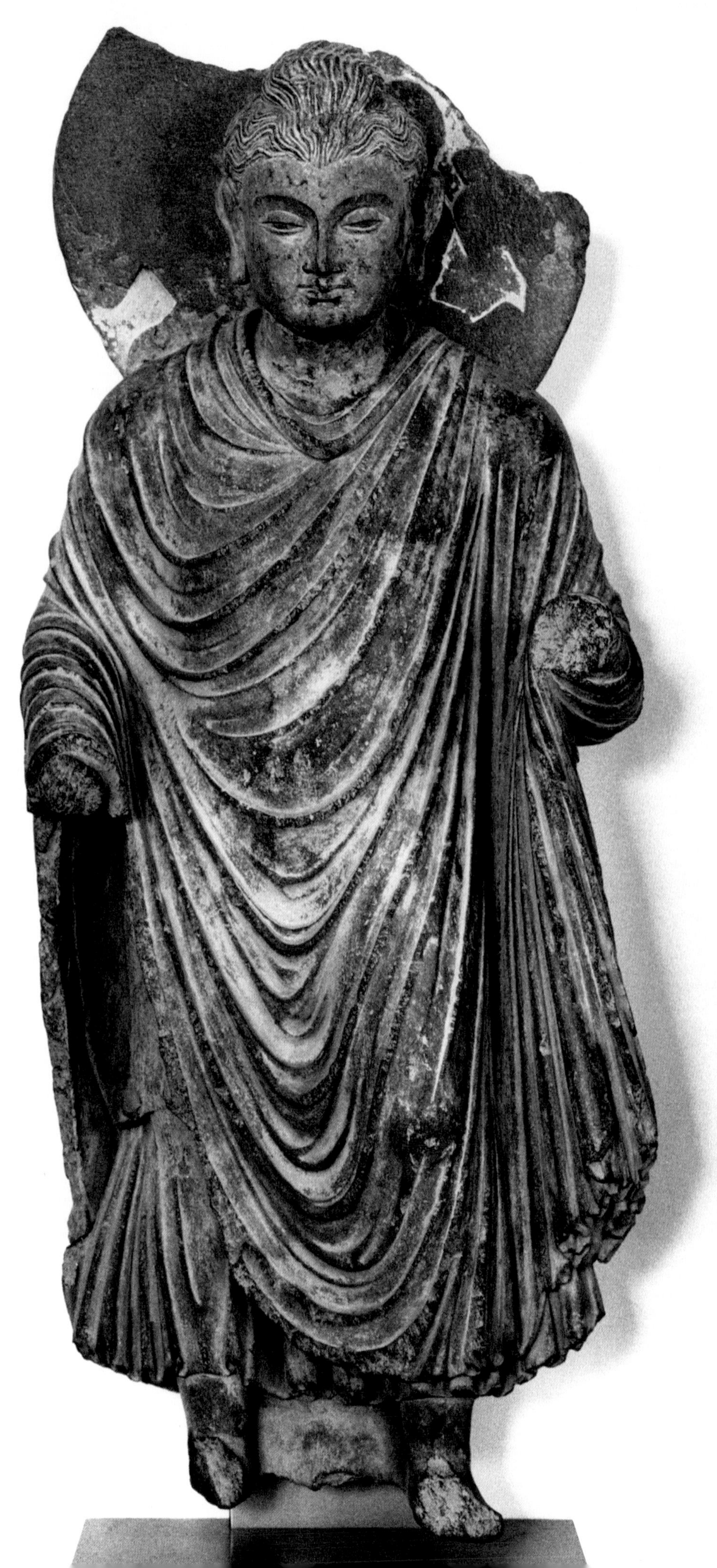

India
Afghanistan
Pakistan

Standing Buddha from the Gandhāra region, at the Musée Guimet, Paris, 2018

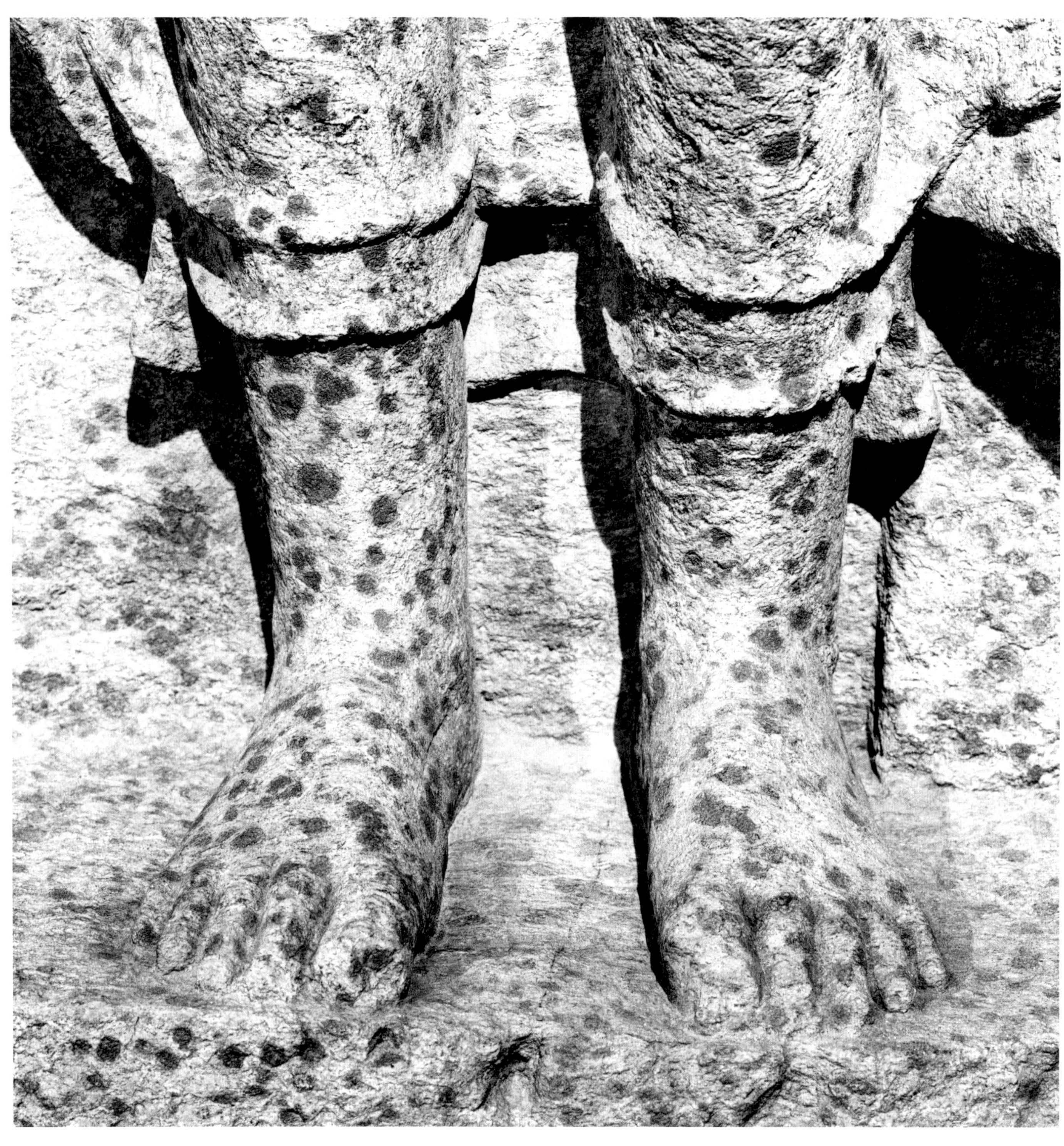

Buddha, presumably from
Lalitgiri, at the Musée Guimet,
Paris, 2018

Tea Estates, Study 1,
Munnar, 2008

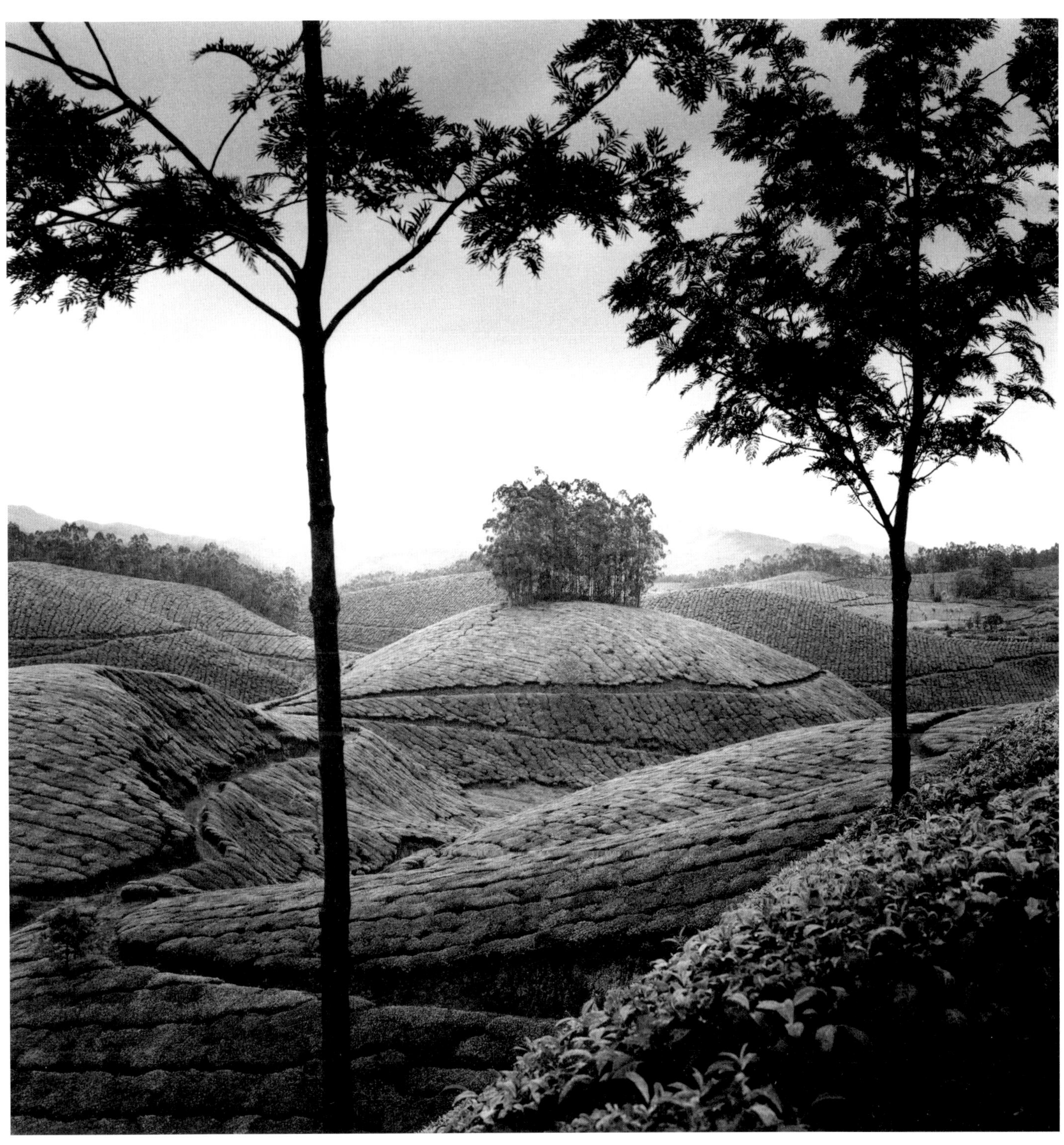

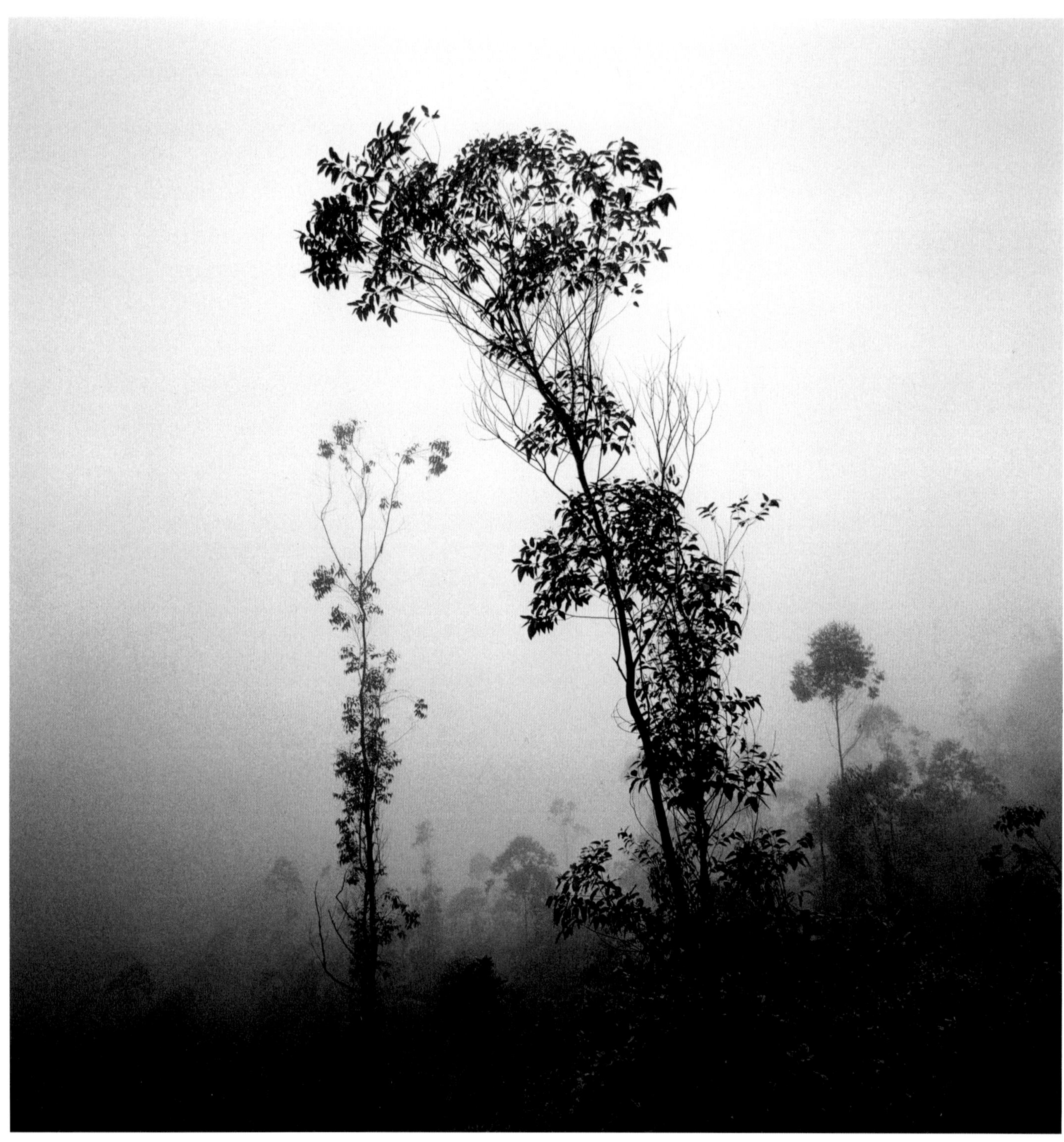

INDIA

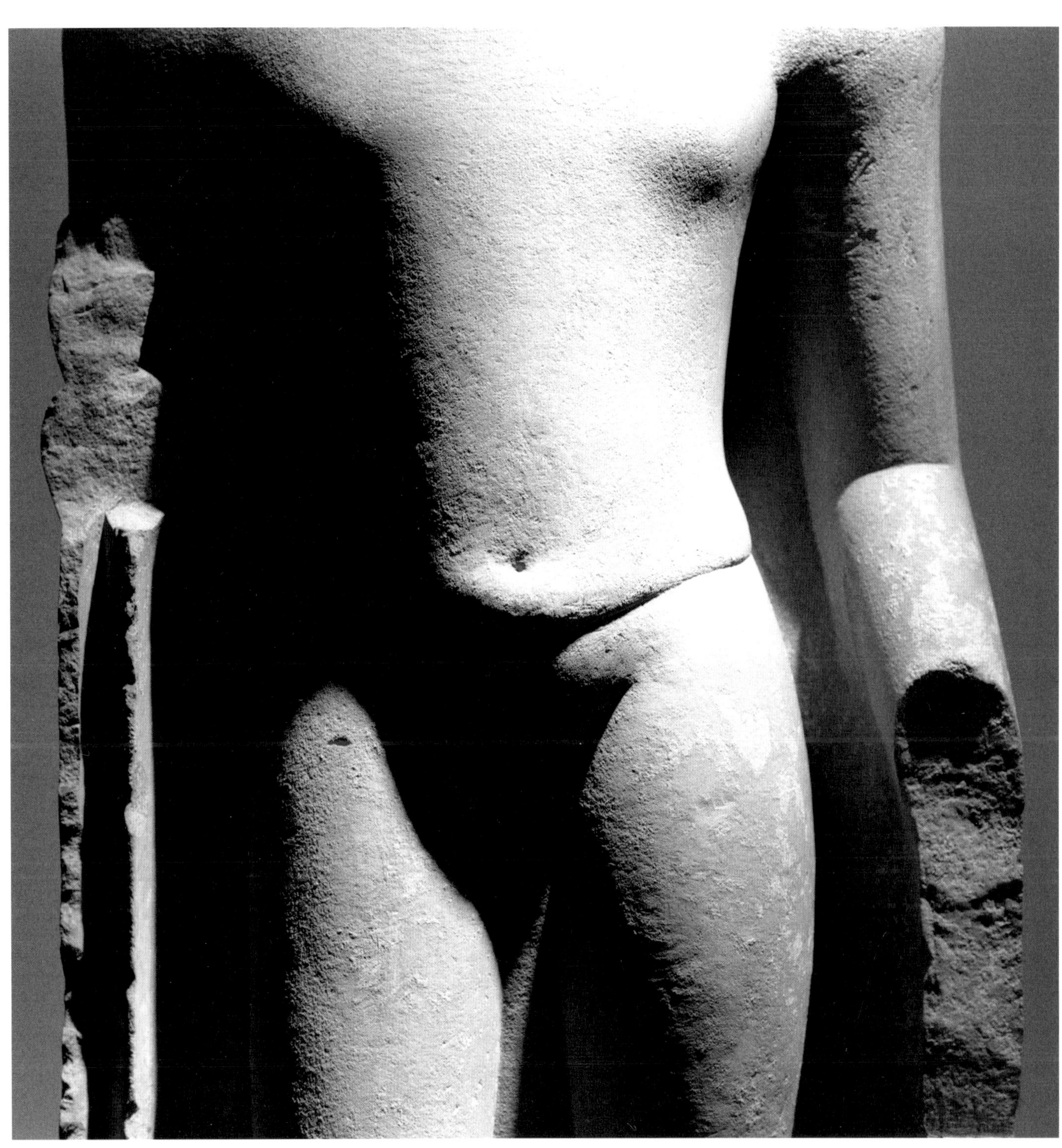

Mountain Trees, Raja Mala,
Munnar, 2008

Standing Buddha, Sarnath,
at the Musée Guimet,
Paris, 2018

AFGHANISTAN

Seated Buddha meditating,
from the Kapisa region,
at the Musée Guimet, Paris, 2018

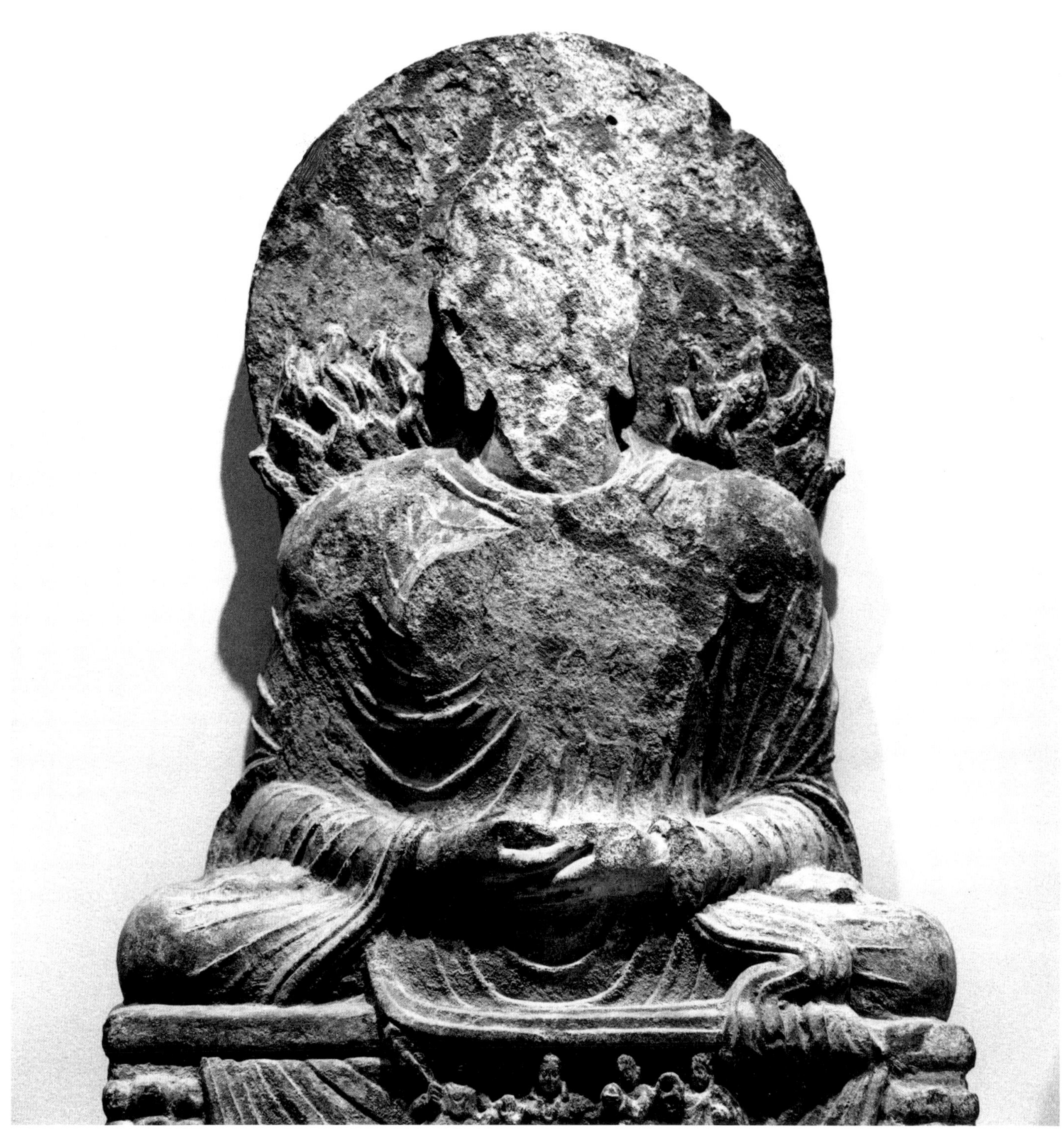

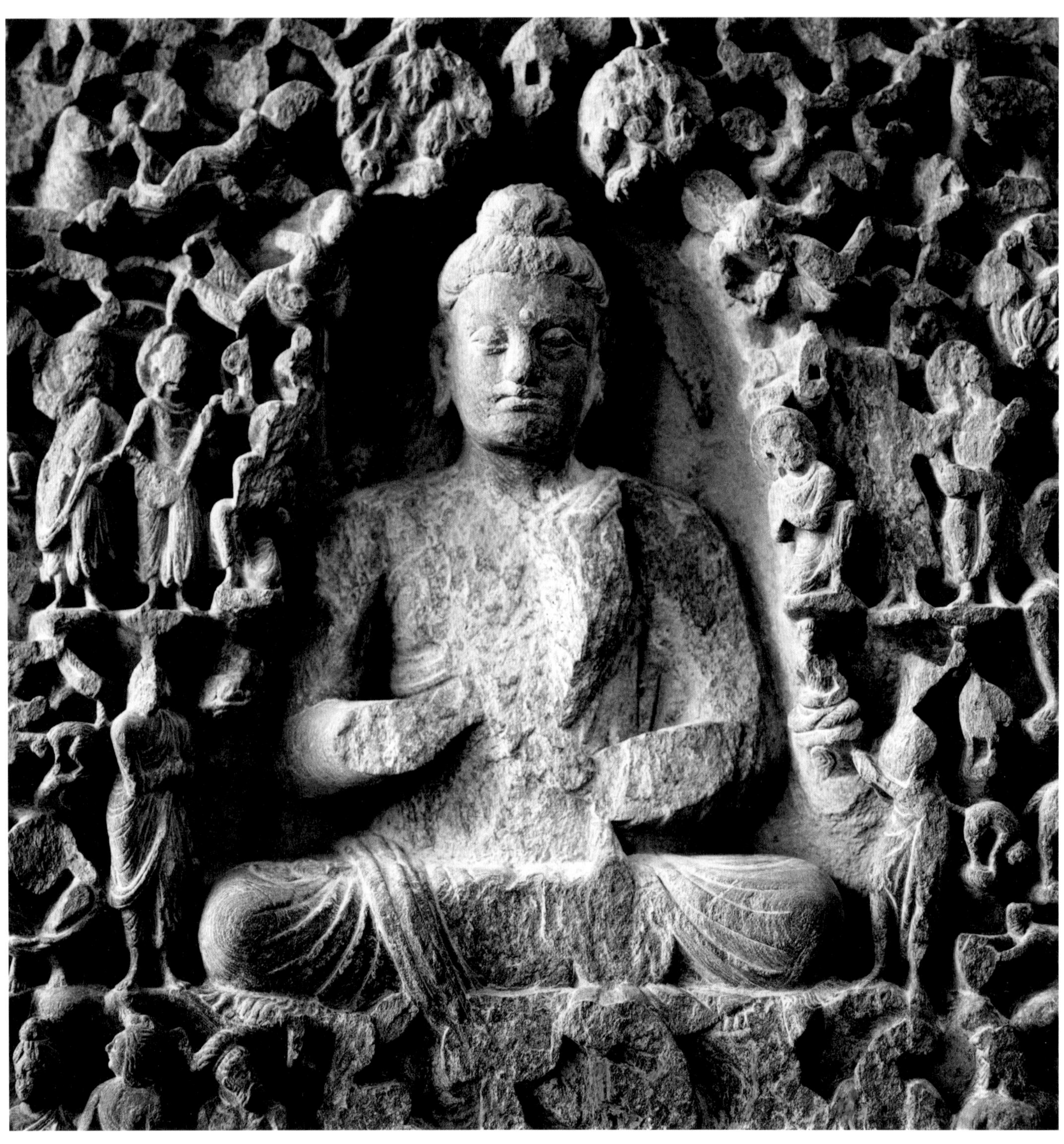

Teaching Buddha from the Gandhāra region, at the Musée Guimet, Paris, 2018

Standing Buddha from the Gandhāra region, at the Musée Guimet, Paris, 2018

PAKISTAN

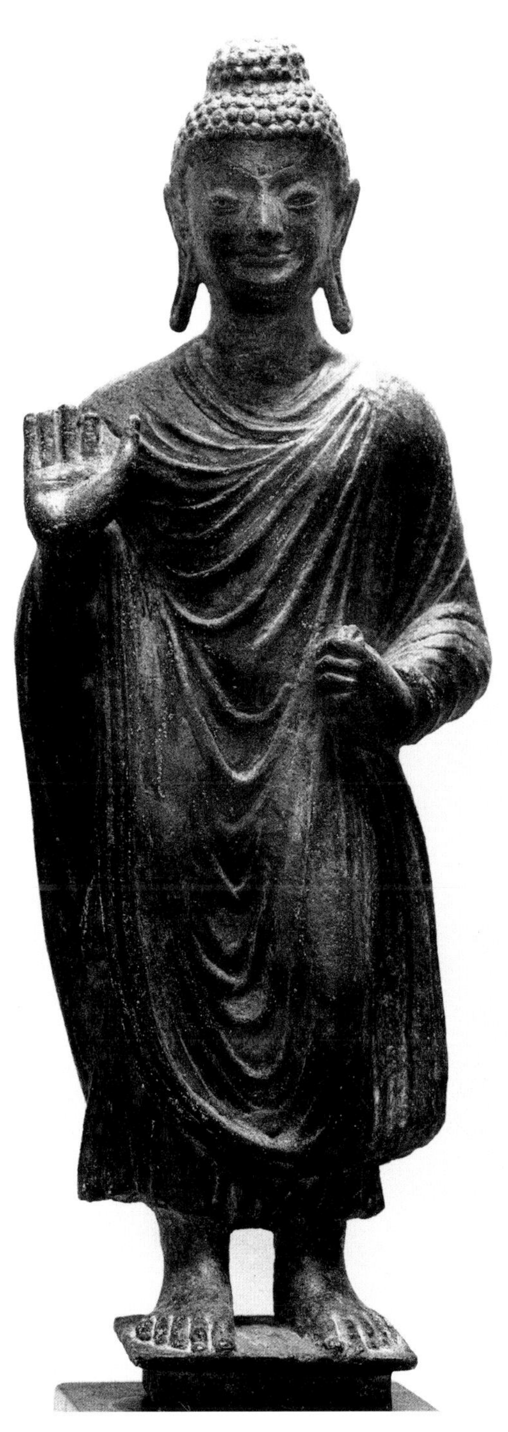

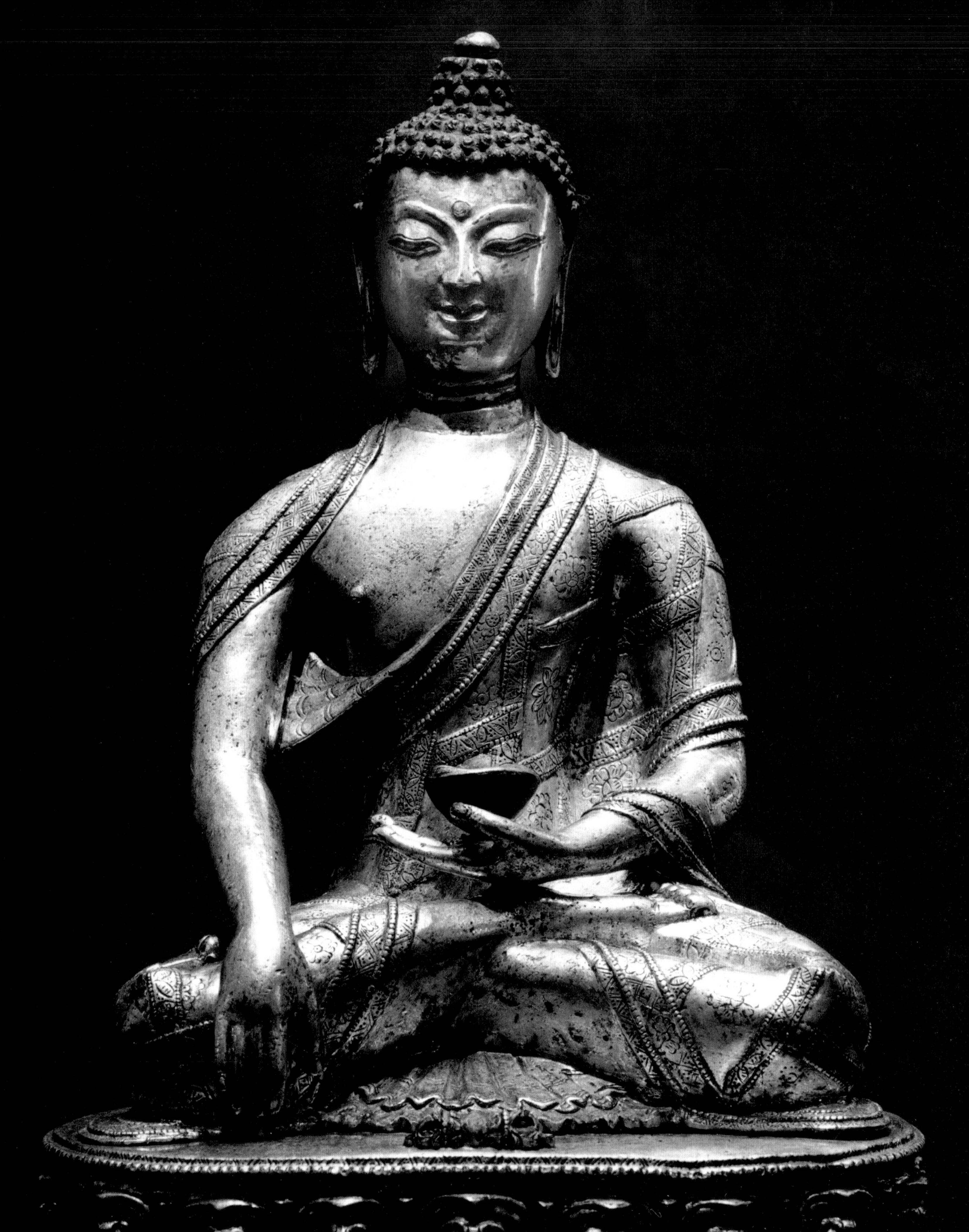

Tibet
Nepal

The Buddha Śākyamuni at the
Musée Guimet, Paris, 2018

TIBET

Bodhisattva Vajrapāṇi at the
Musée Guimet, Paris, 2018

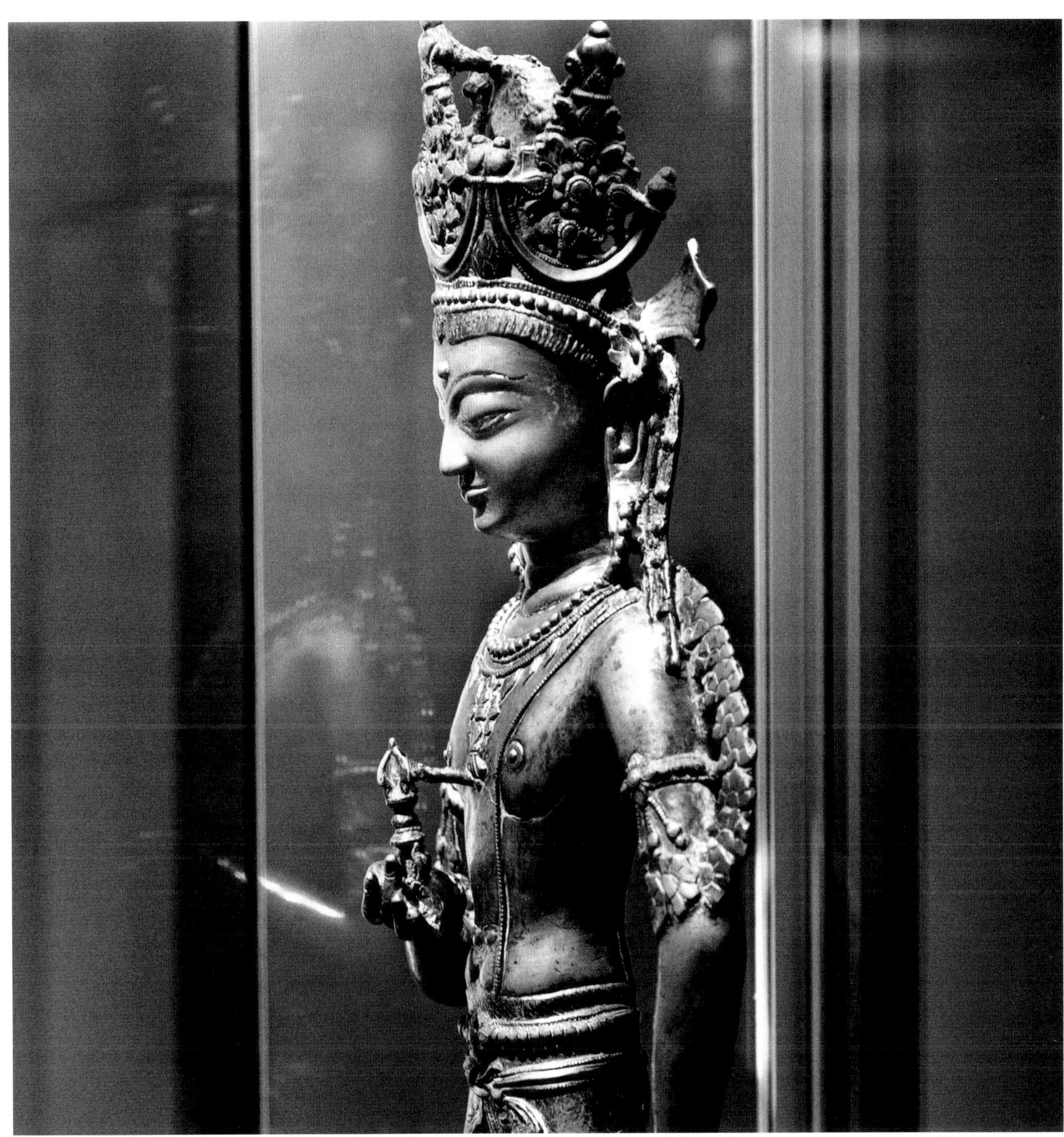

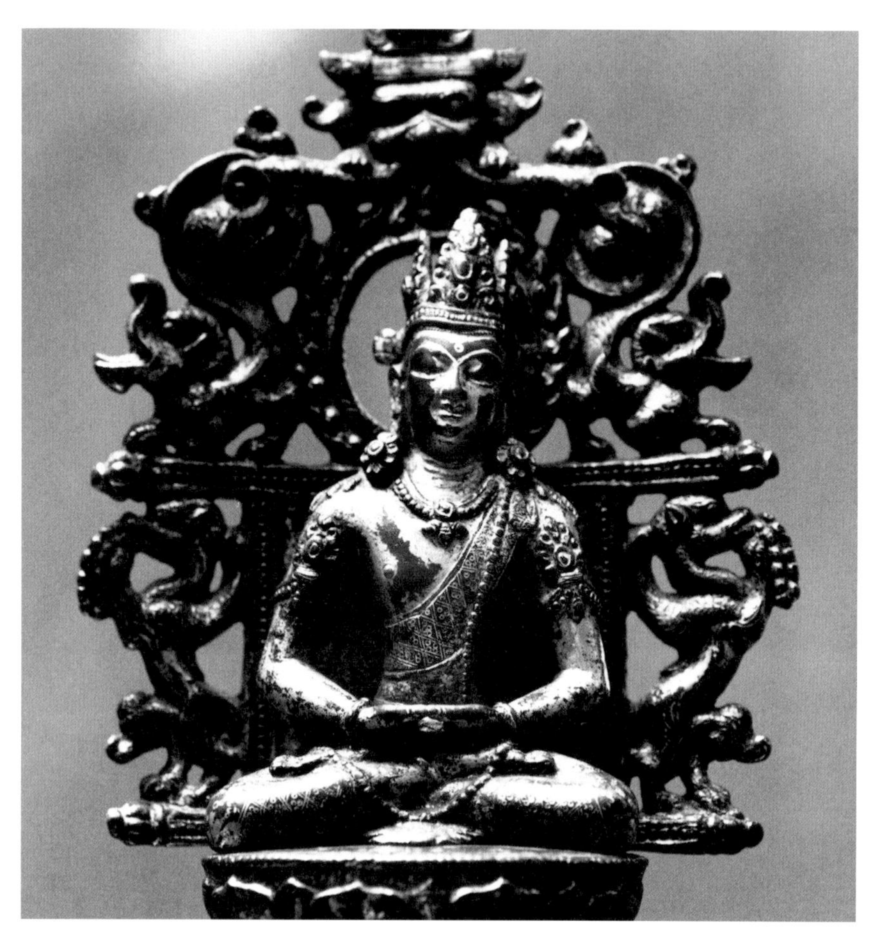

Bodhisattva Mañjuśrī
at the Musée Guimet,
Paris, 2018

Amoghasiddhi Buddha
at the Musée Guimet,
Paris, 2018

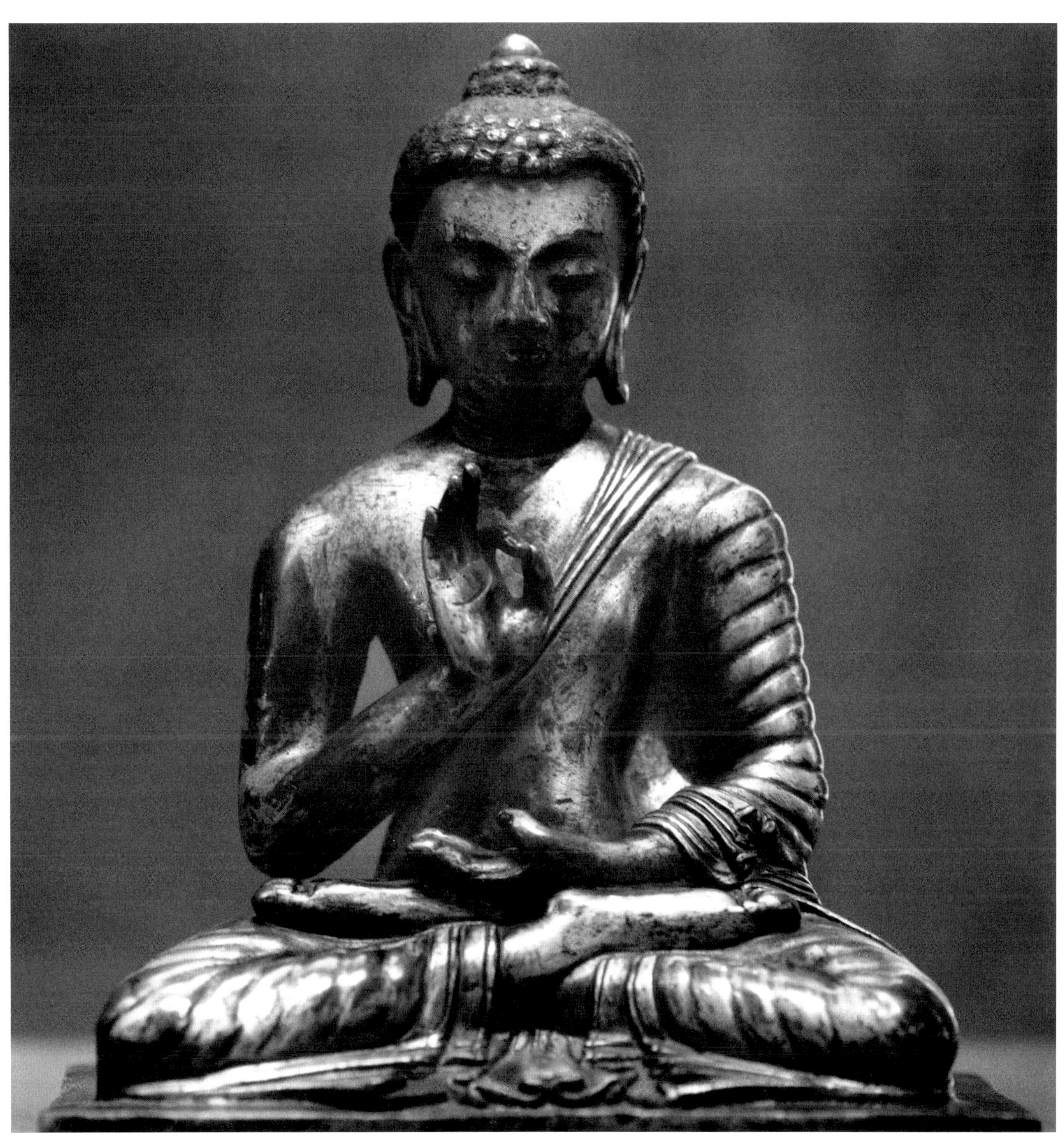

Nepalese Medicine Buddha,
Seattle, USA. 2019

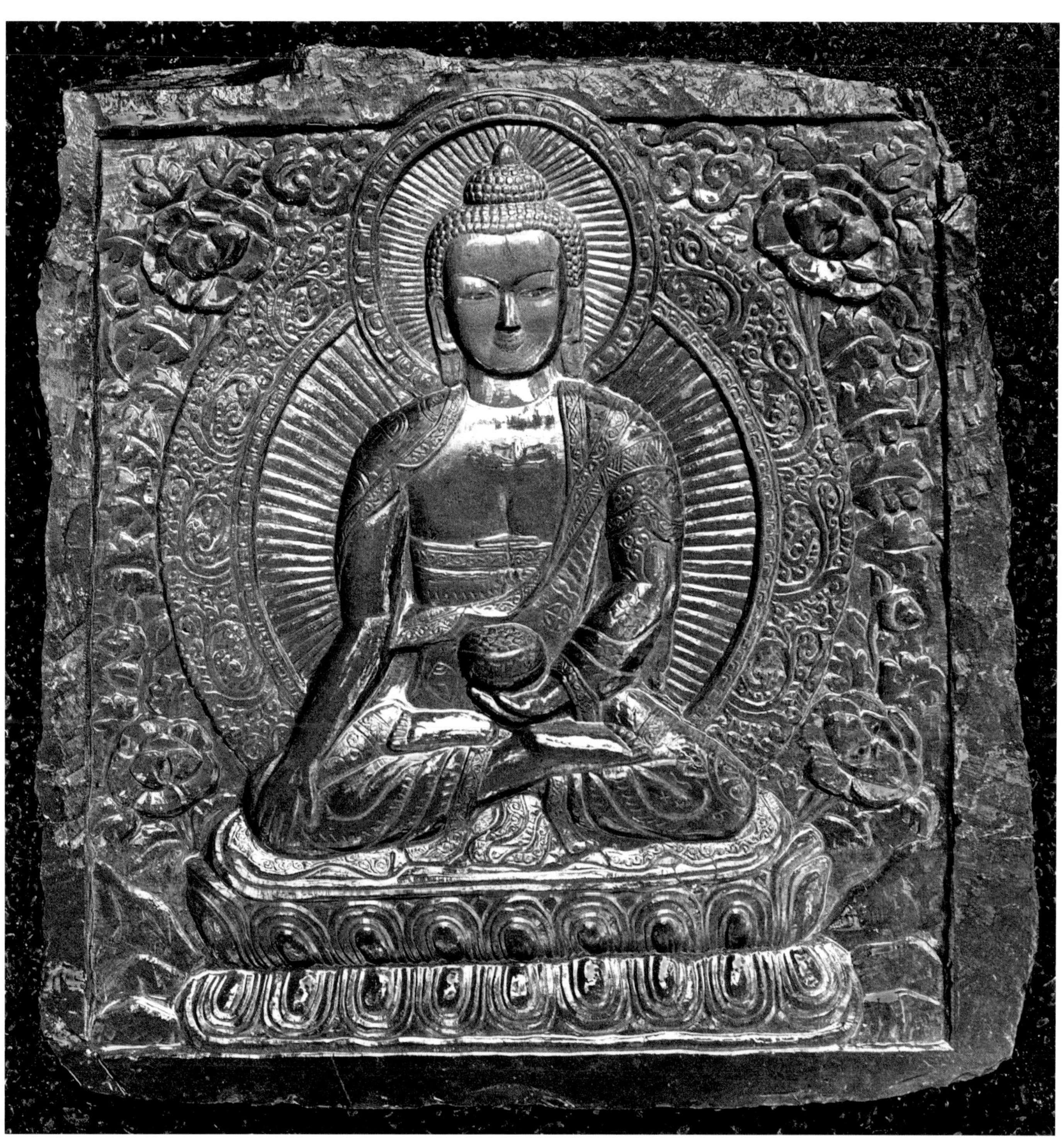

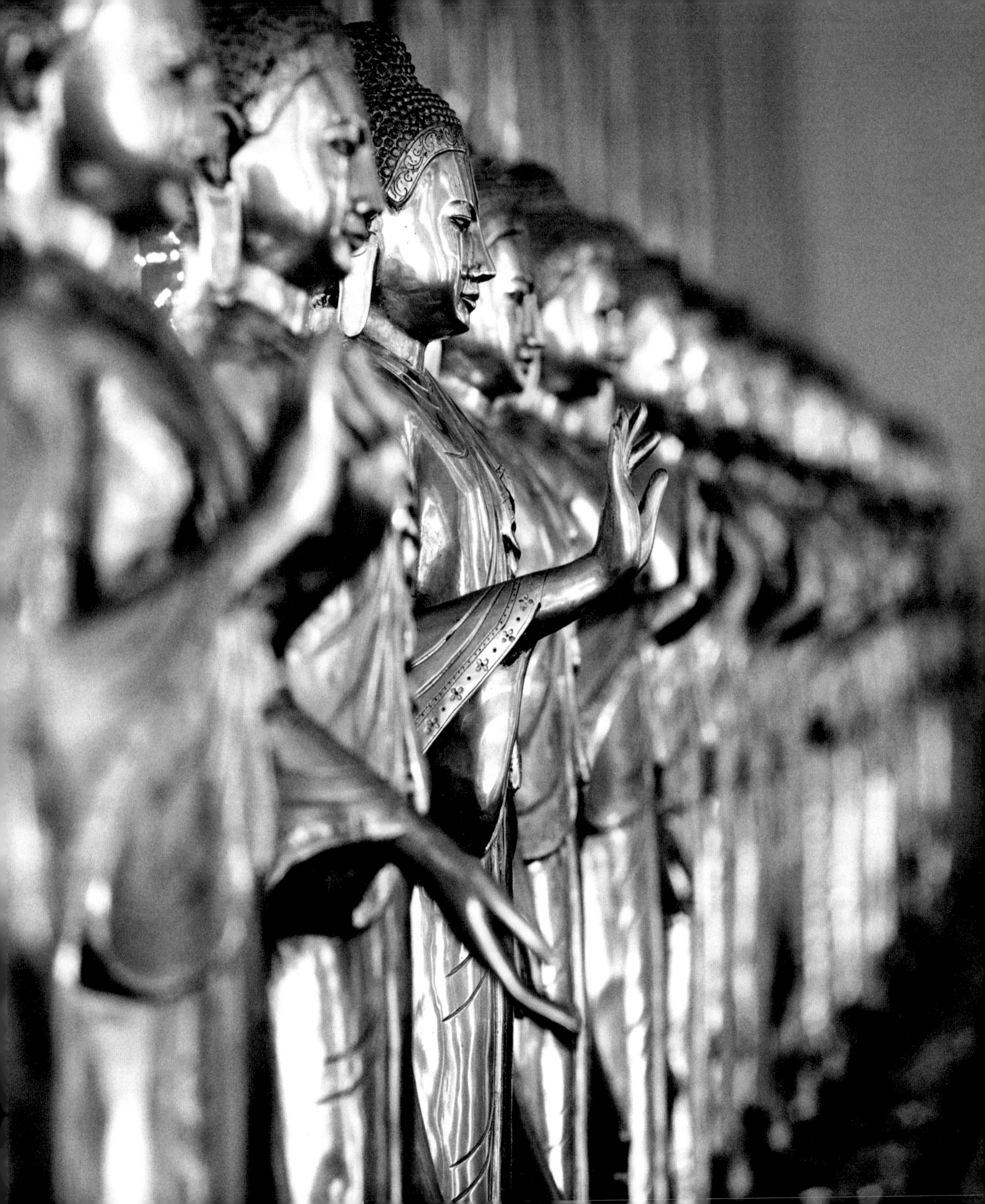

Myanmar

Hand Gestures, Yangon, 2019

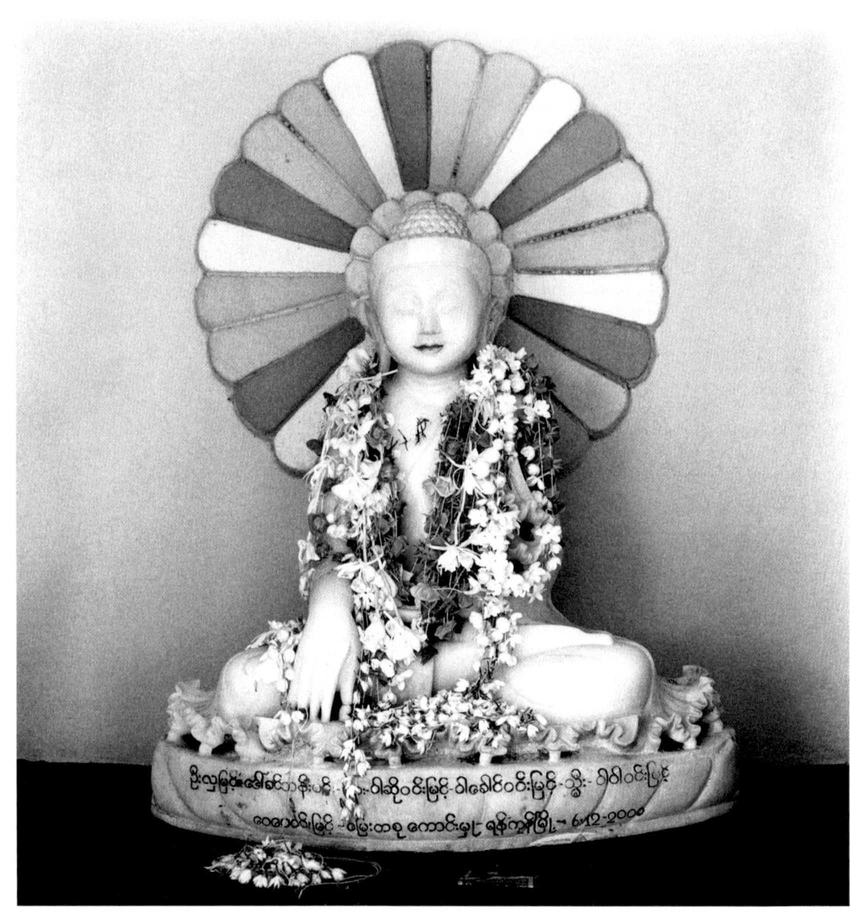

Garlanded Buddha,
Sagaing, 2019

Mountaintop Buddha,
Pindaya, 2019

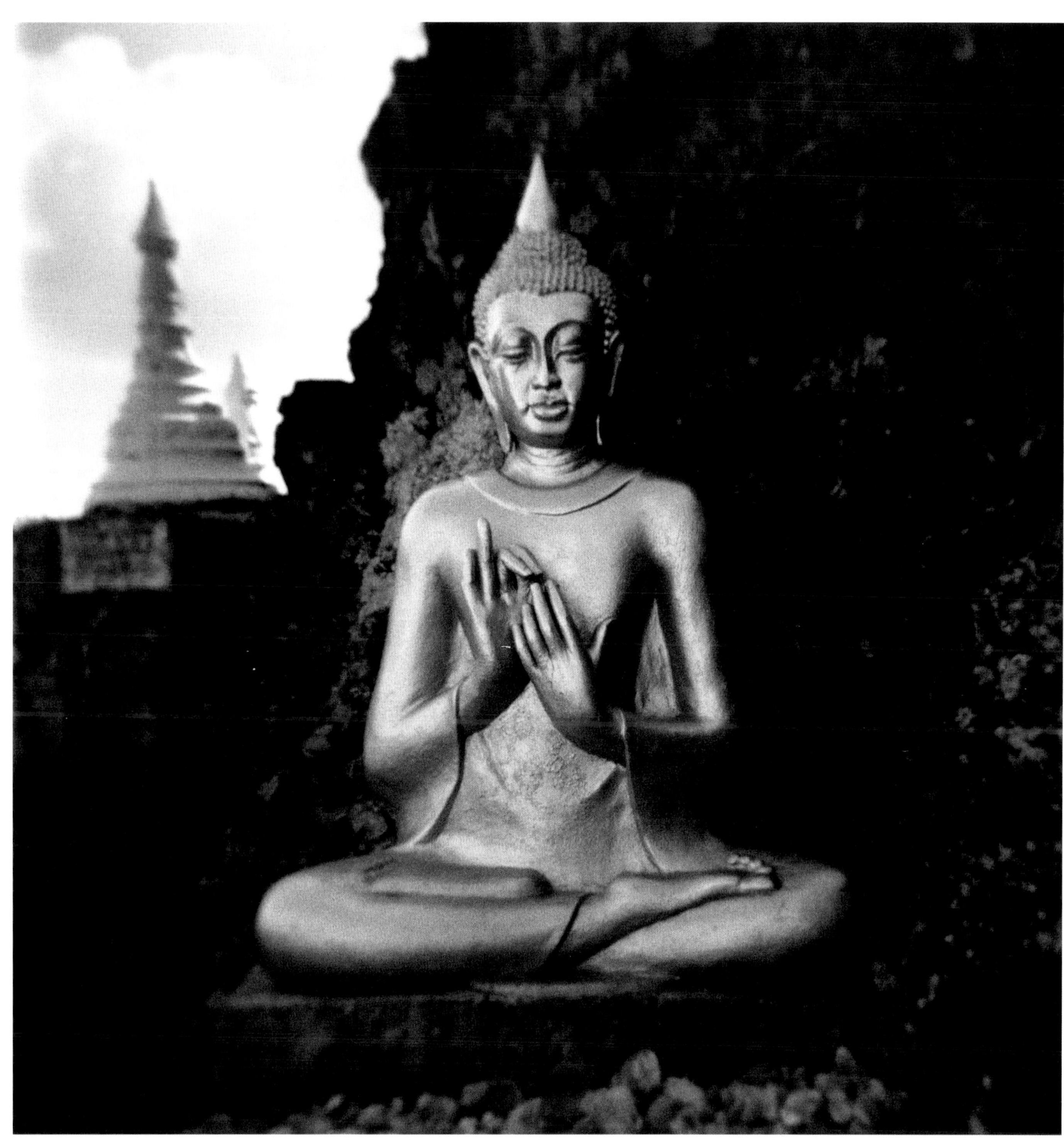

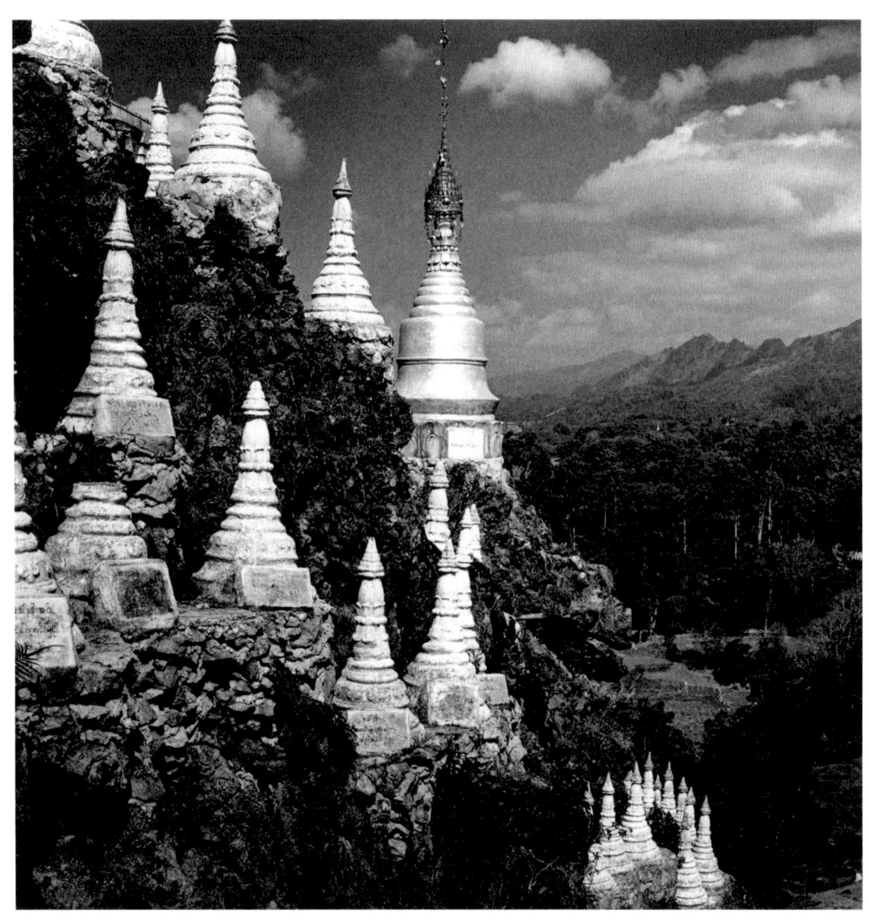

Mountain Pagodas,
Main Ma Ye Thakinma Tuang
Temple, Pindaya, 2019

Buddha Cave, Pindaya, 2019

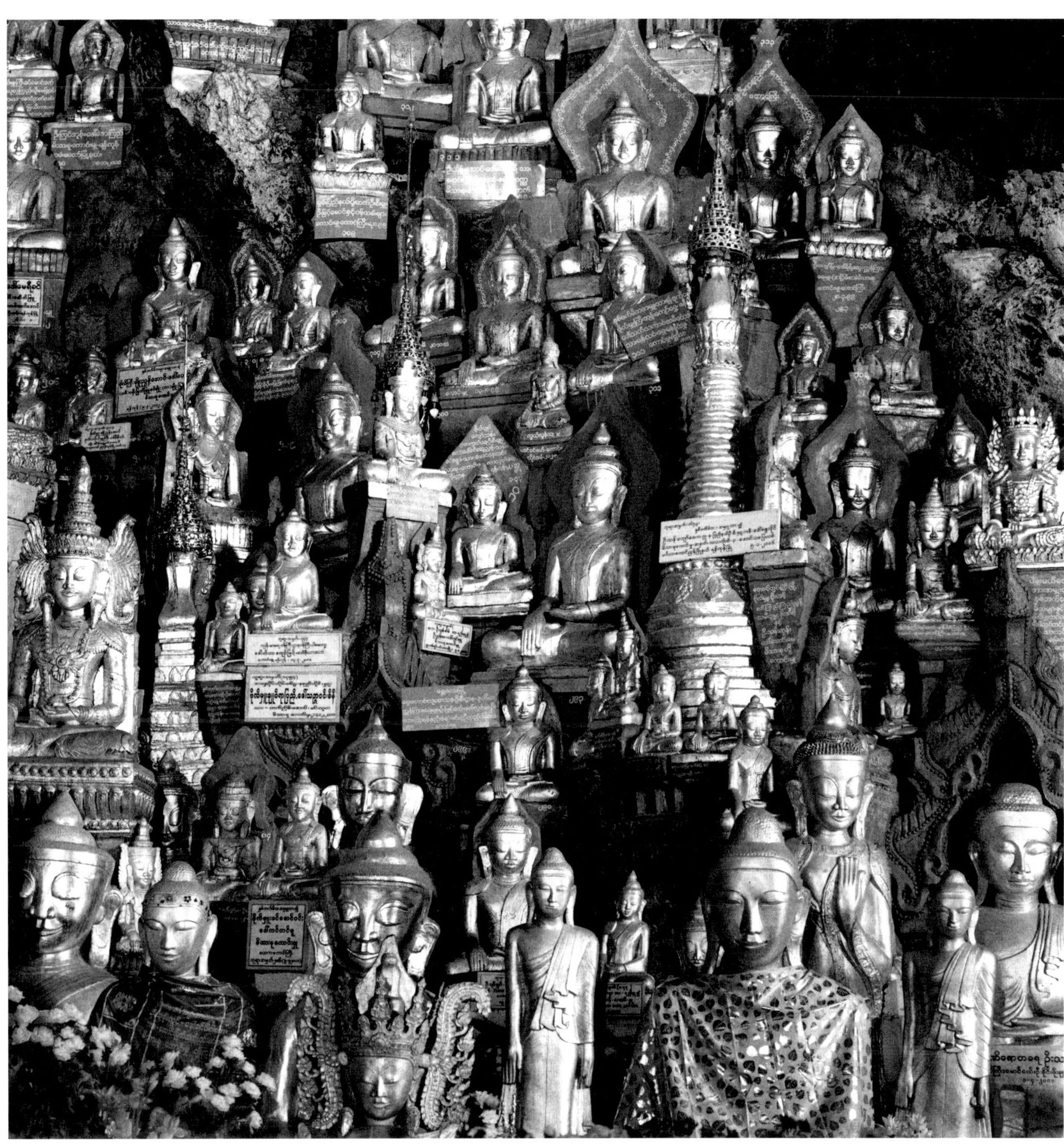

MYANMAR

Tuan Tsu Reclining Buddha,
Yangon, 2019

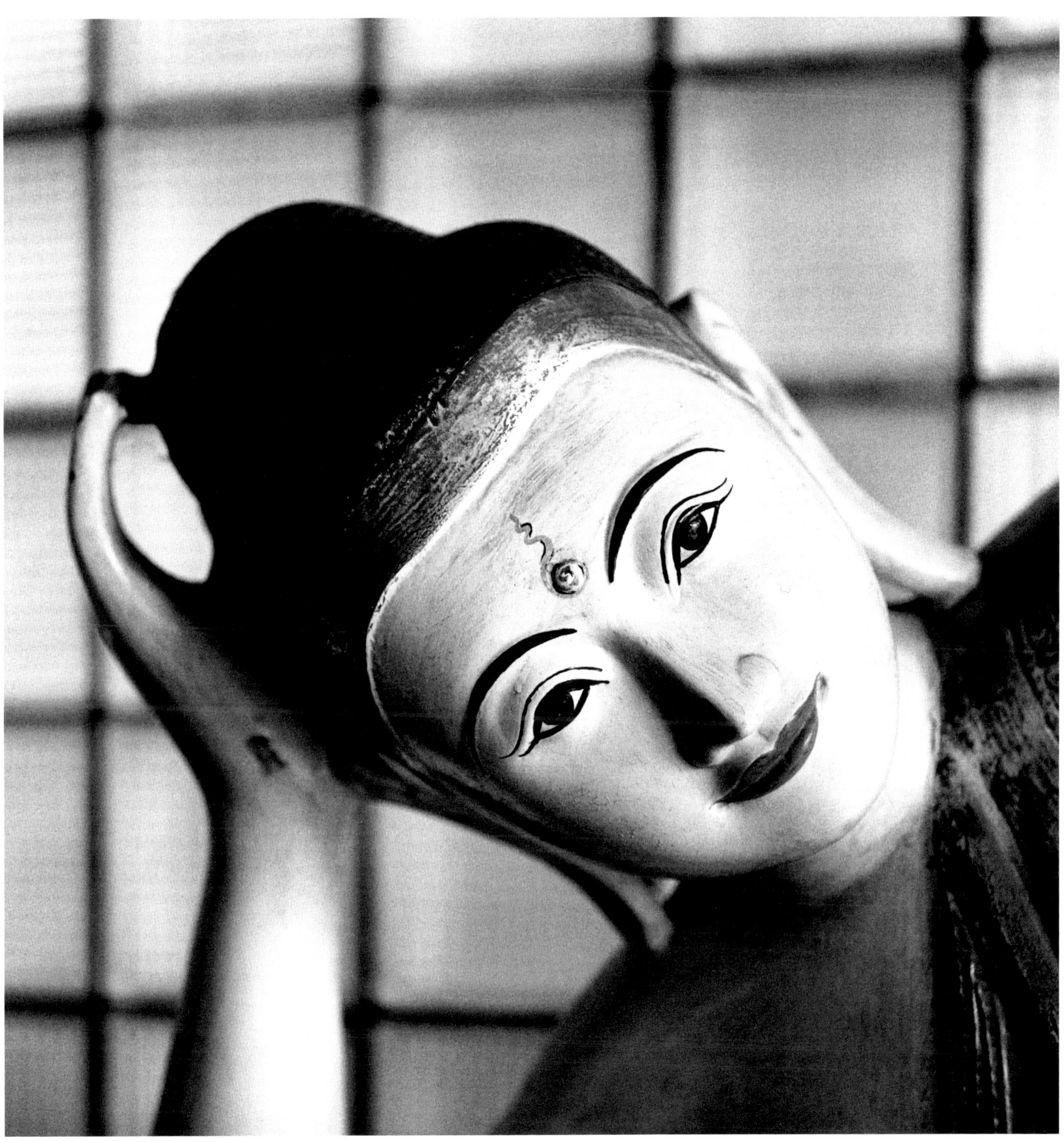

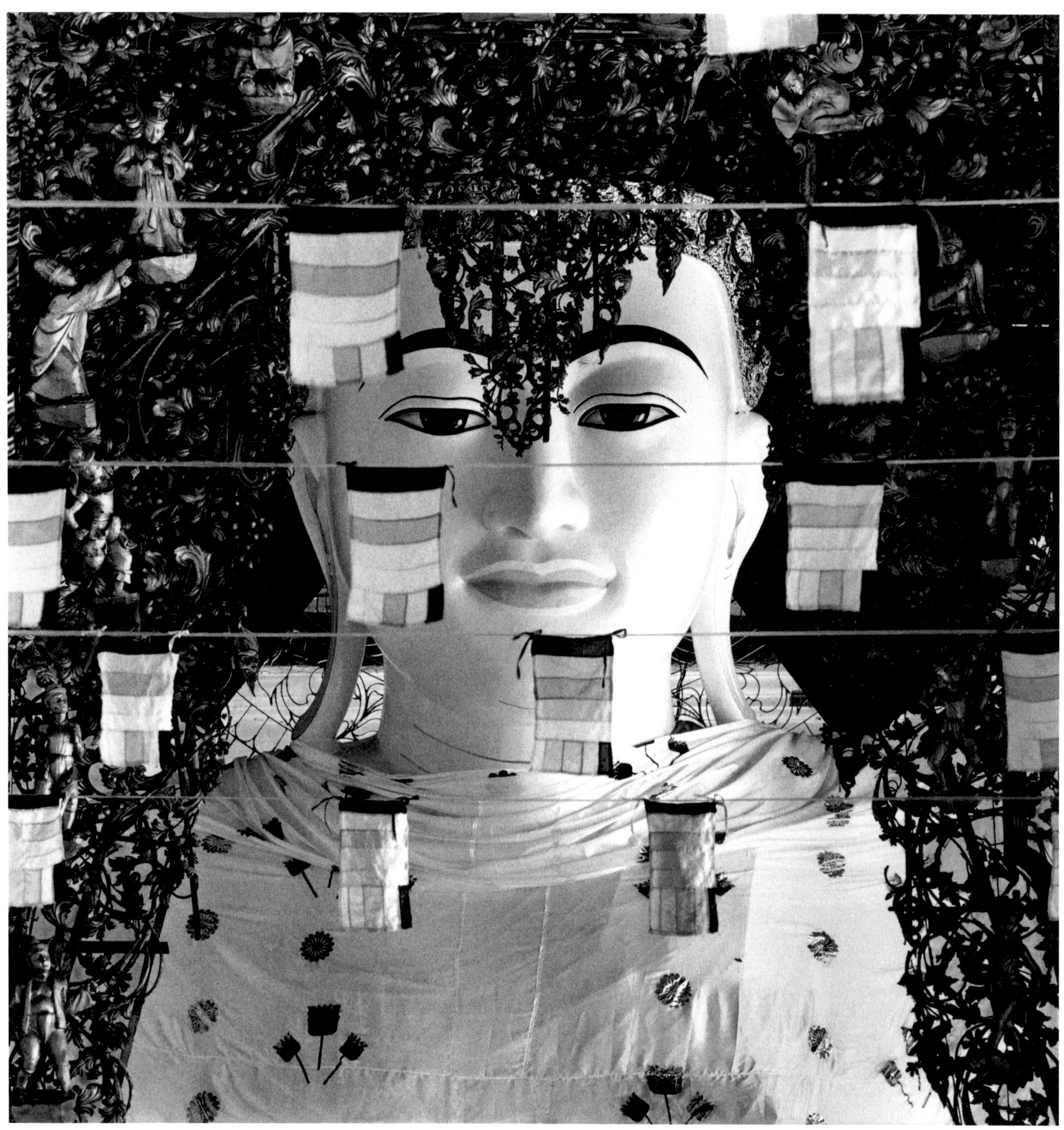

MYANMAR

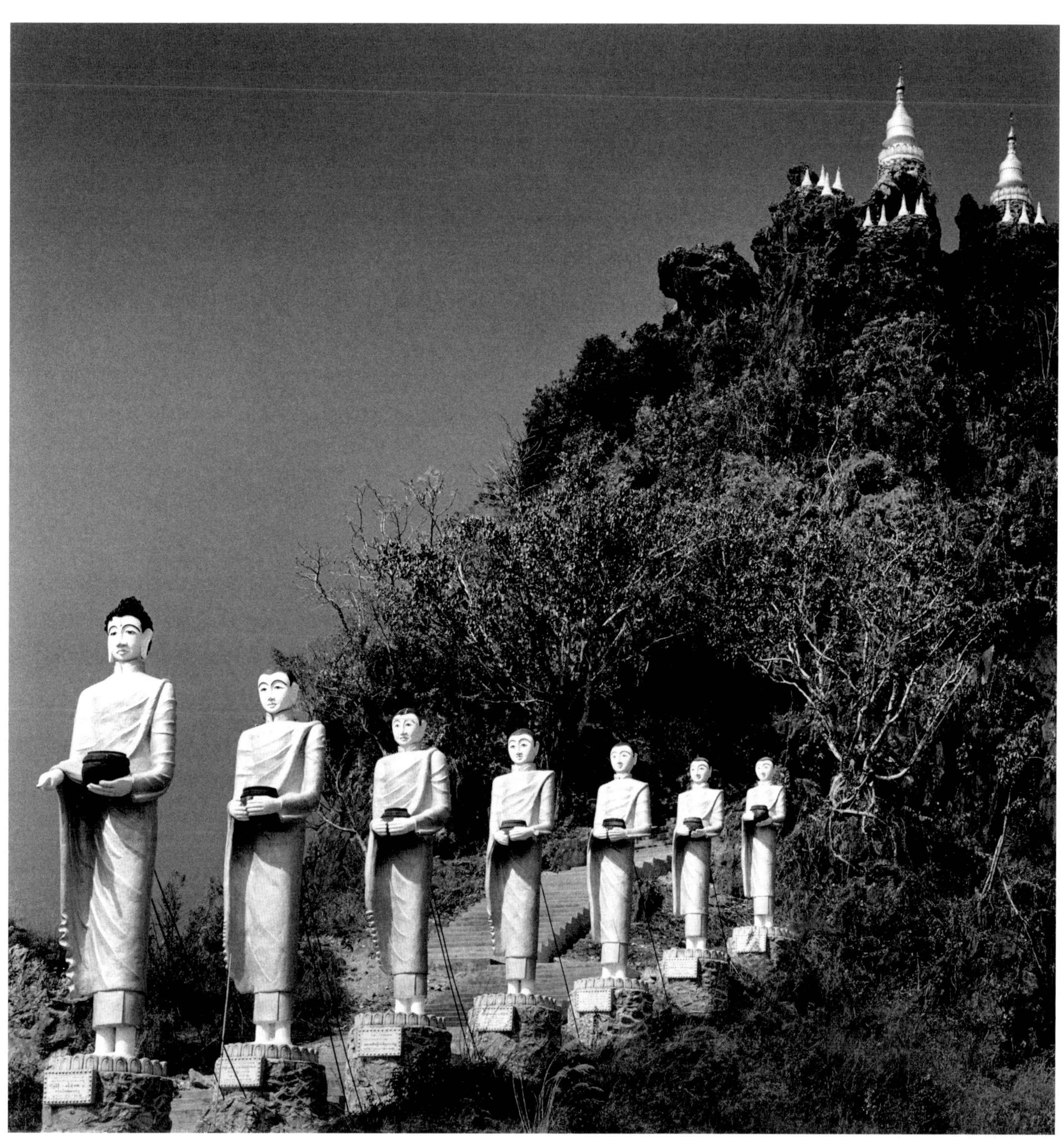

Chanthagyi Buddha,
Yangon, 2019

Buddha Procession,
Pindaya, 2019

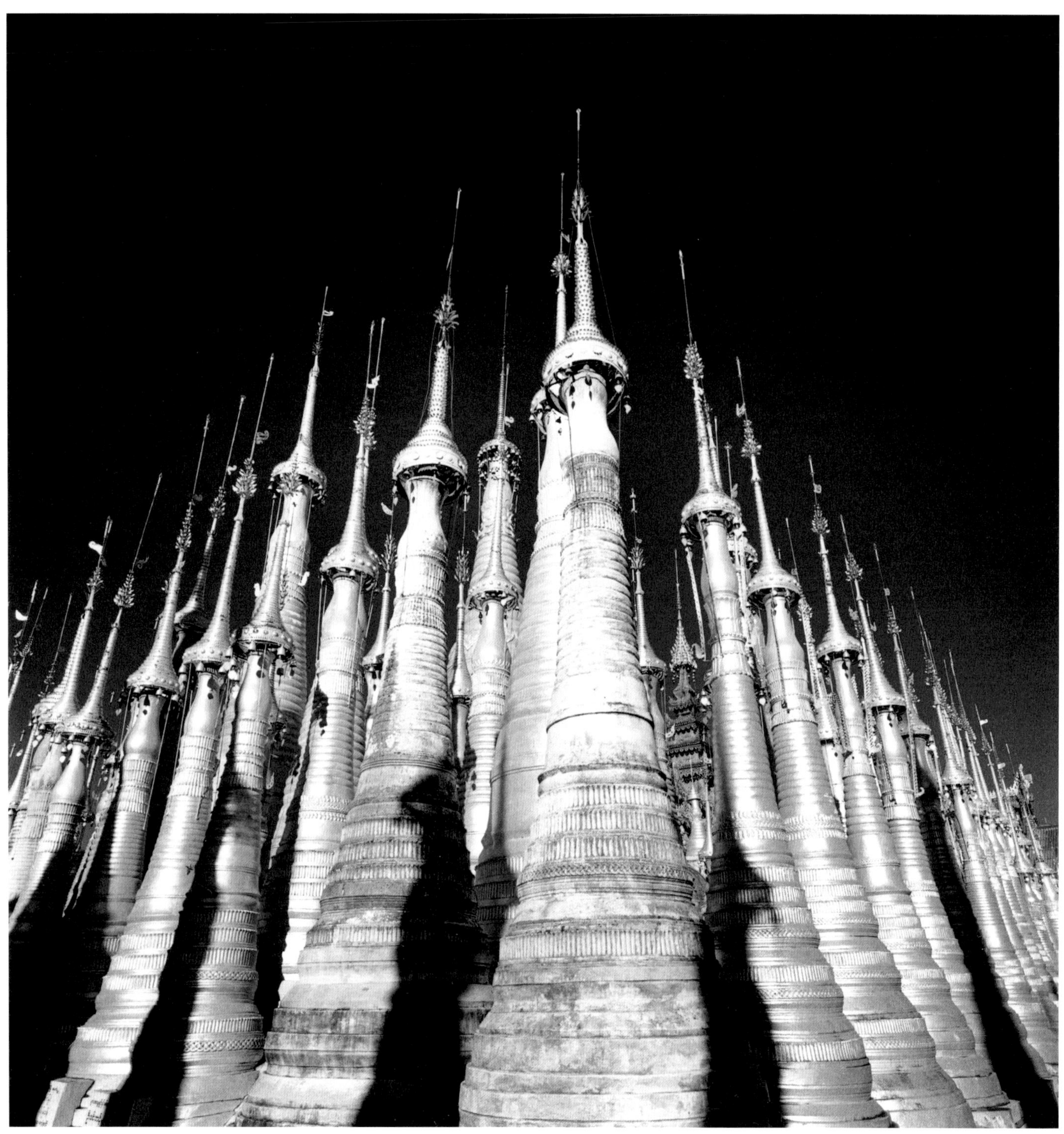

MYANMAR

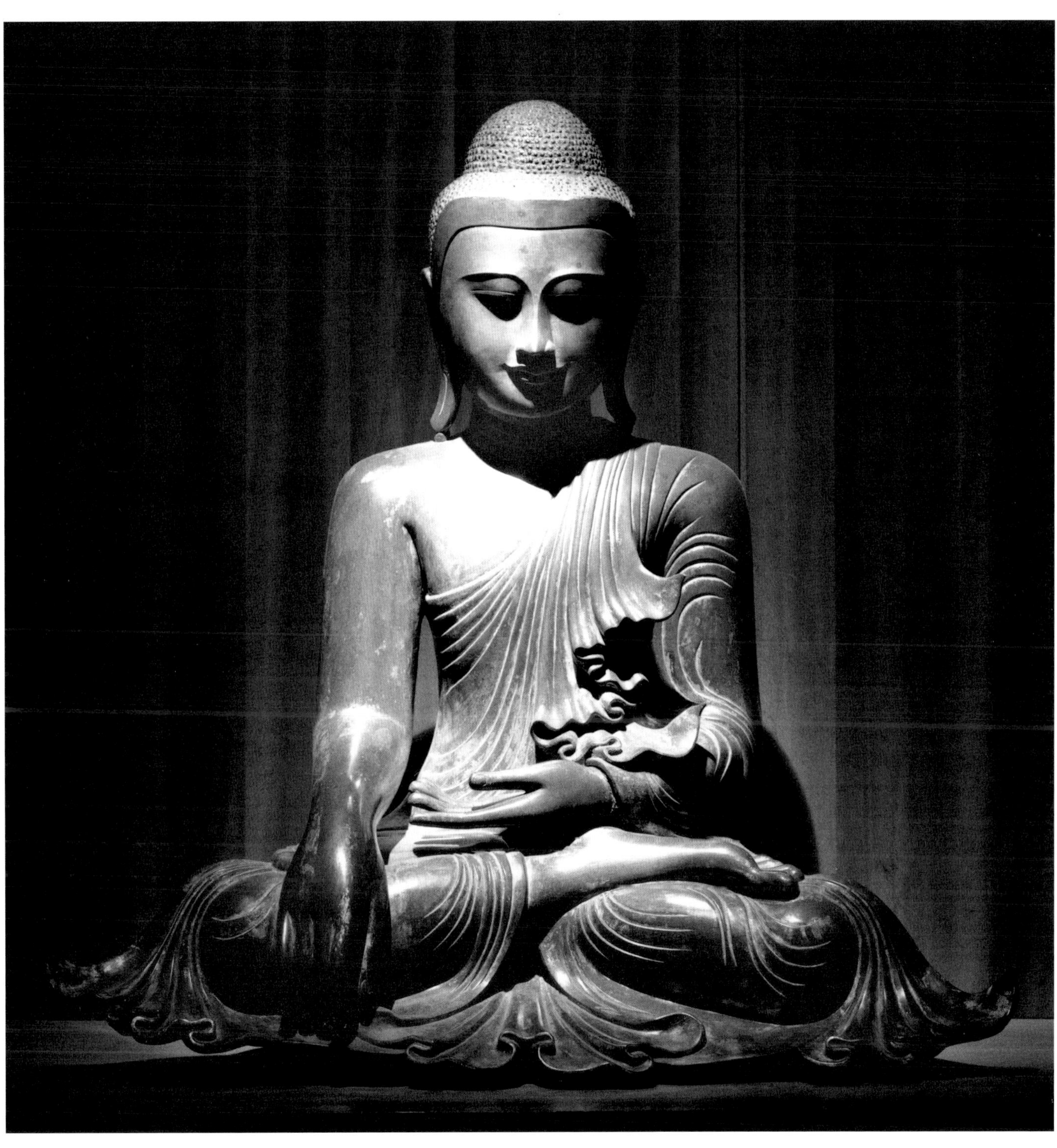

Temple Pagodas,
Shan State, 2019

Māravijaya Buddha
at the Musée Guimet,
Paris, 2018

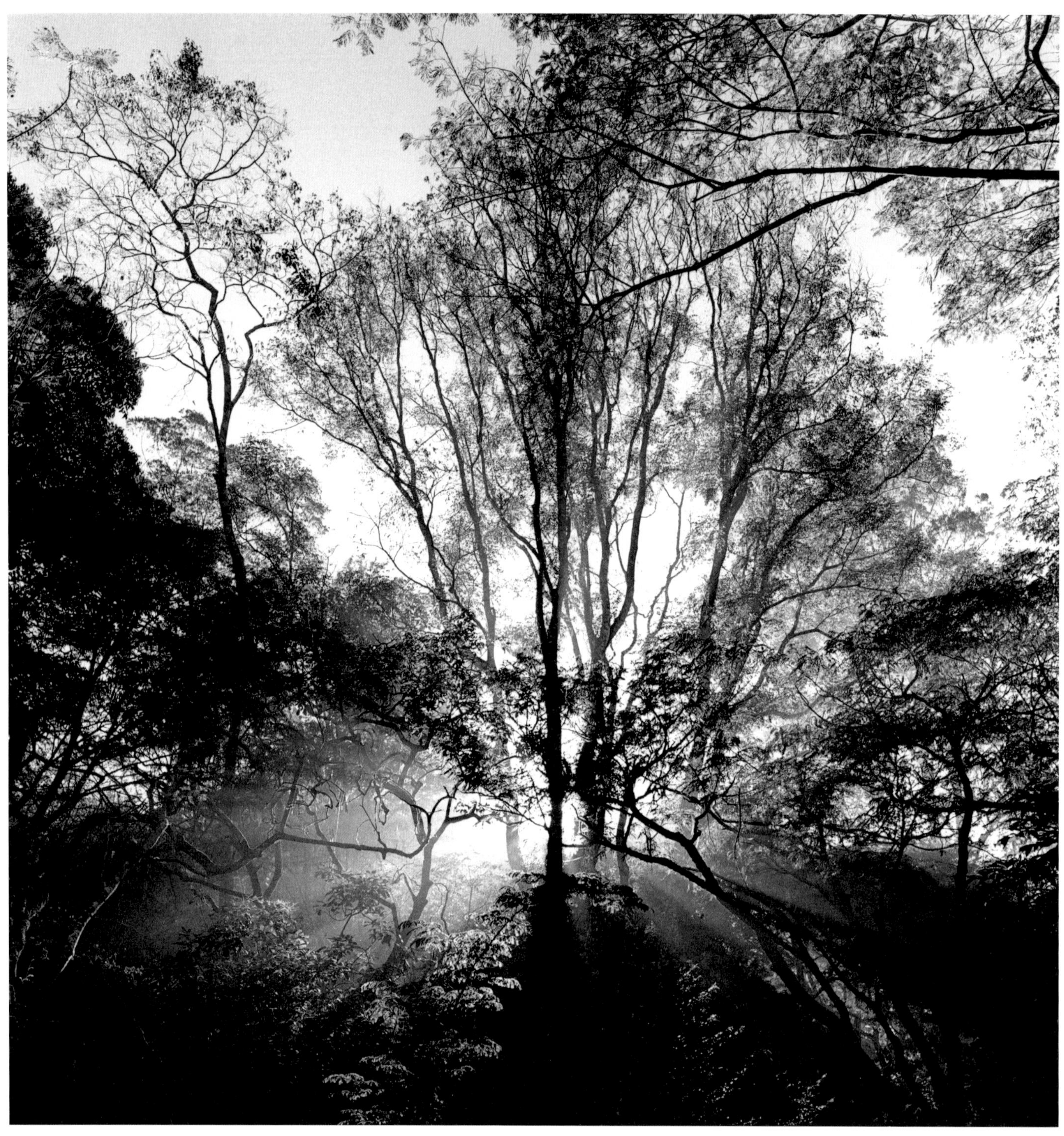

MYANMAR

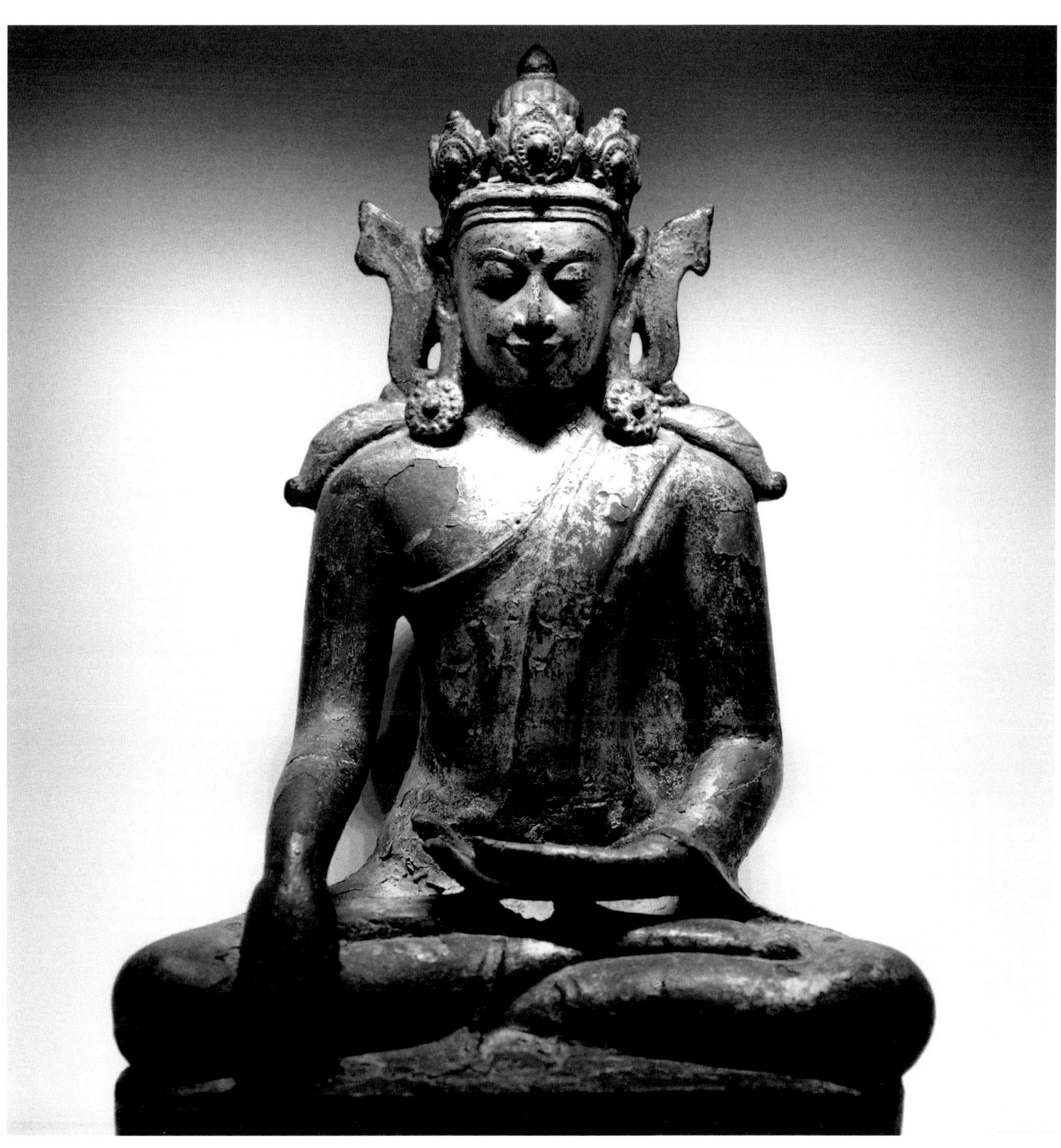

Sun Rays in Trees, Study 1,
Pyin U Lwin, 2019

Māravijaya Buddha
at the Musée Guimet,
Paris, 2018

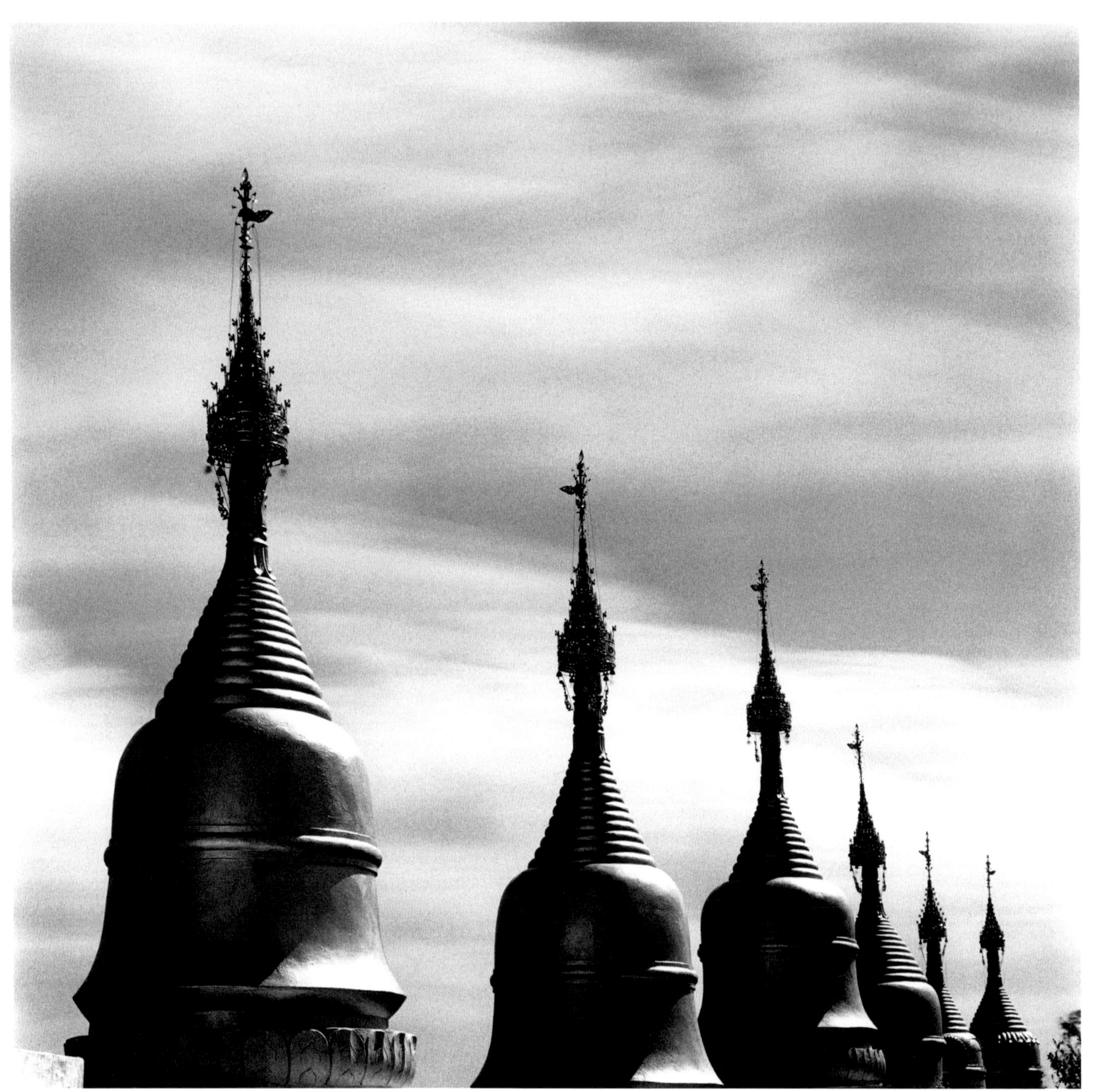

MYANMAR

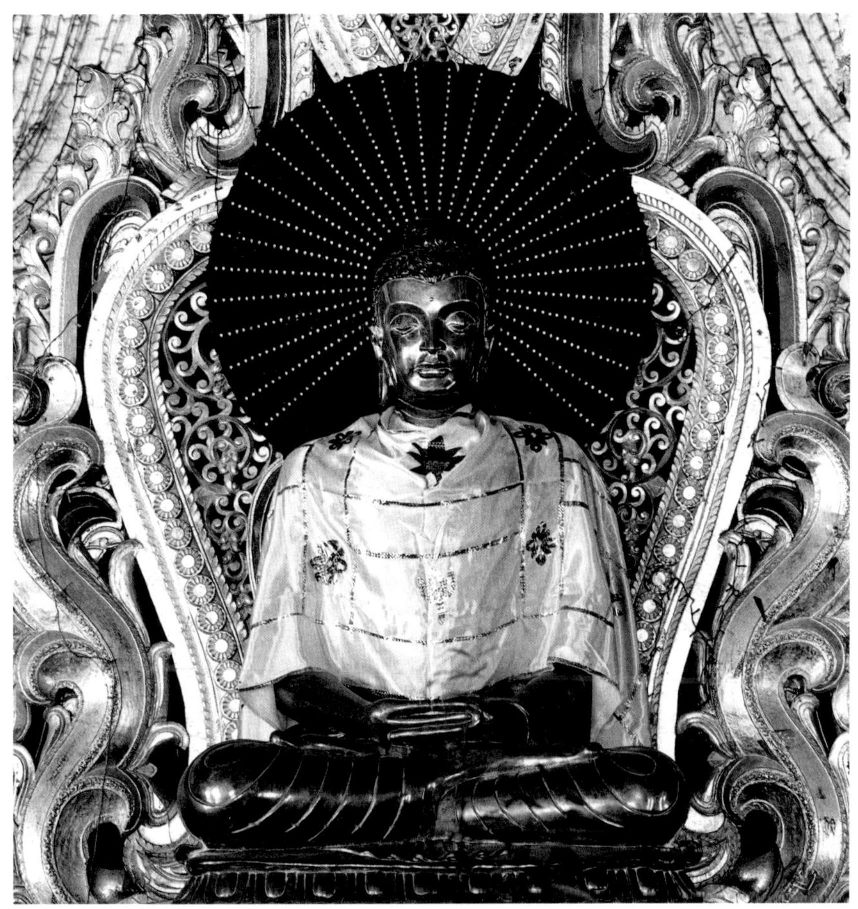

Six Pagodas, Main Ma Ye Thakinma
Tuang Temple, Pindaya, 2019

Black Buddha, Mandalay, 2019

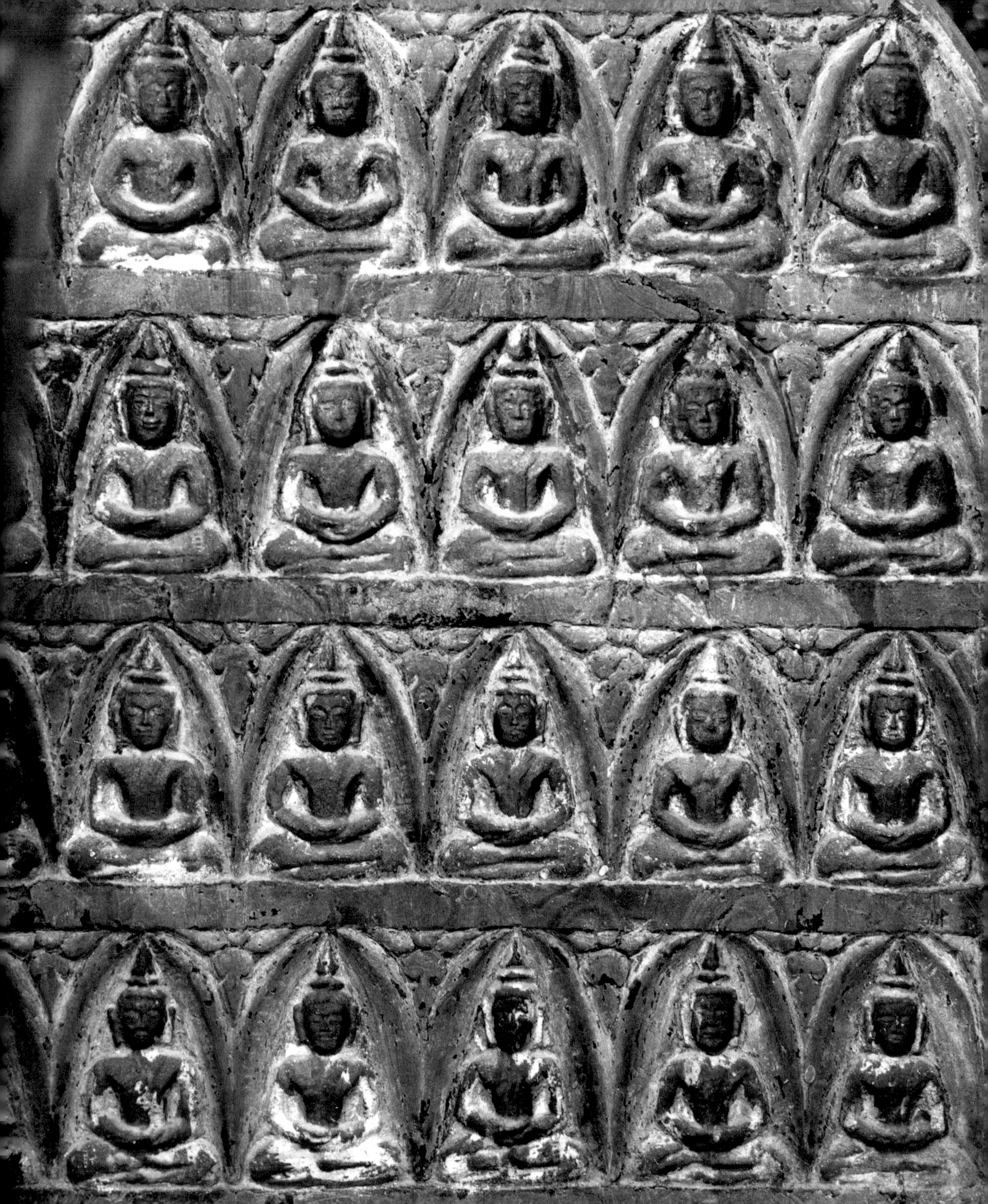

Laos

Screen of Buddhas,
Luang Prabang, 2015

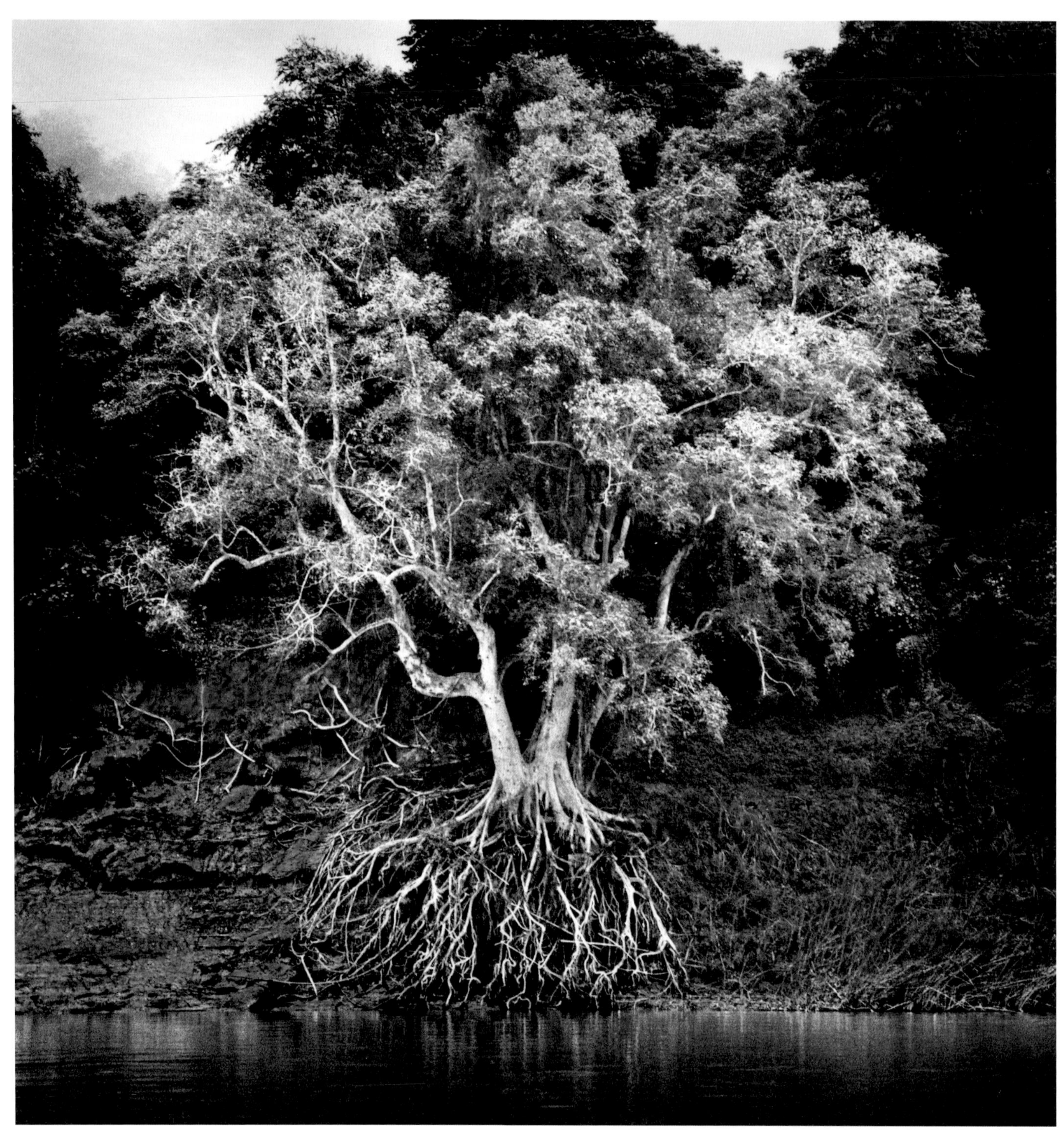

Kokdua Tree with
Exposed Roots, Mekong River,
Luang Prabang, 2015

Buddha and Cobwebs,
Luang Prabang, 2015

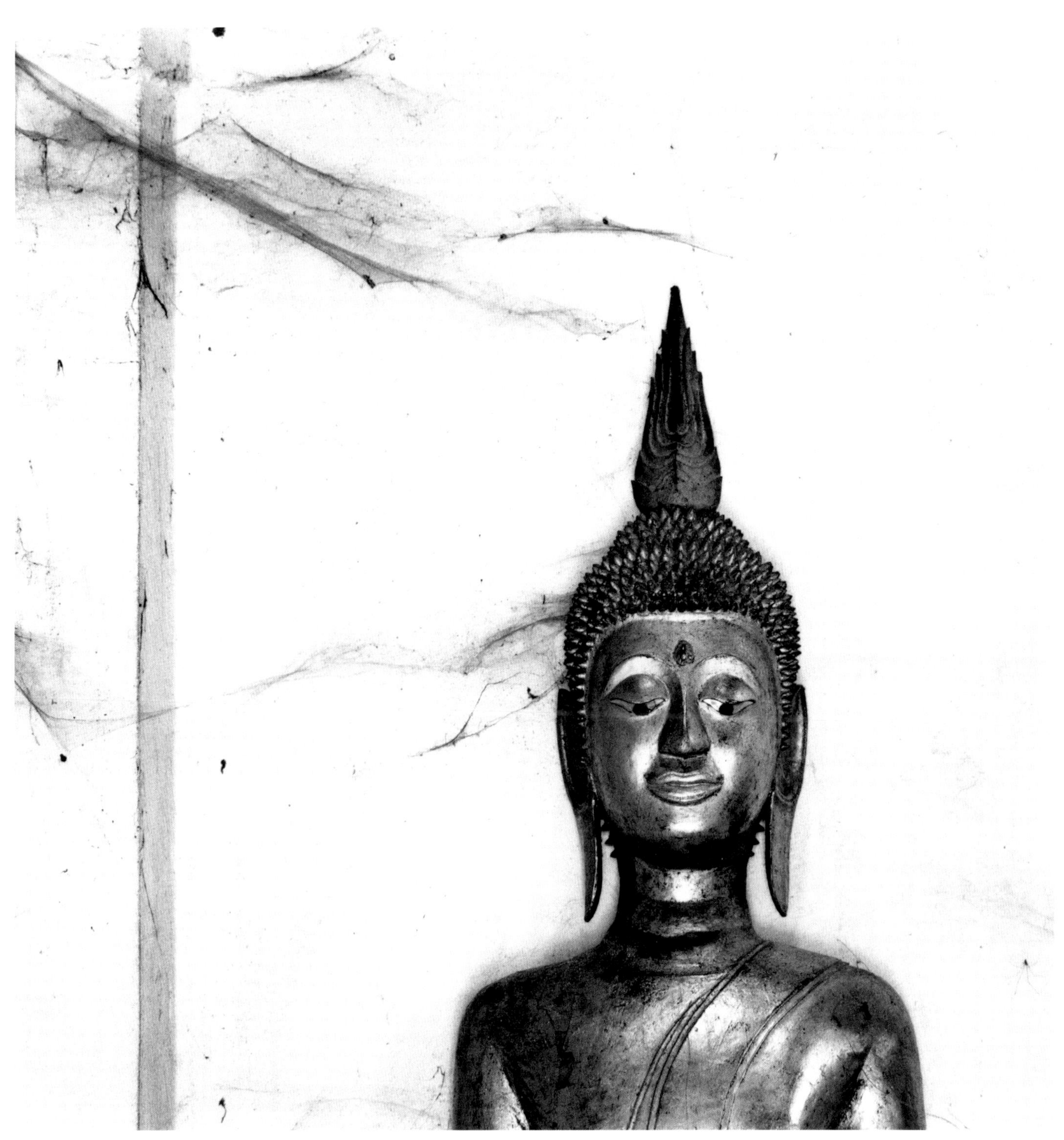

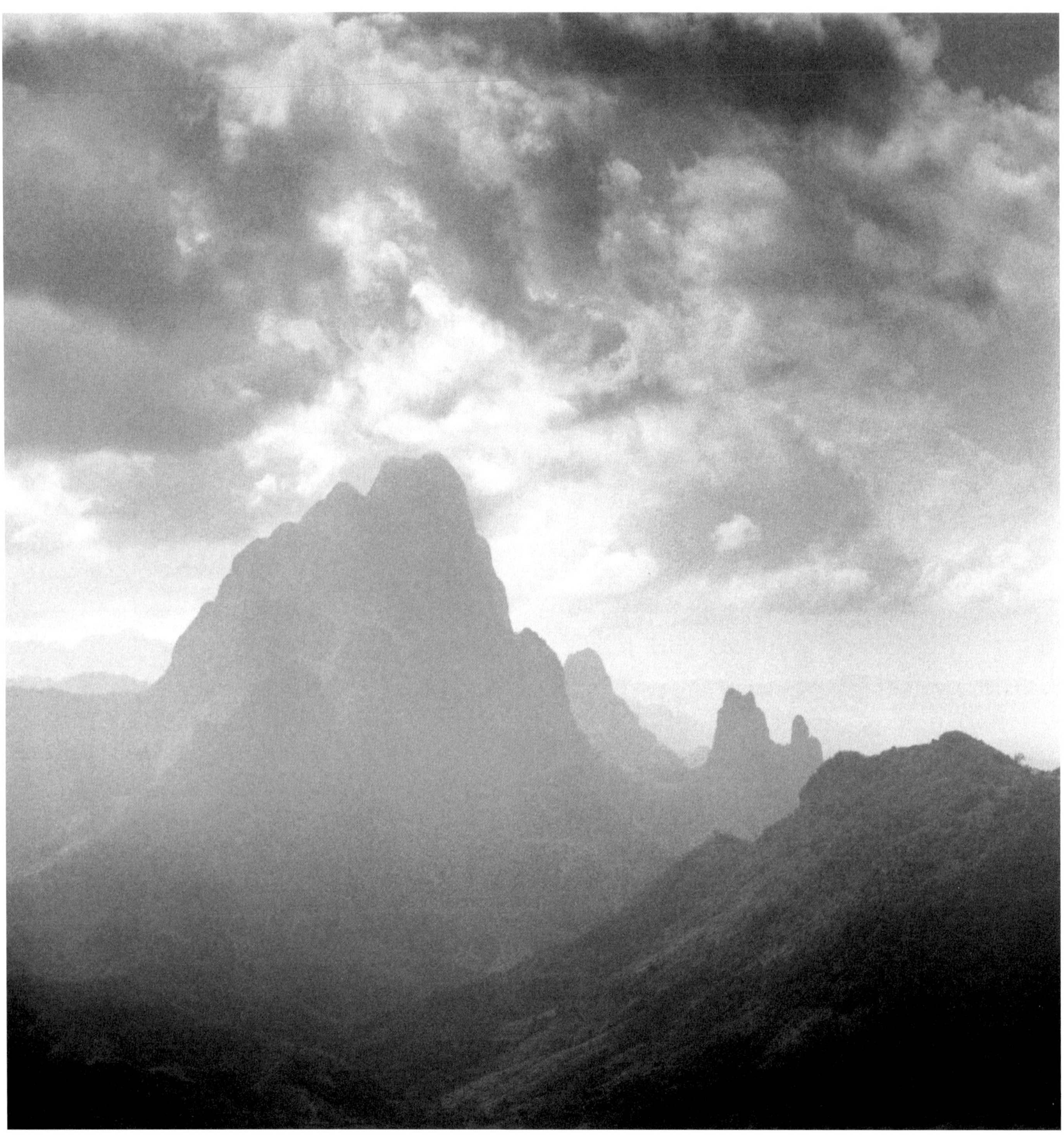

LAOS

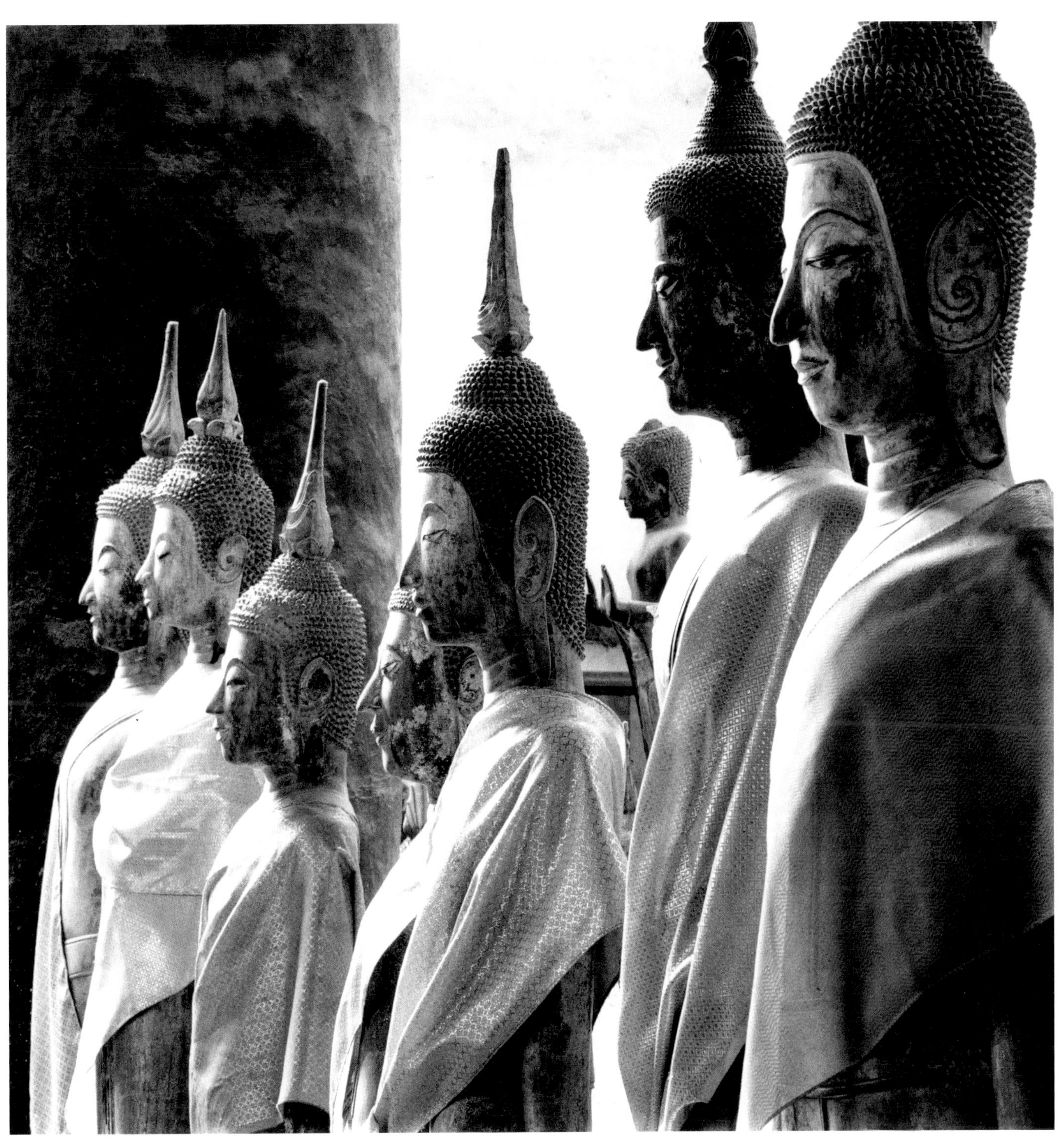

Phachao Mountain Viewed from
Phu Phieng Fa, Kasi, 2015

Eight Buddha Statues,
Wat Visounarat, Luang Prabang, 2015

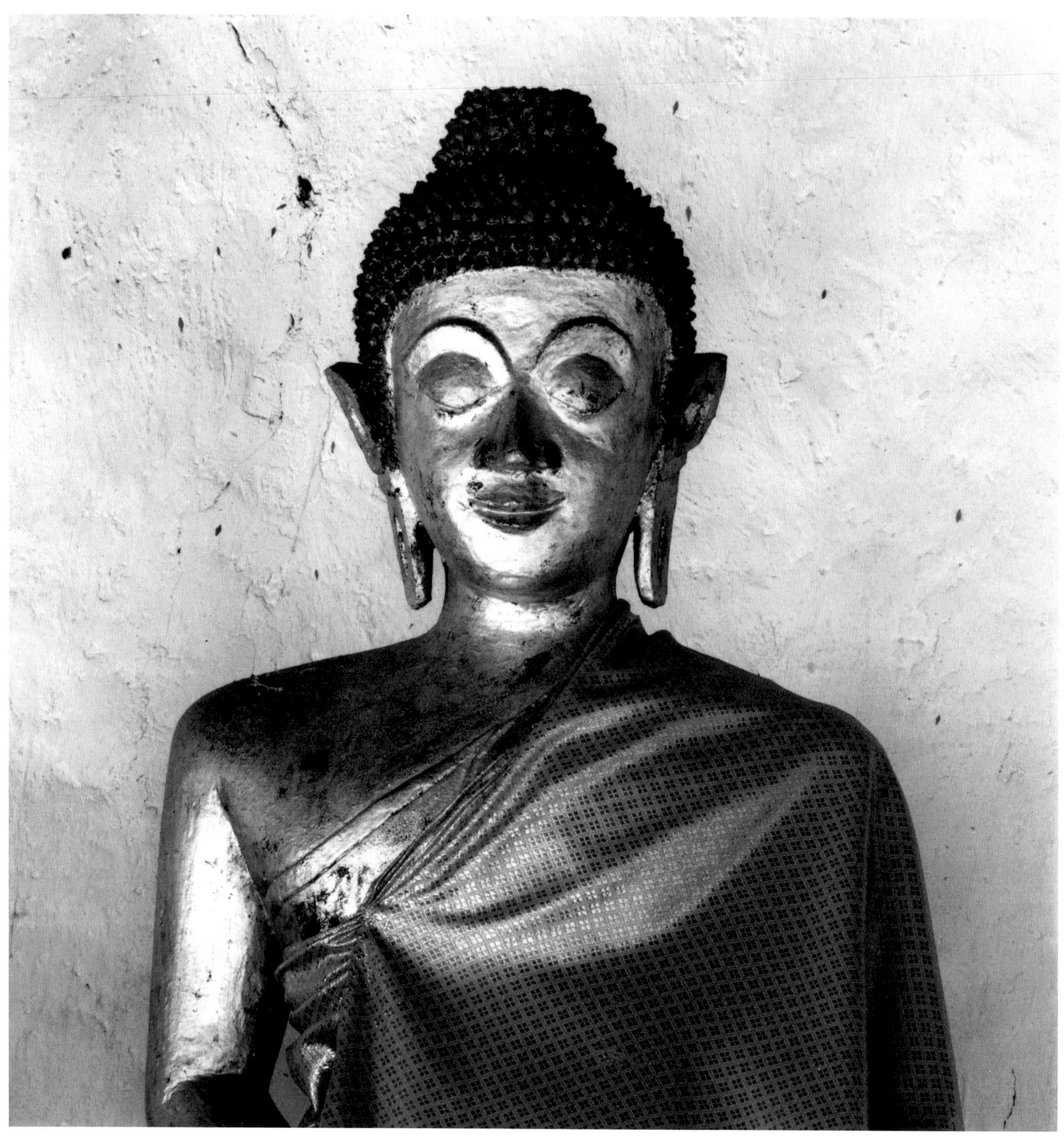

LAOS

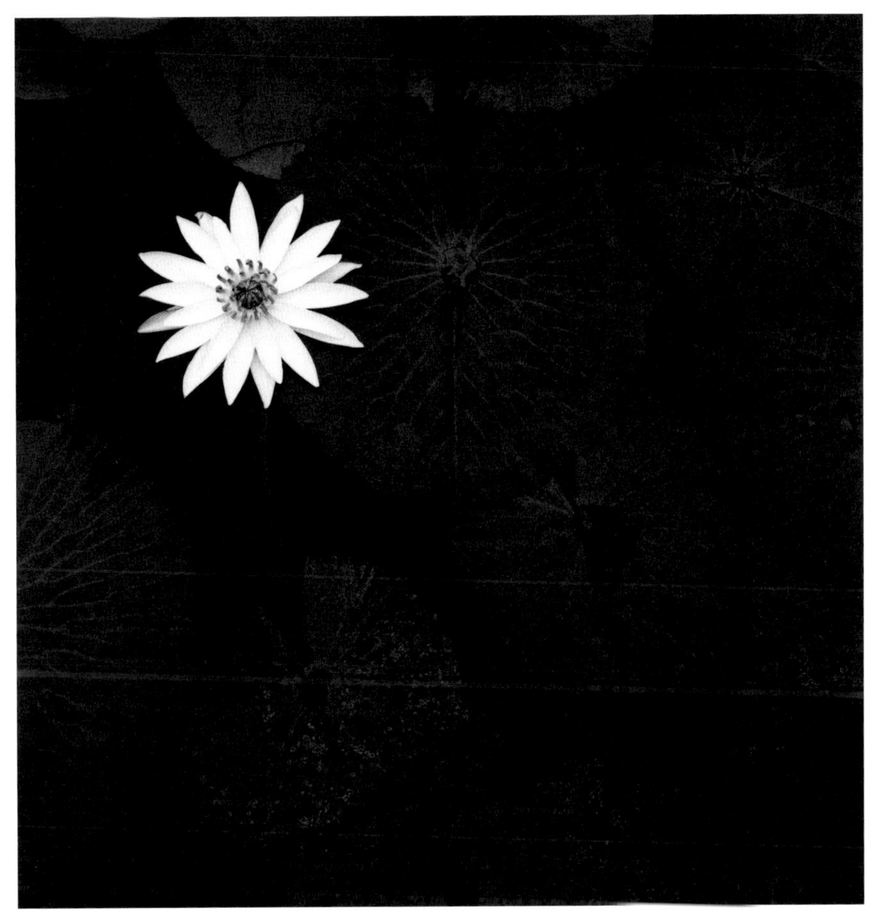

Buddha Portrait,
Luang Prabang, 2015

Mamta's Lotus Flower,
Ban Viengkeo,
Luang Prabang, 2015

LAOS

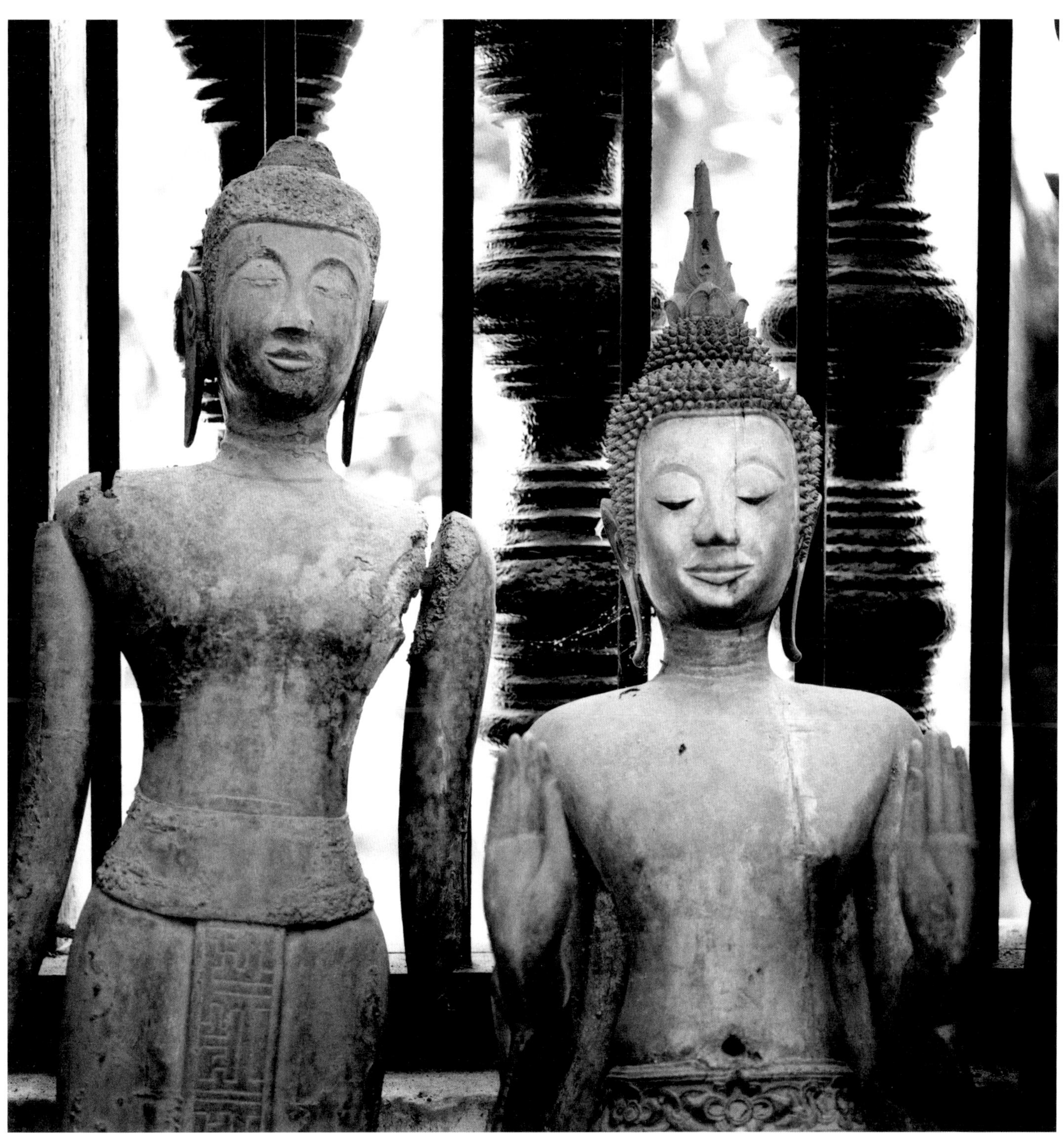

Morning Rain Clouds, Phou Chaleng
Mountain, Muang Ngoi, 2015

Two Buddha Statues,
Wat Visounarat, Luang Prabang, 2015

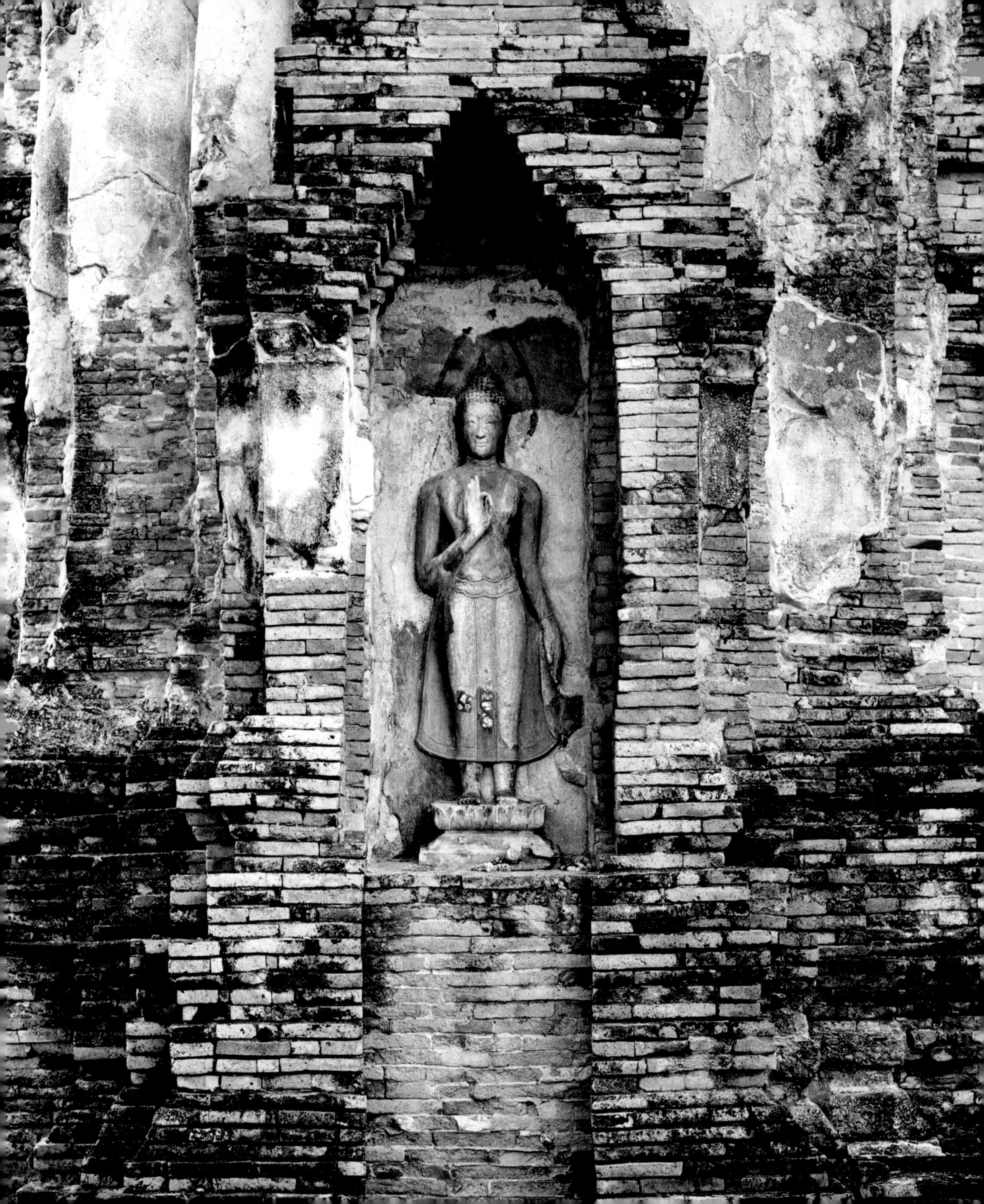

Thailand

Wat Mahathat Standing Buddha,
Ayutthaya, 2019

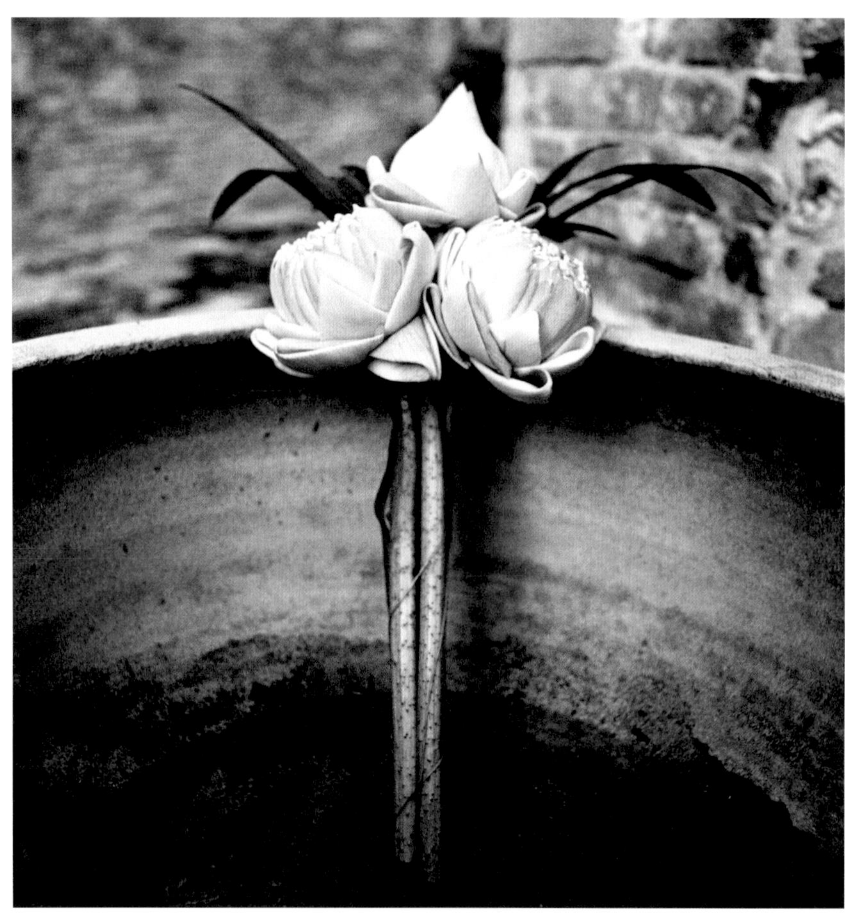

Three Lotus Flowers,
Ayutthaya, 2019

Wat Mahathat Buddha Head,
Ayutthaya, 2019

THAILAND

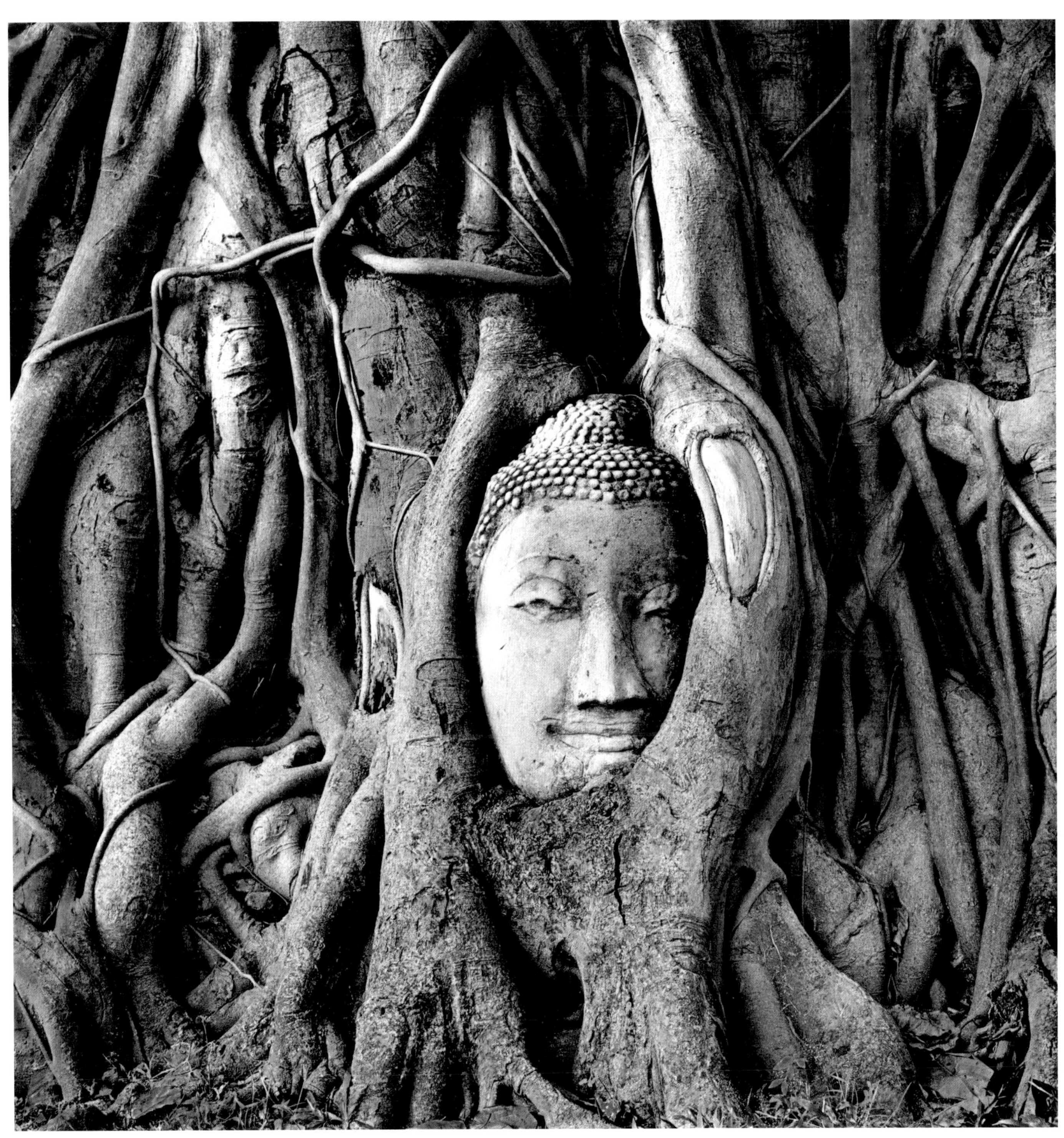

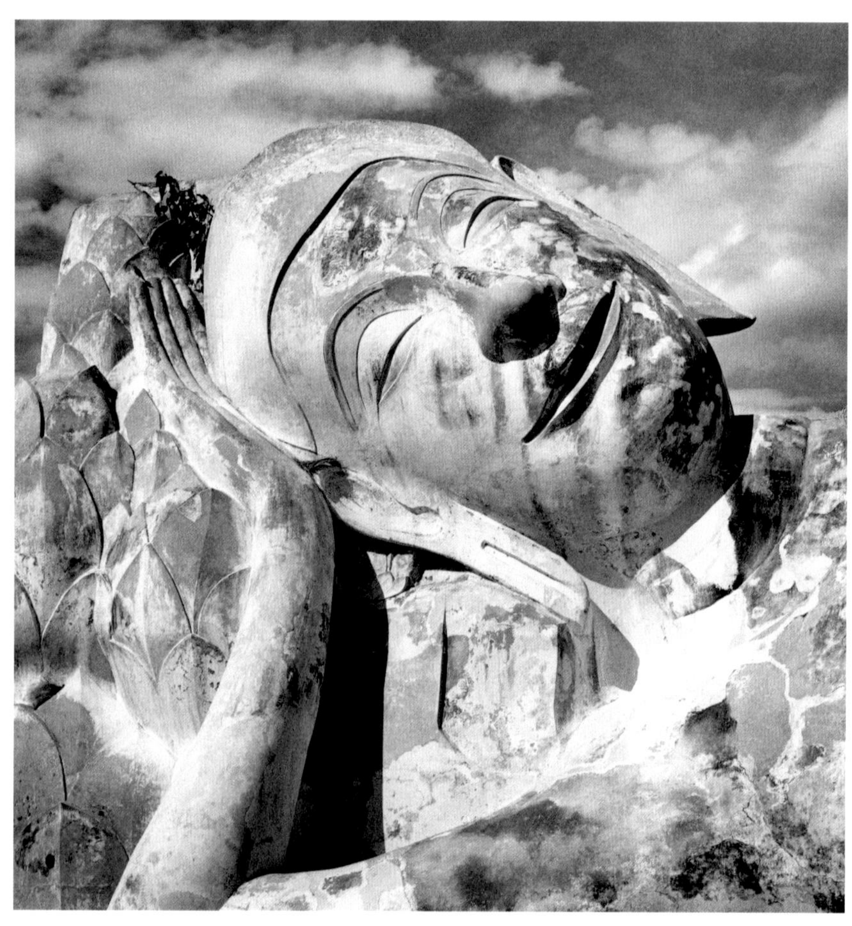

Sai Yat Reclining Buddha,
Ayutthaya, 2019

Wat Mahathat Seated Buddha,
Ayutthaya, 2019

THAILAND

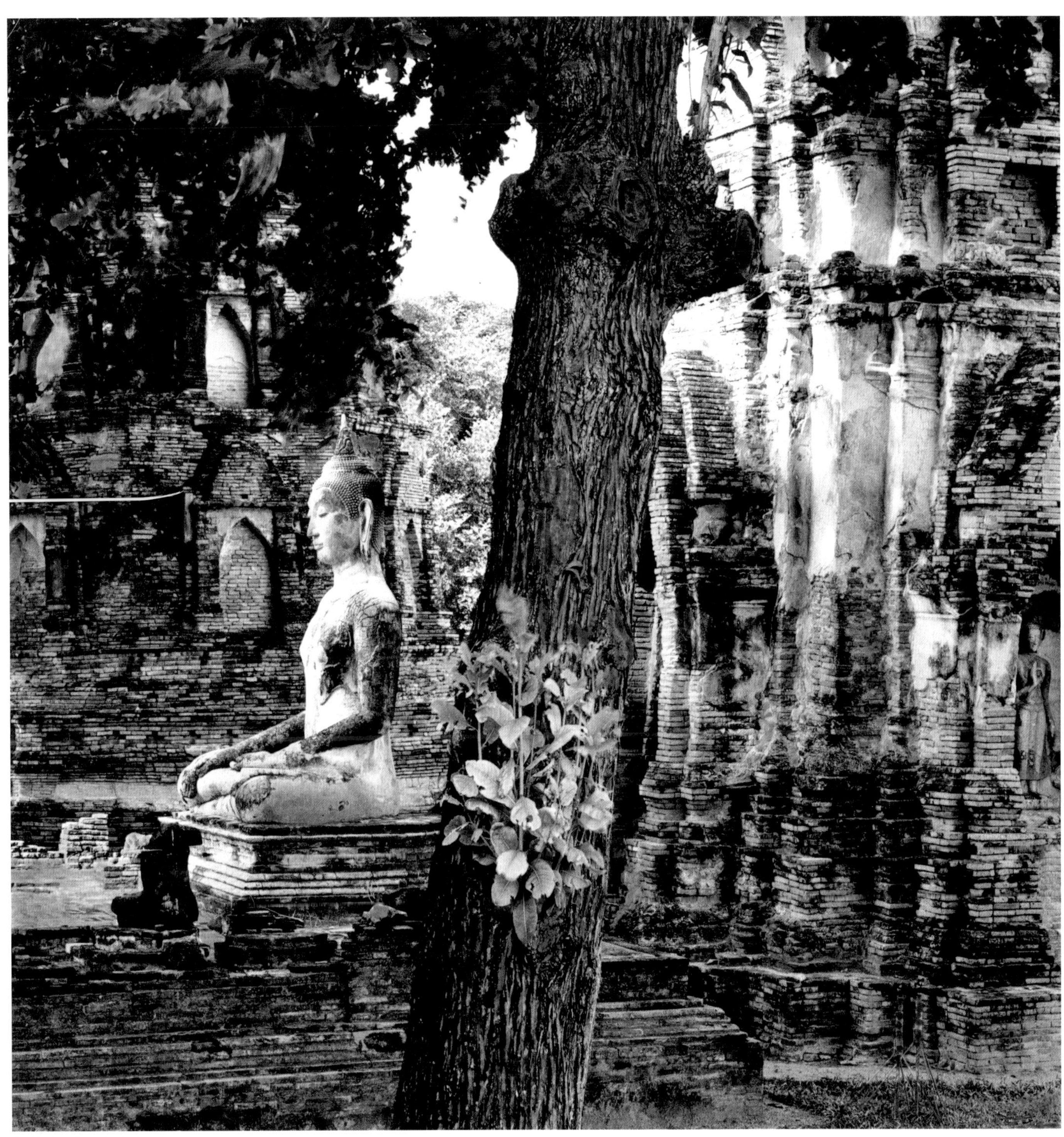

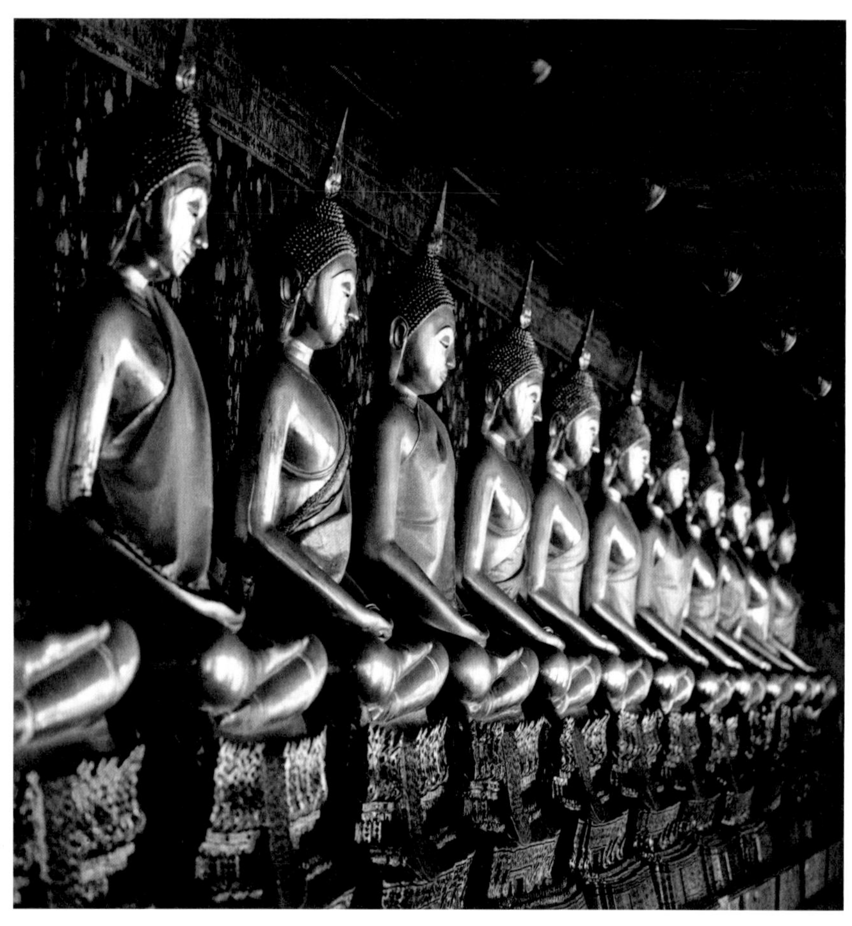

THAILAND

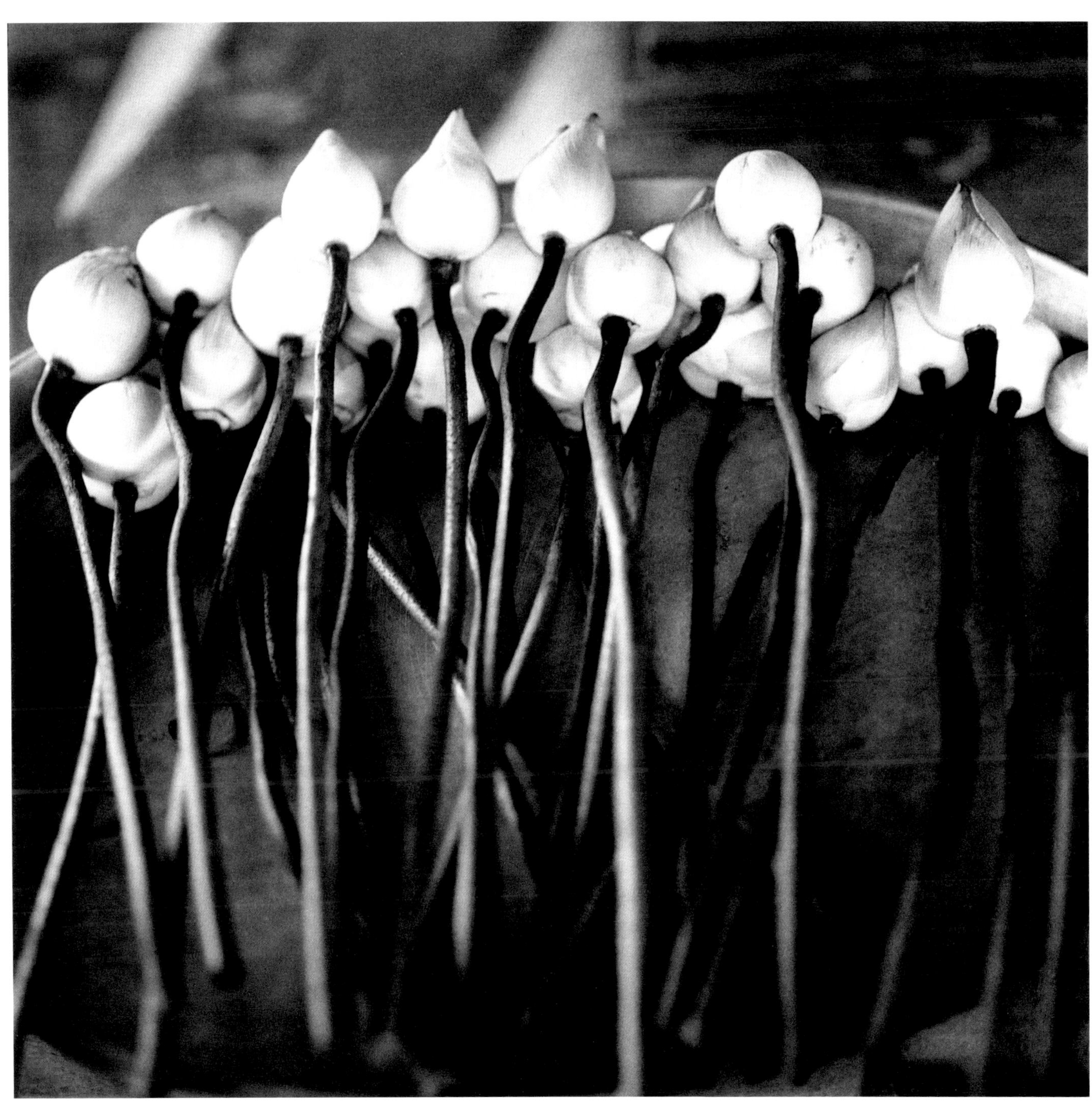

Wat Suthat Buddhas,
Bangkok, 2018

Temple Lotus Flowers,
Ayutthaya, 2019

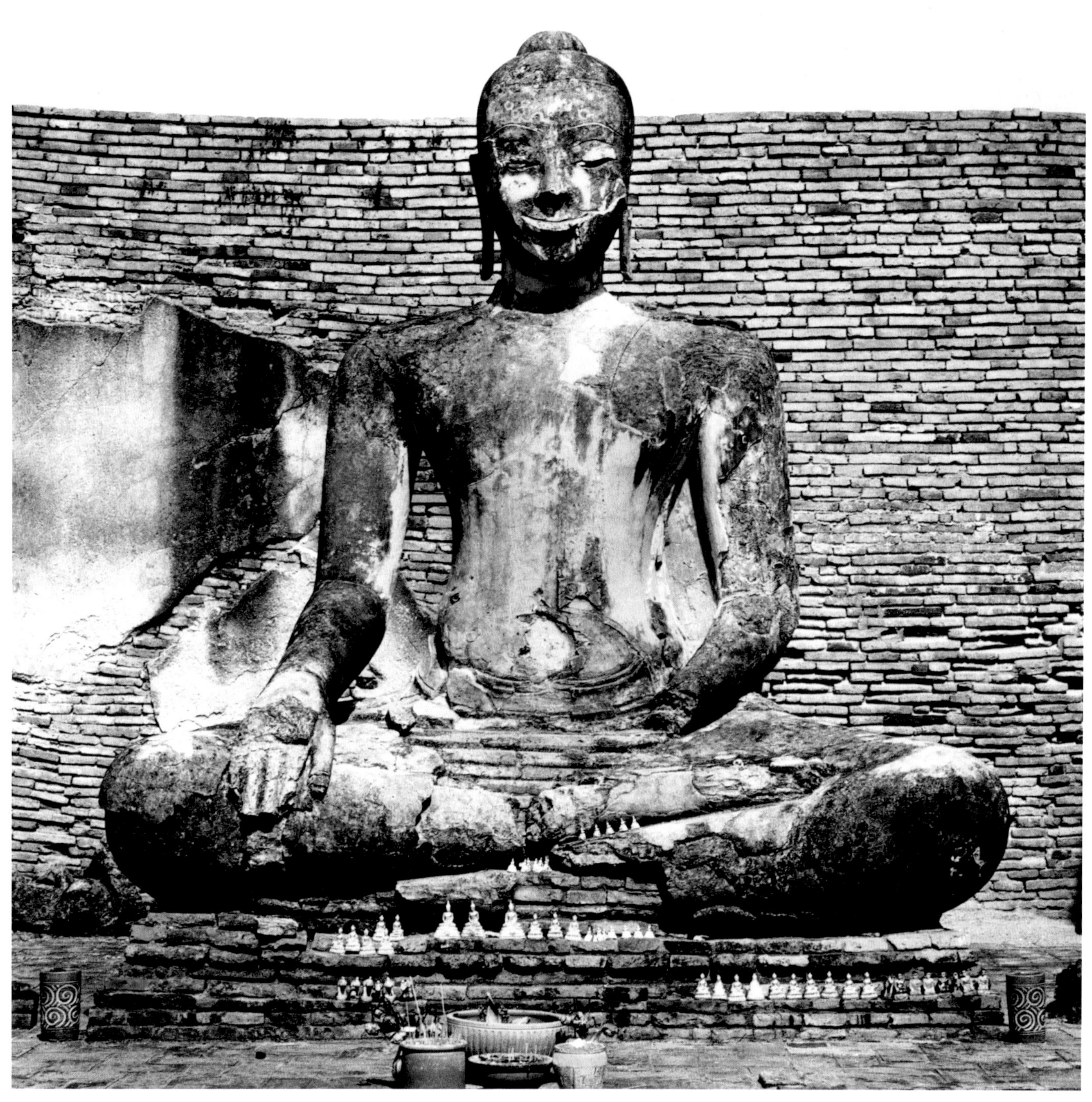

THAILAND

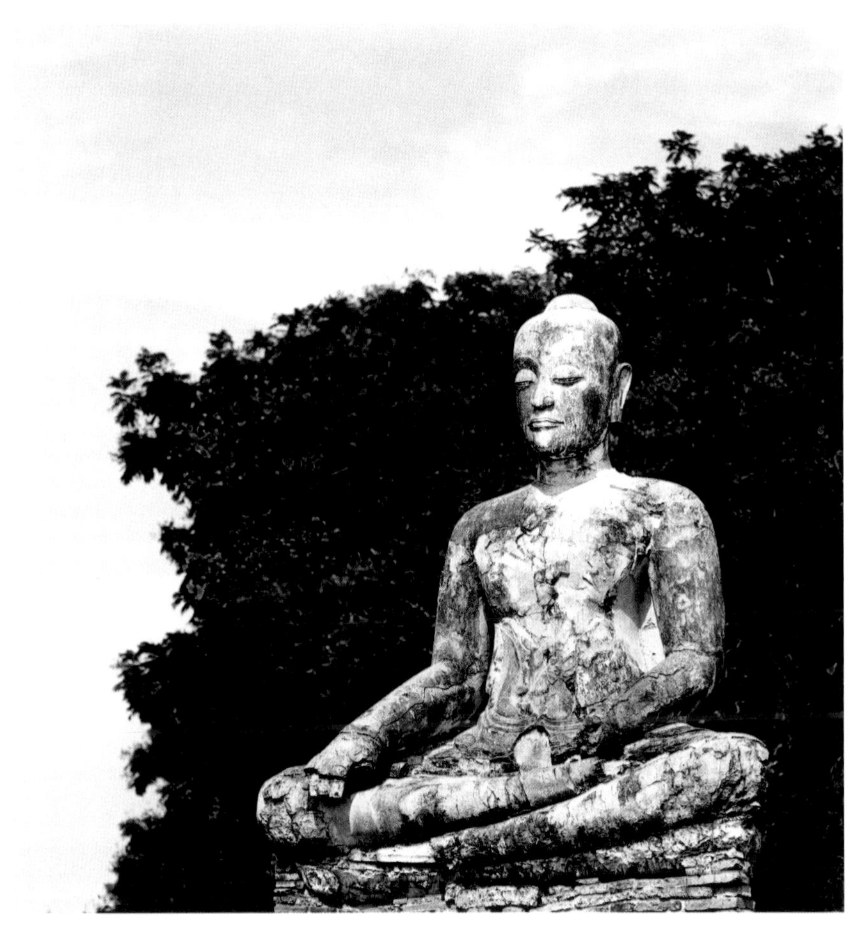

Wat Worachet Tharam Buddha,
Ayutthaya, 2019

Wat Worachet Taram Seated Buddha,
Ayutthaya, 2019

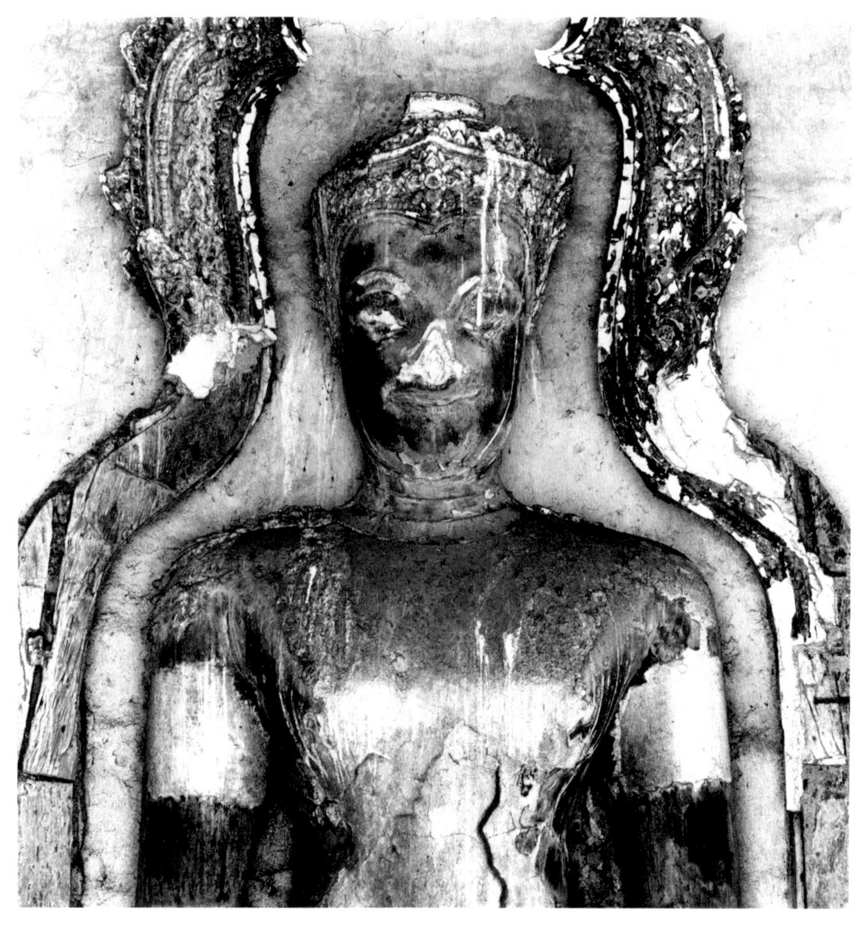

THAILAND

Wat Chaiwatthanaram Buddha
Remains, Ayutthaya, 2019

Wat Chaiwatthanaram Seated
Buddhas, Ayutthaya, 2019

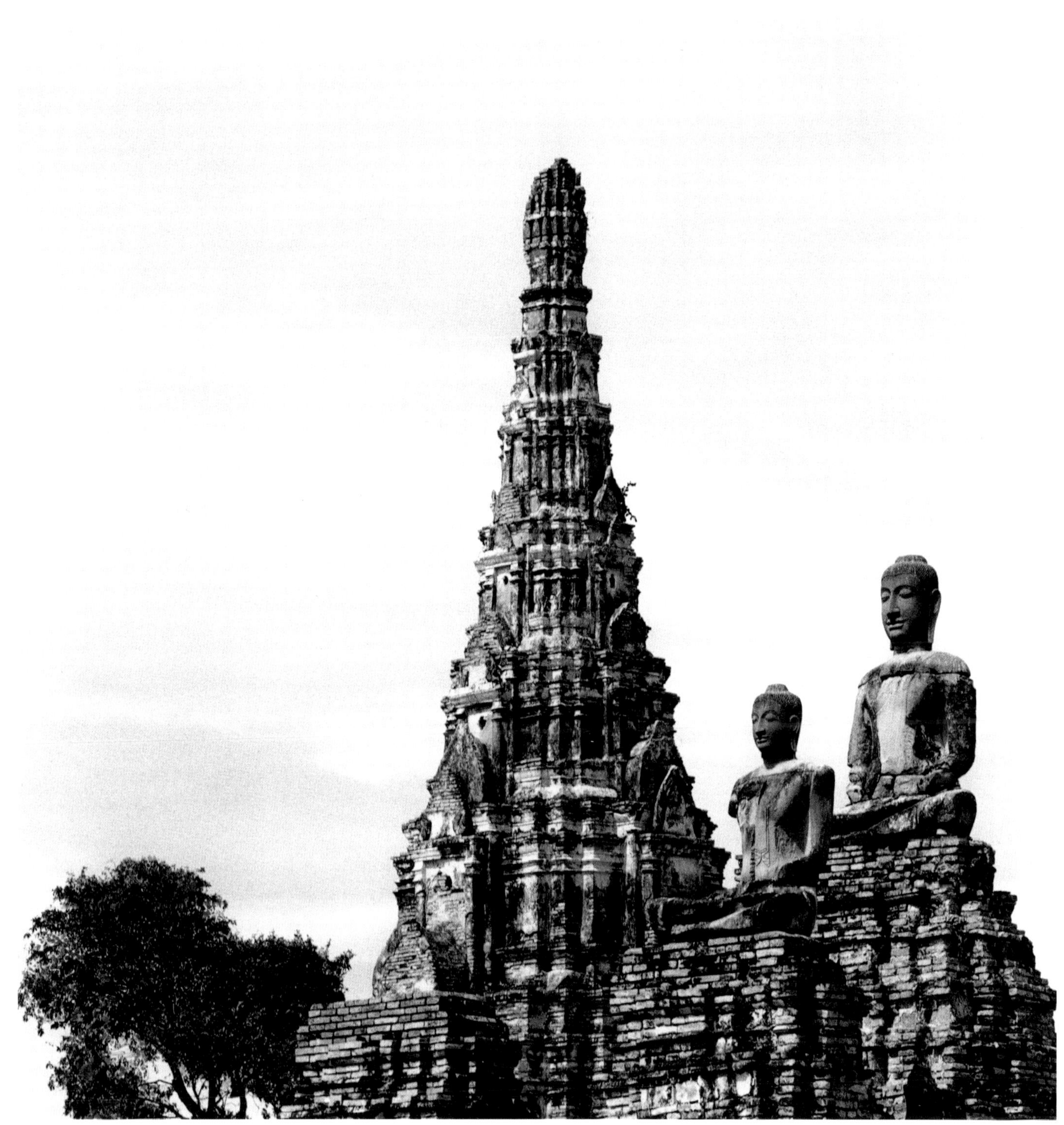

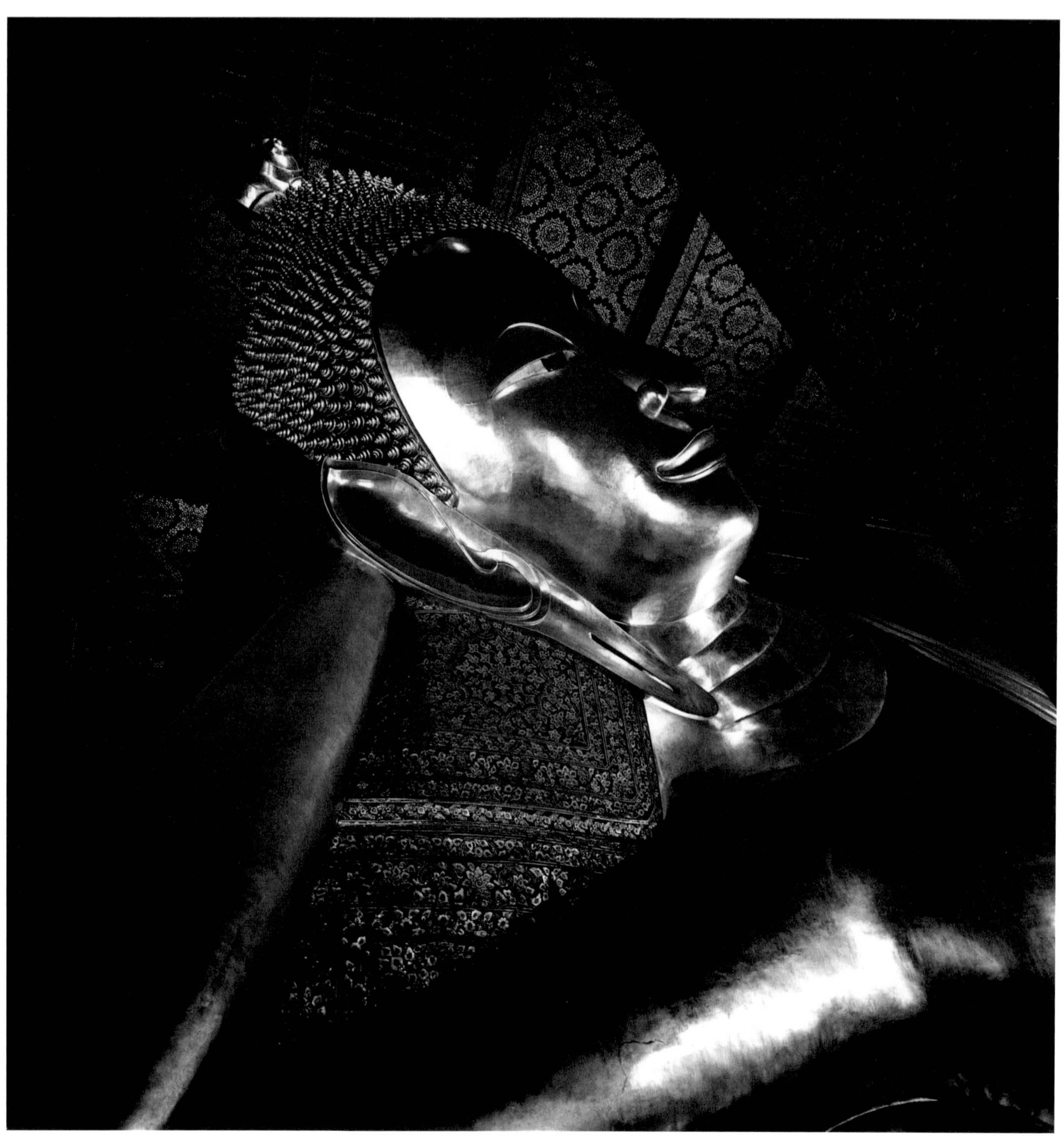

THAILAND

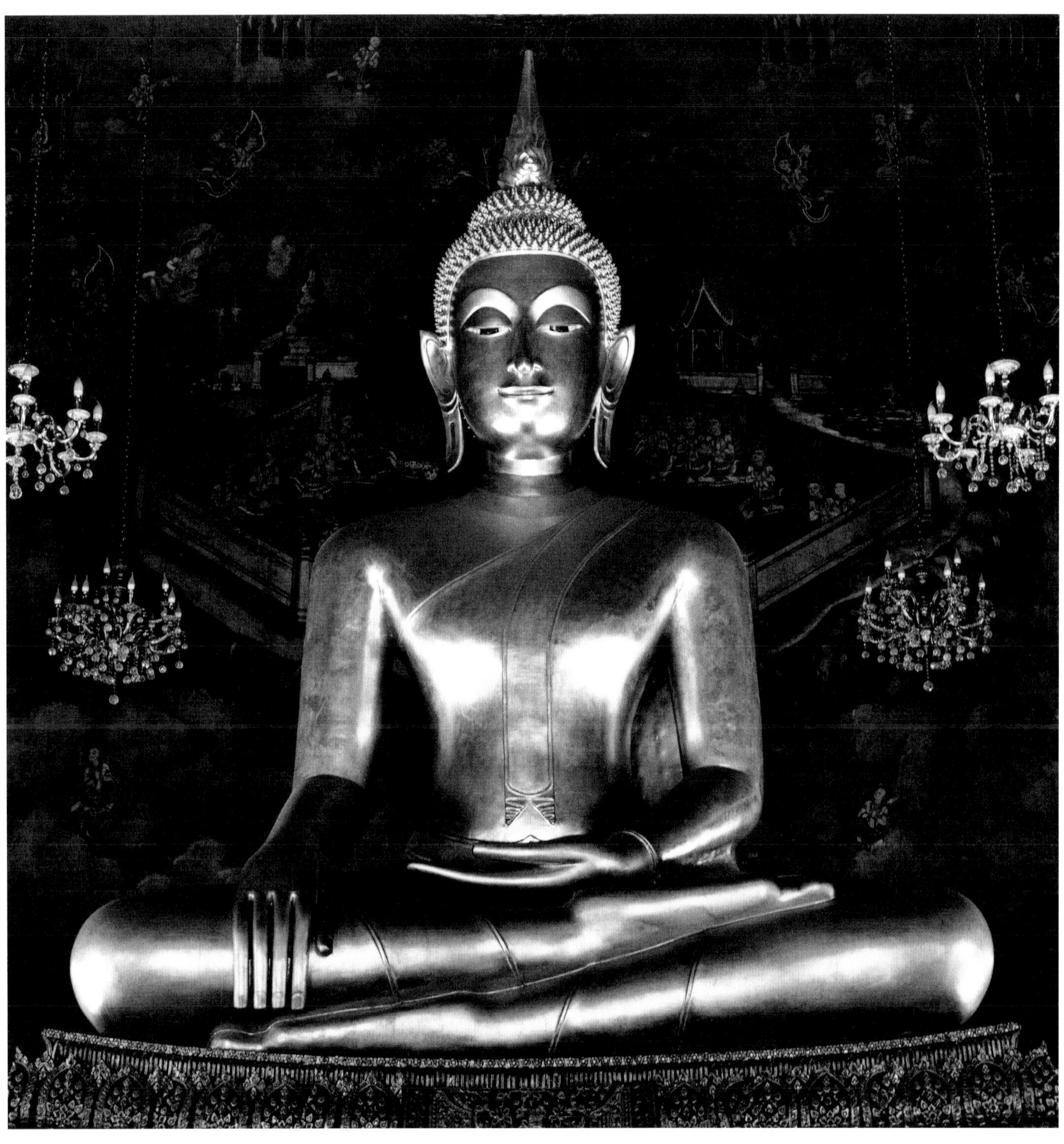

Wat Pho Reclining Buddha,
Bangkok, 2018

Samran Rat Buddha, Bangkok, 2018

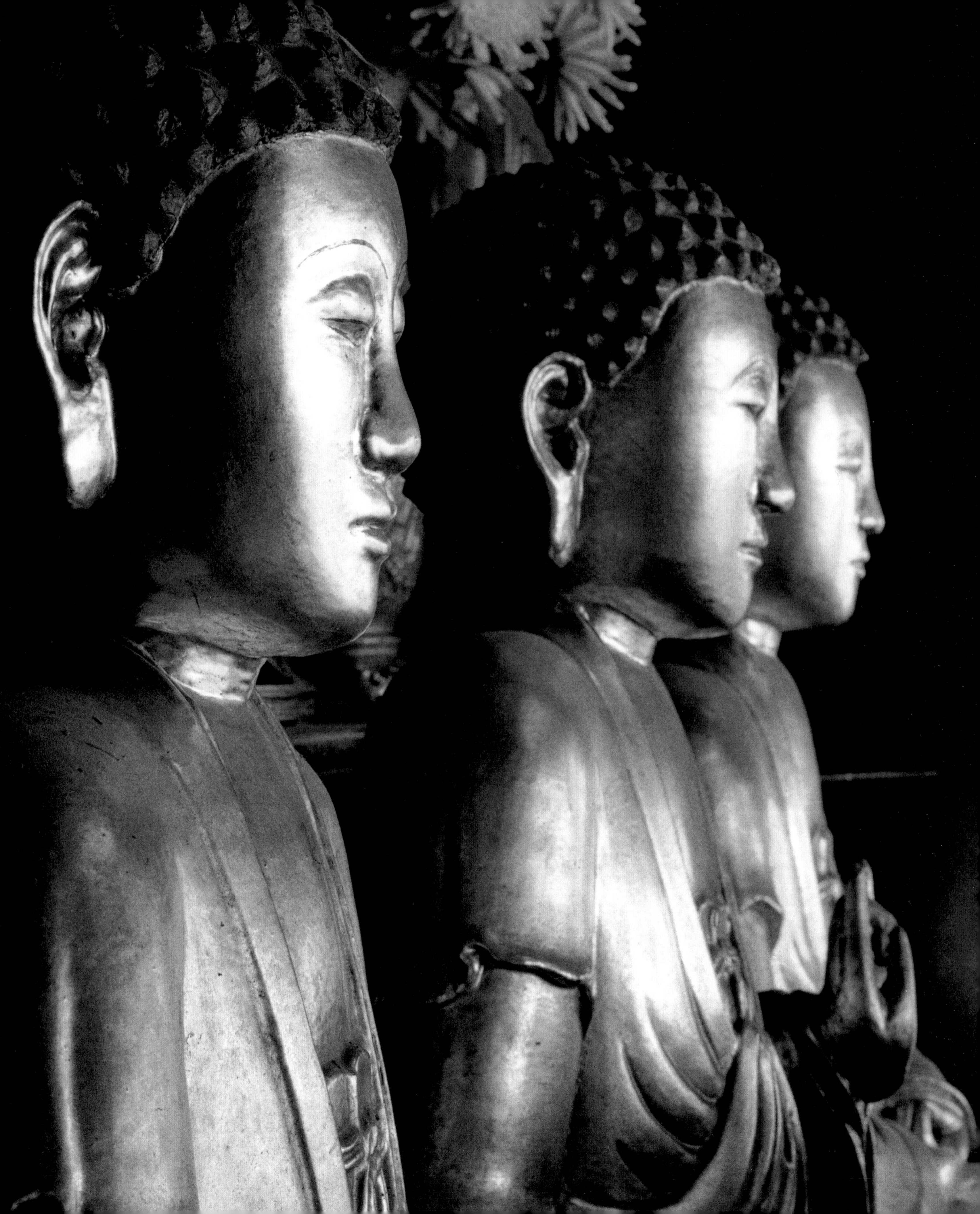

Vietnam

Tu Hieu Buddhas,
Hue, 2019

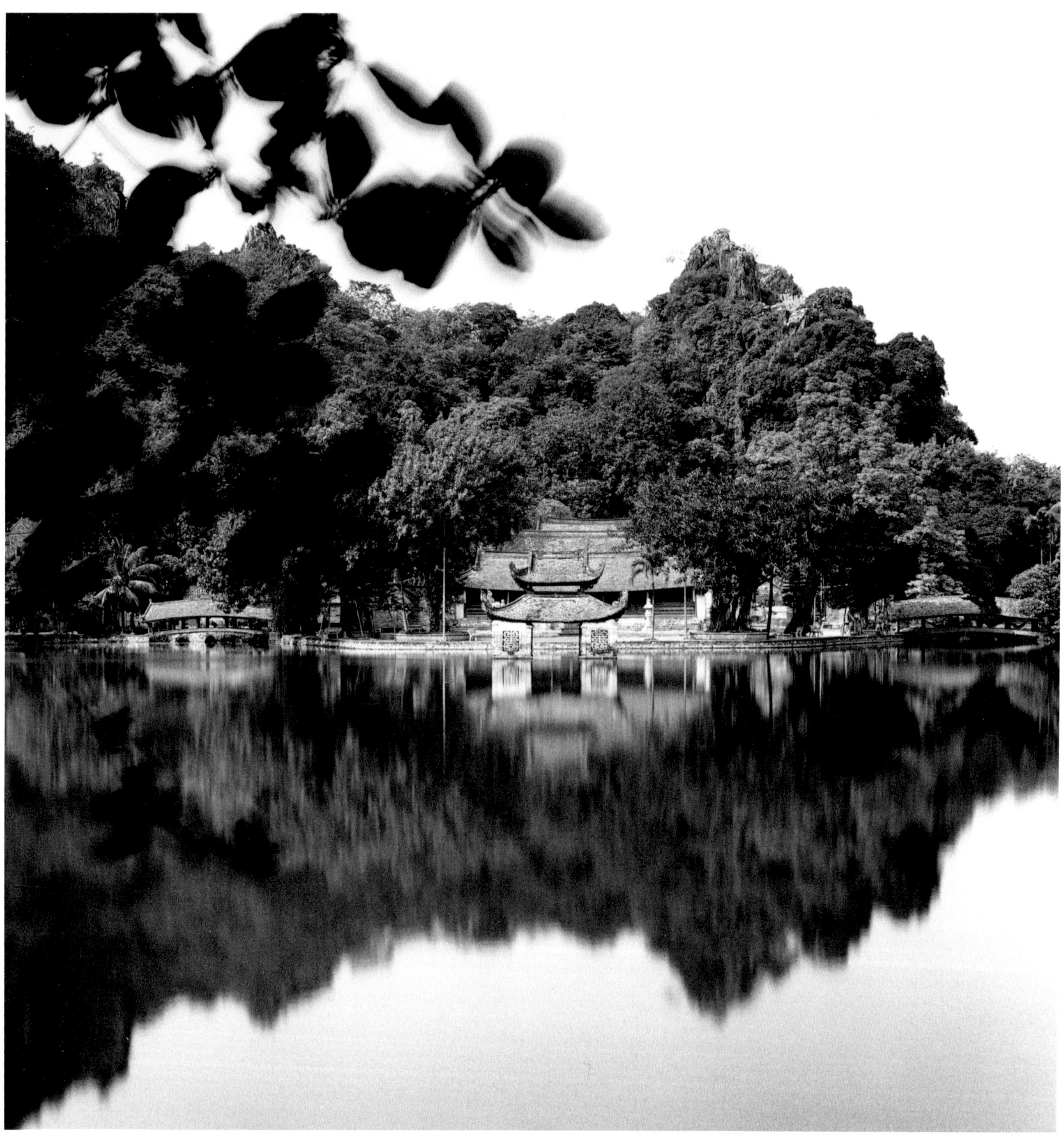

VIETNAM

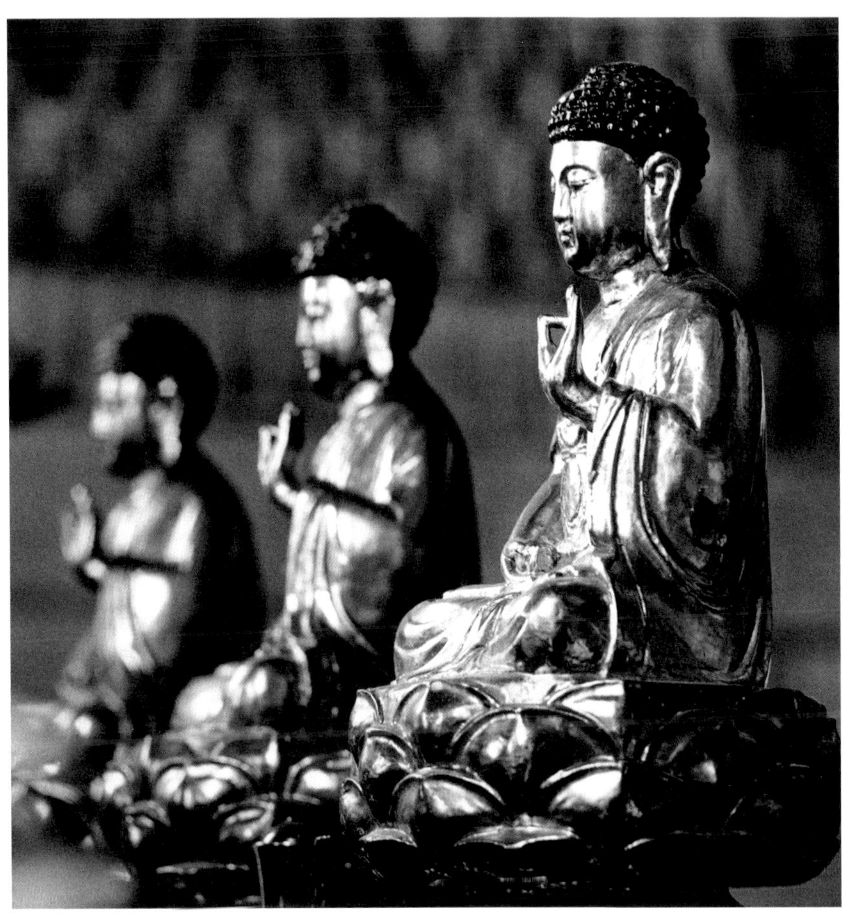

Tay Pagoda, Hanoi, 2019

Three Buddhas, Hanoi, 2019

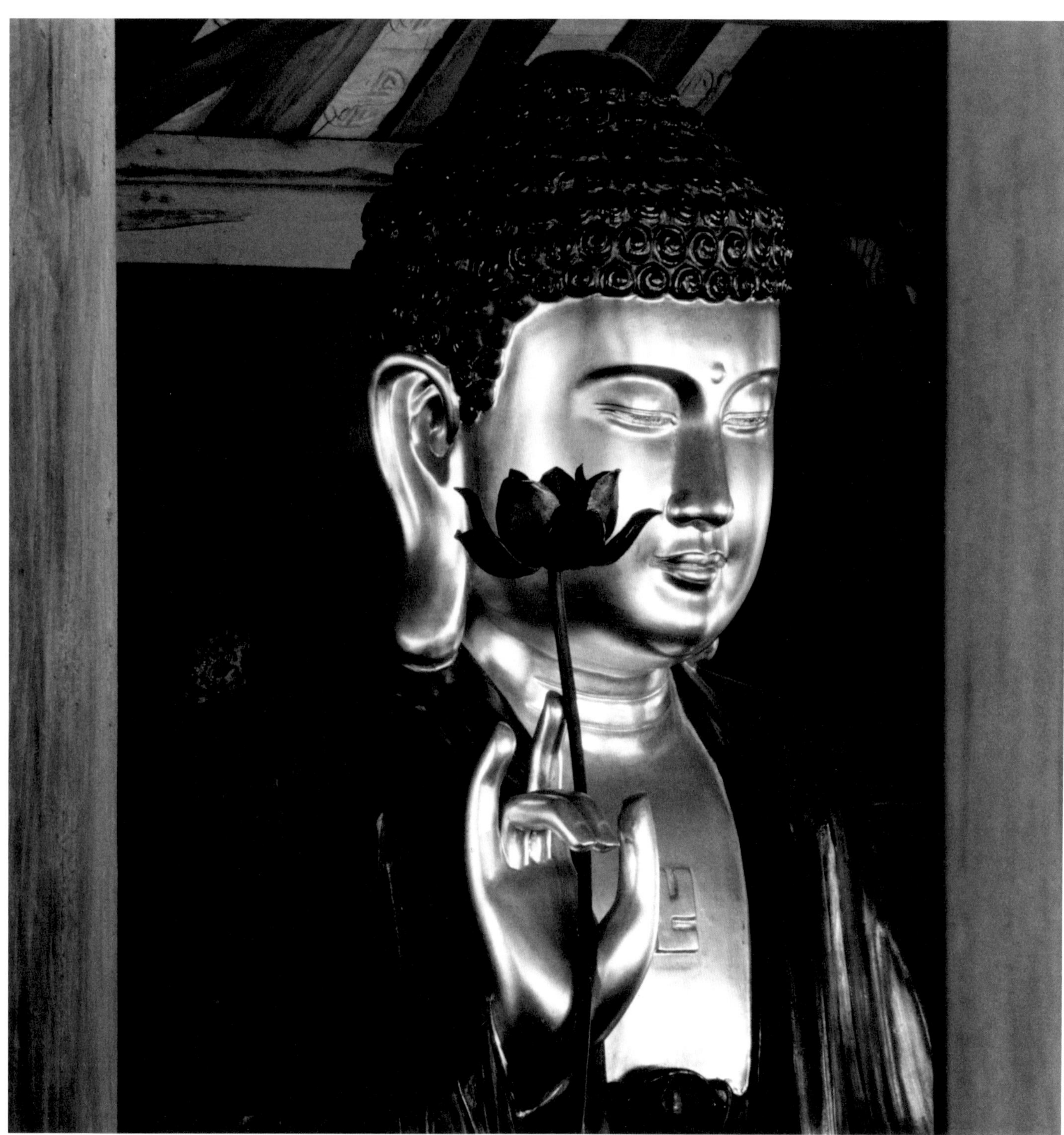

VIETNAM

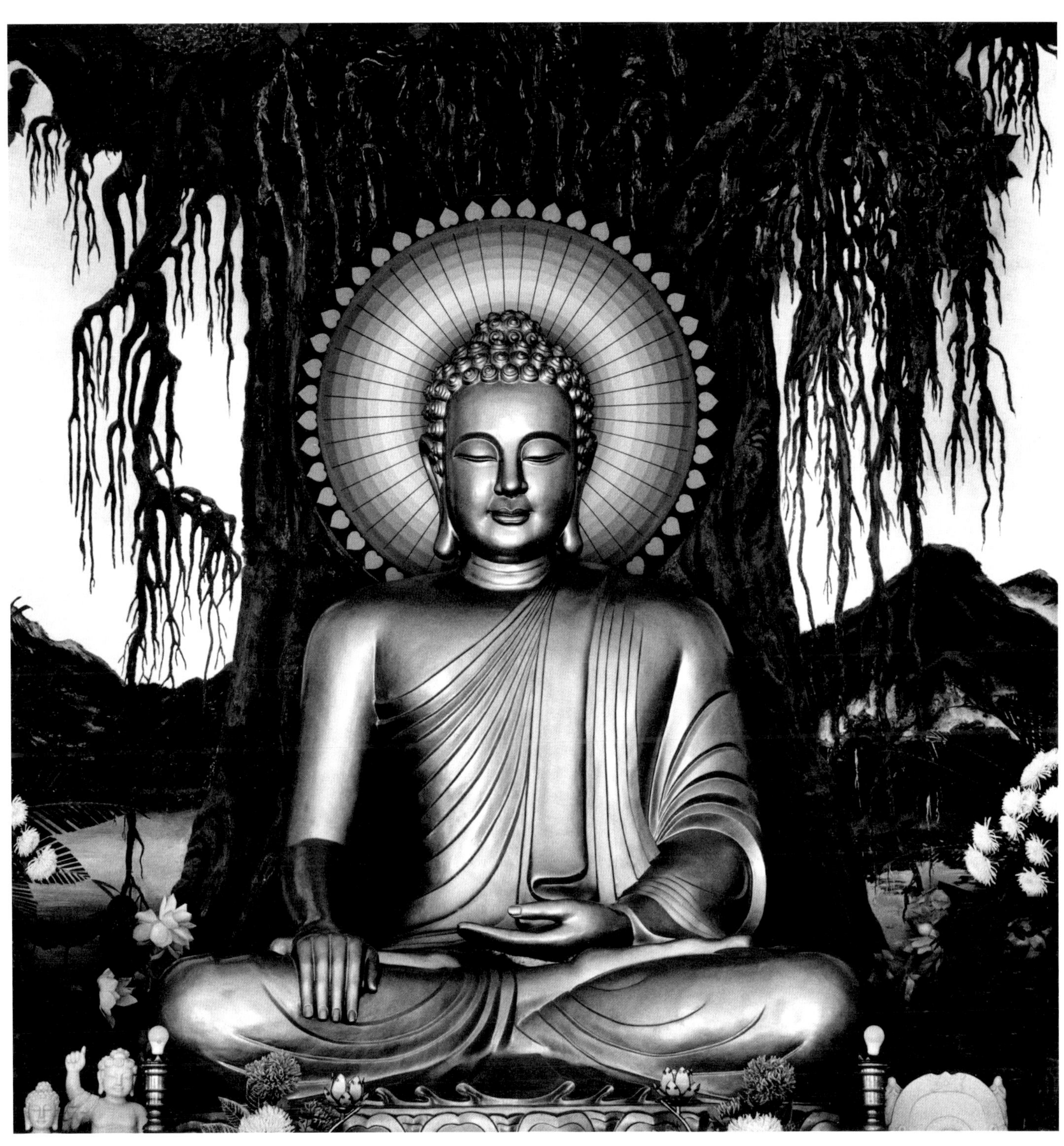

Buddha and Lotus Flower,
Hanoi, 2019

Buddha and Bodhi Tree,
Hue, 2019

VIETNAM

Marble Mountain Buddha,
Danang, 2019

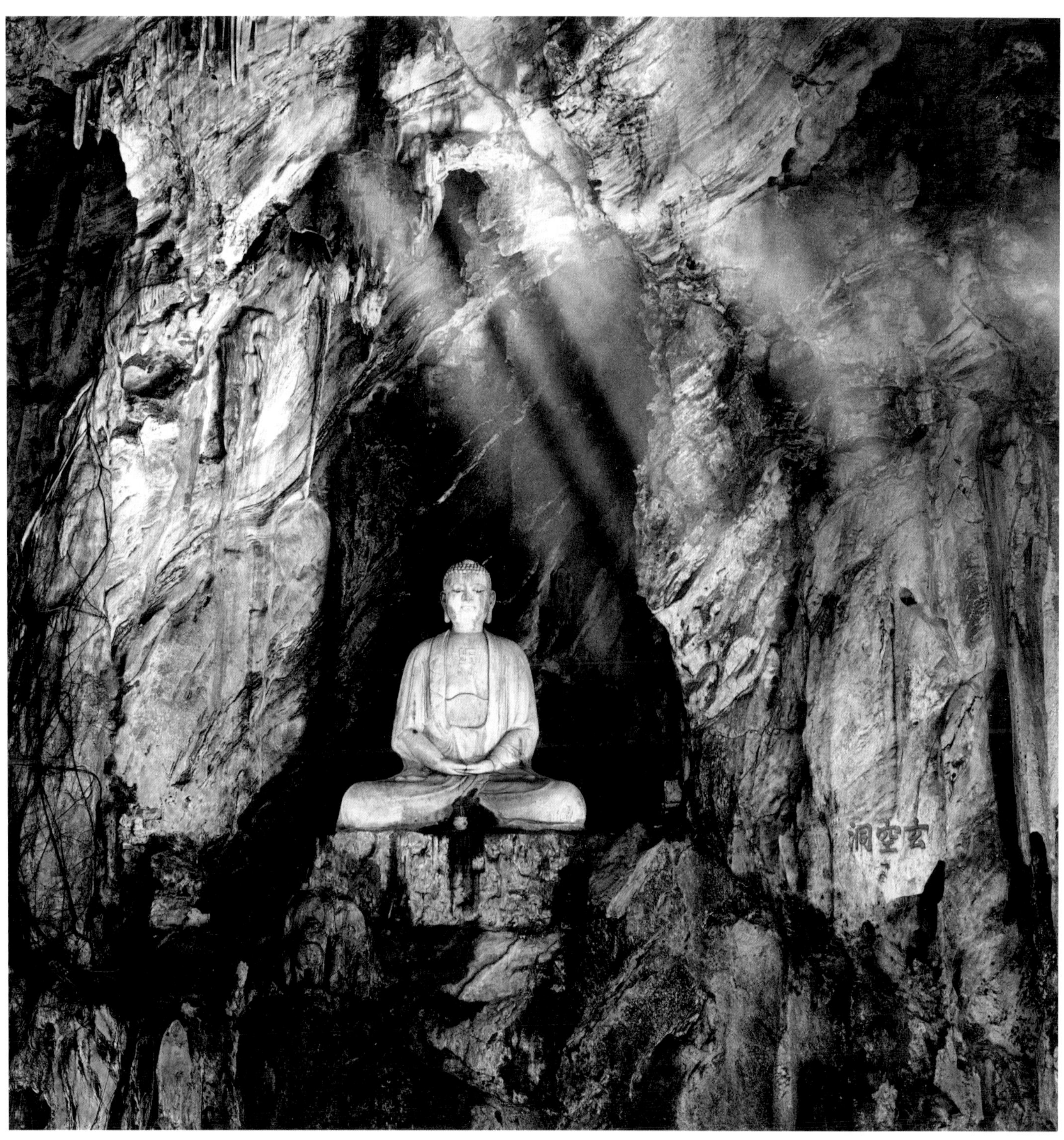
玄空洞

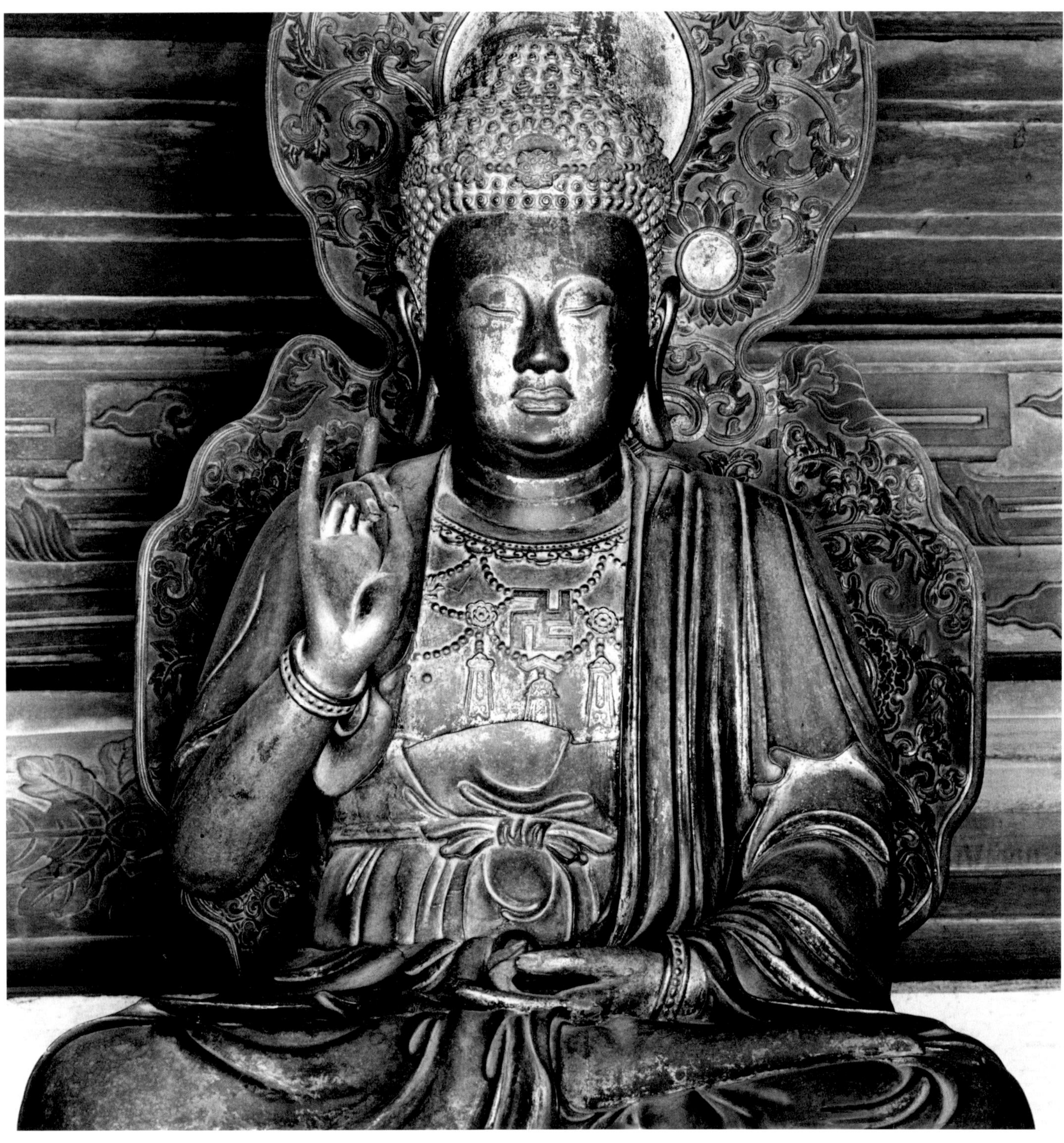

Tay Phuang Buddha,
Hanoi, 2019

Humid Landscape,
Ninh Binh, 2019

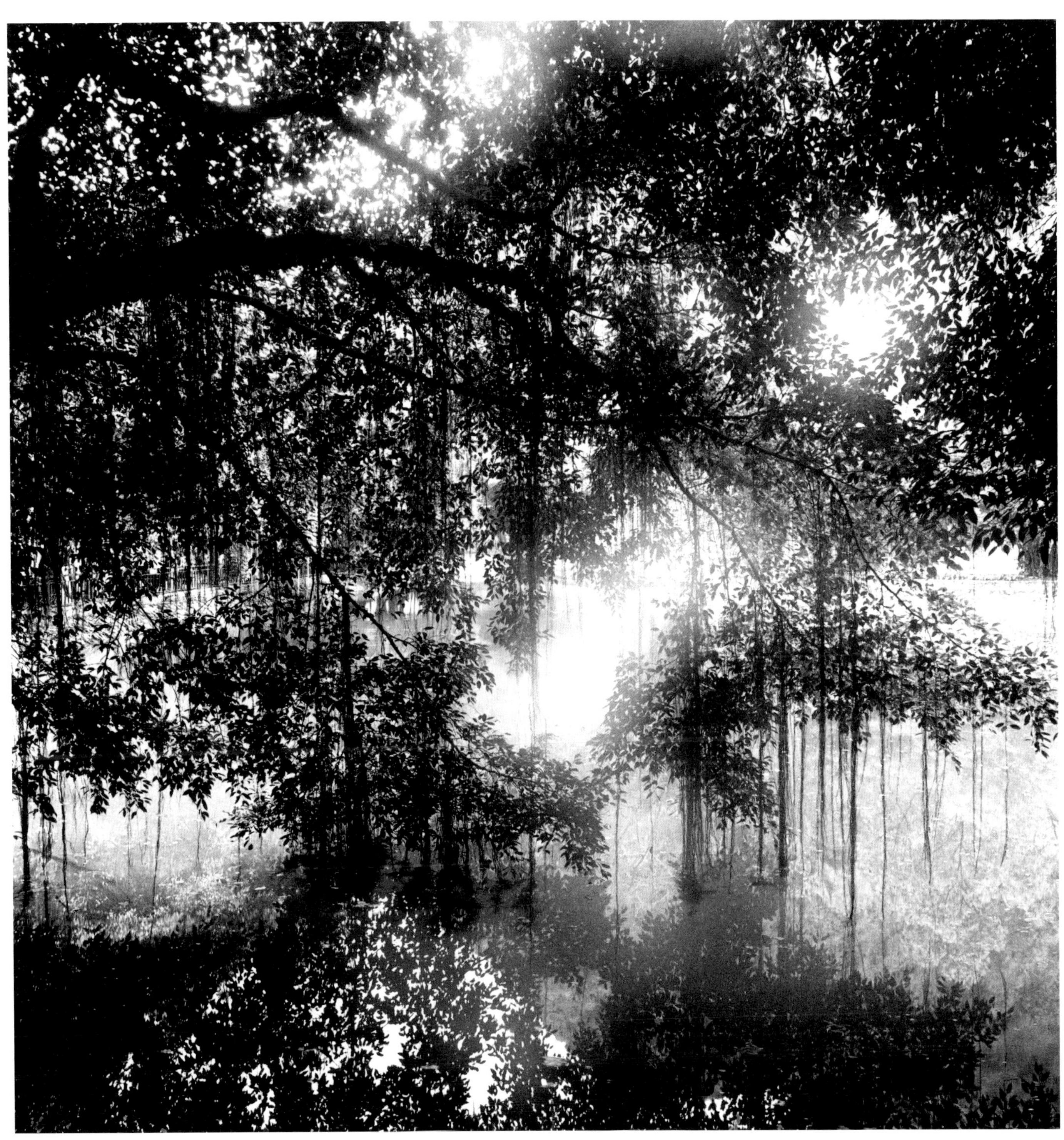

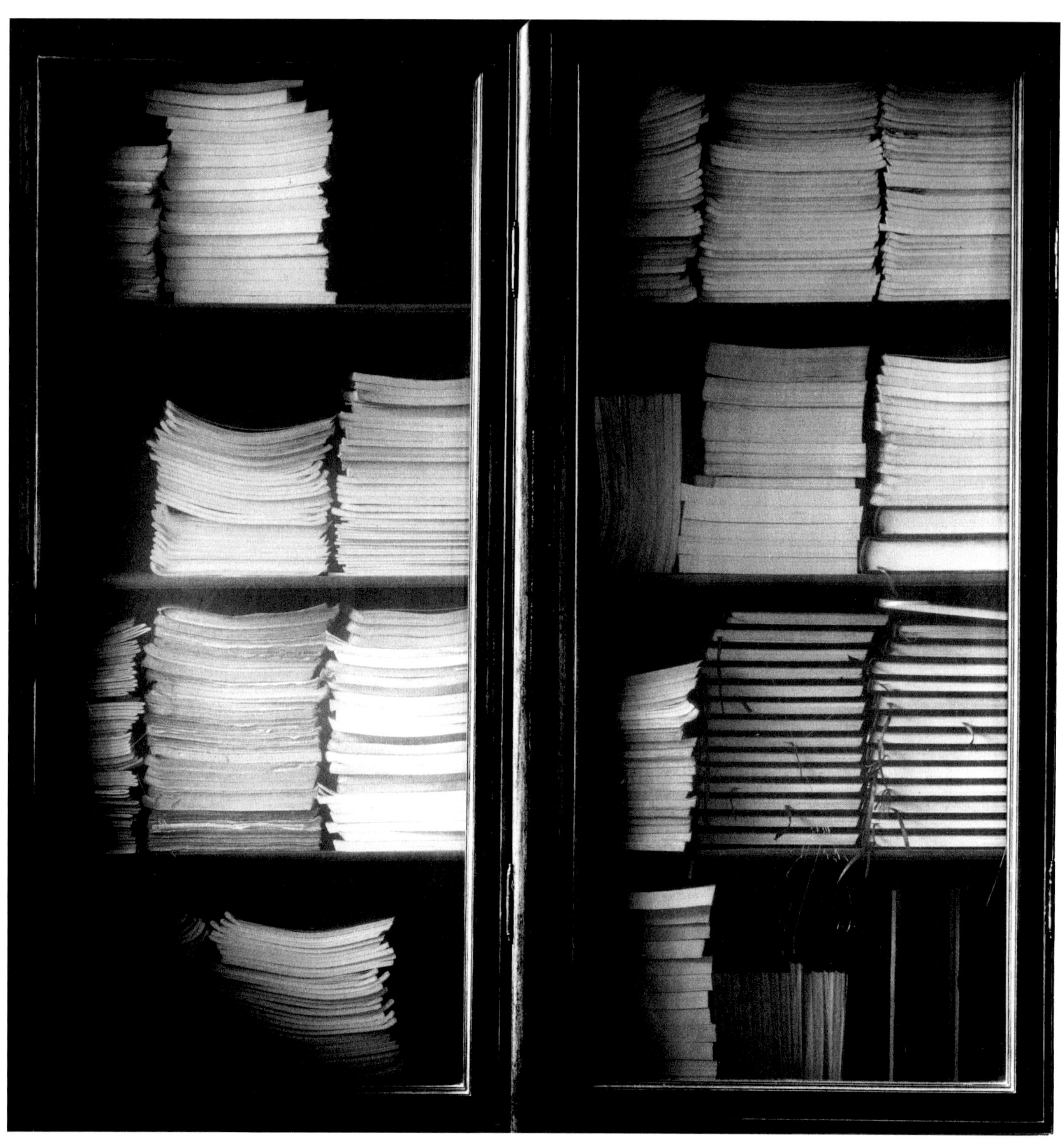

VIETNAM

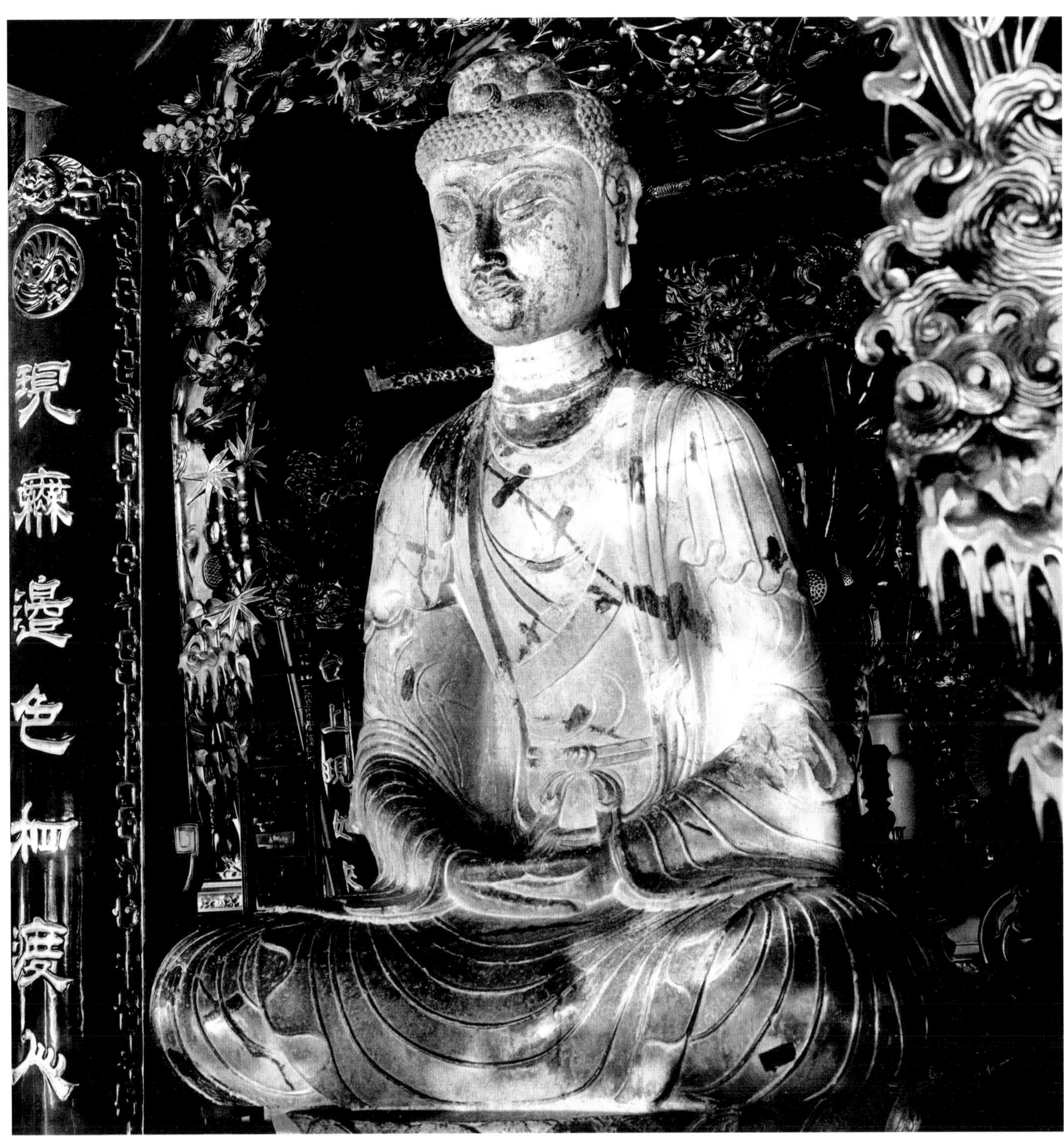

Prayer Books, Tay Pagoda,
Hanoi, 2019

Jade Buddha, Hanoi, 2019

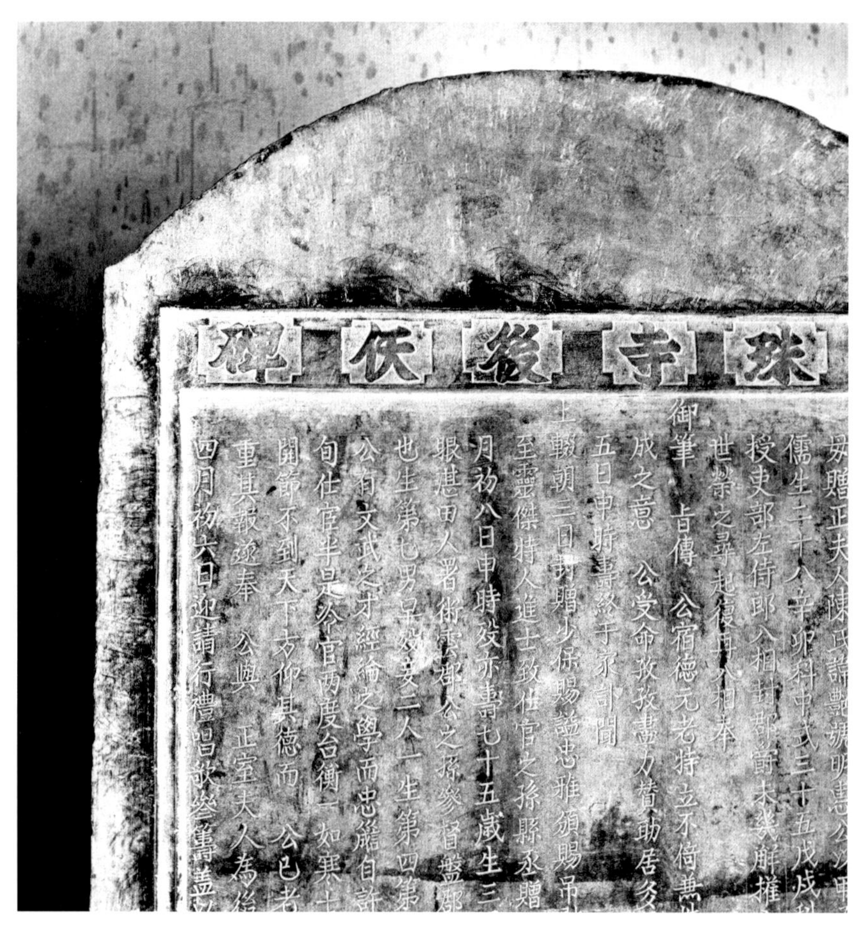

Monk's Epitaph,
Hanoi, 2019

Phat Tich Buddha,
Bac Ninh, 2019

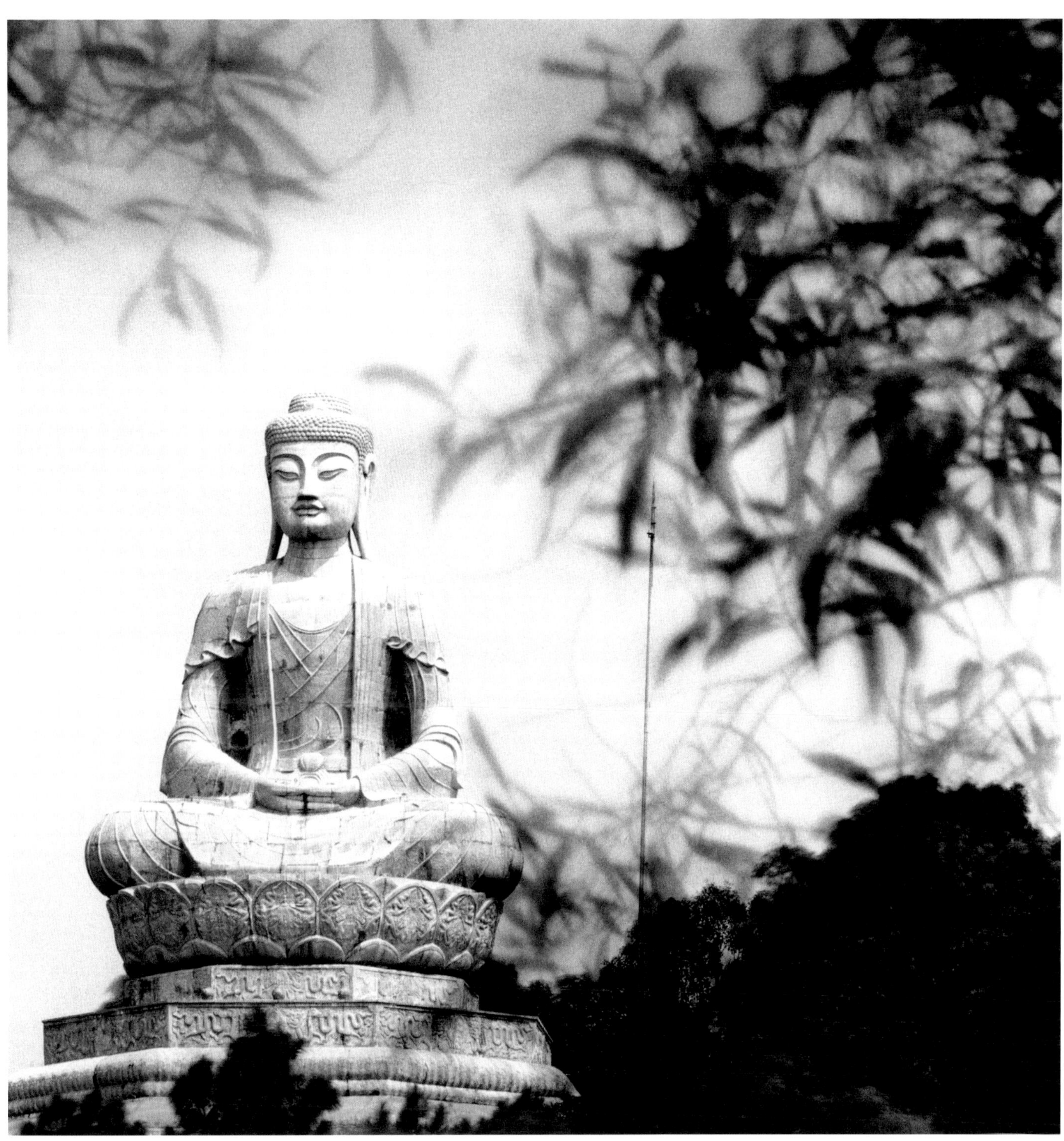

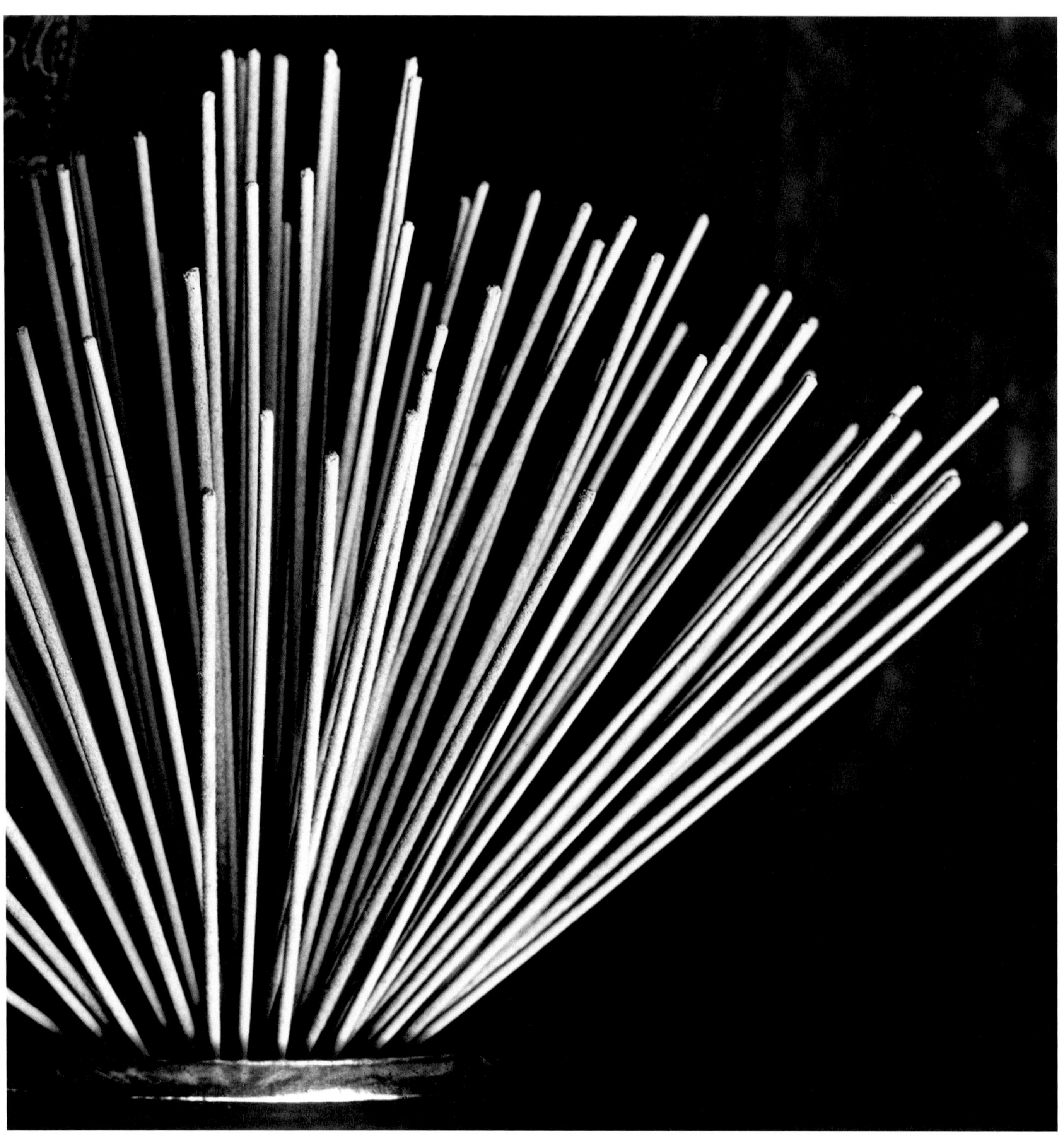

VIETNAM

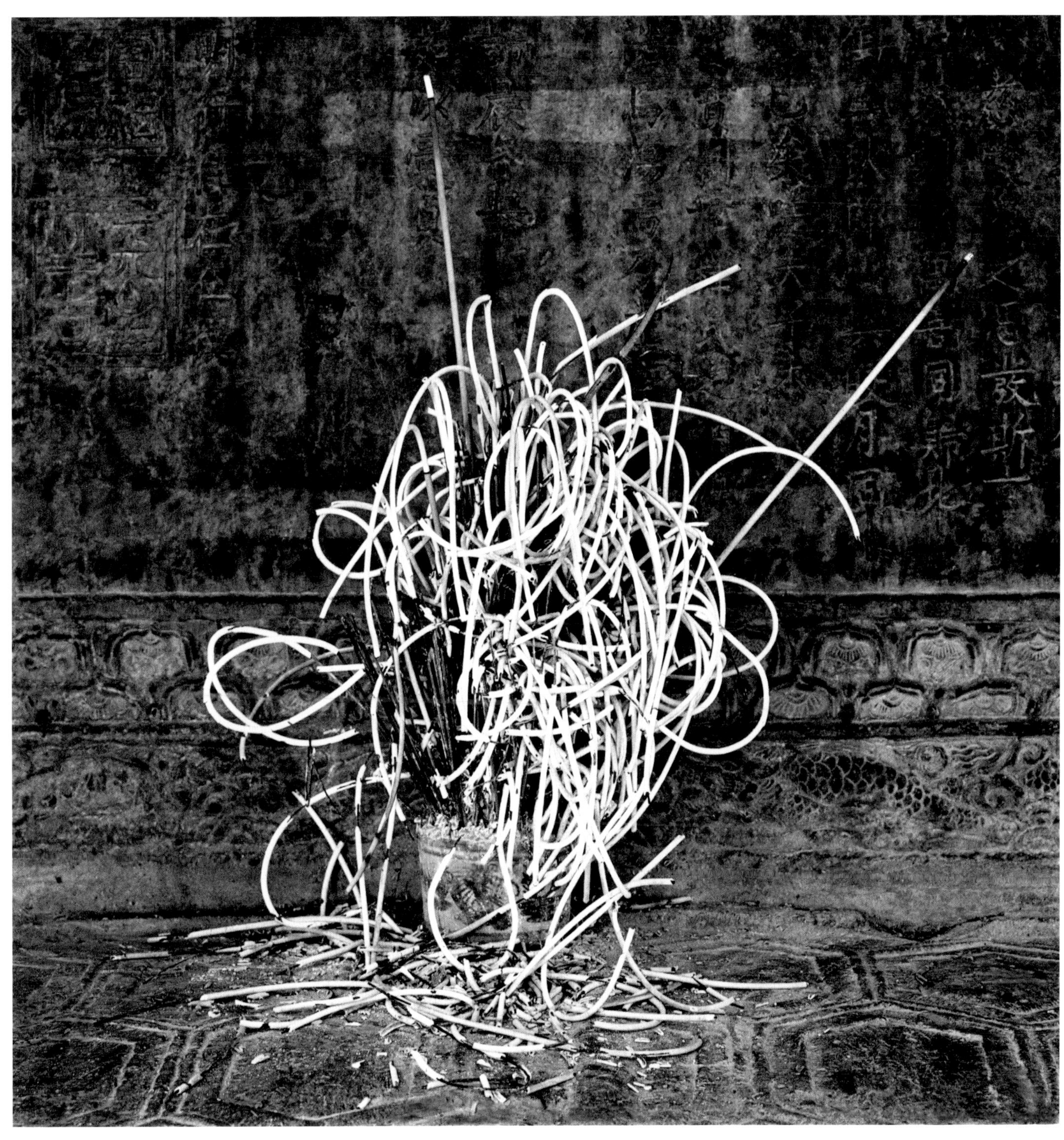

But Phap Incense Sticks,
Bach Ninh, 2019

Burnt Incense Sticks, Hanoi, 2019

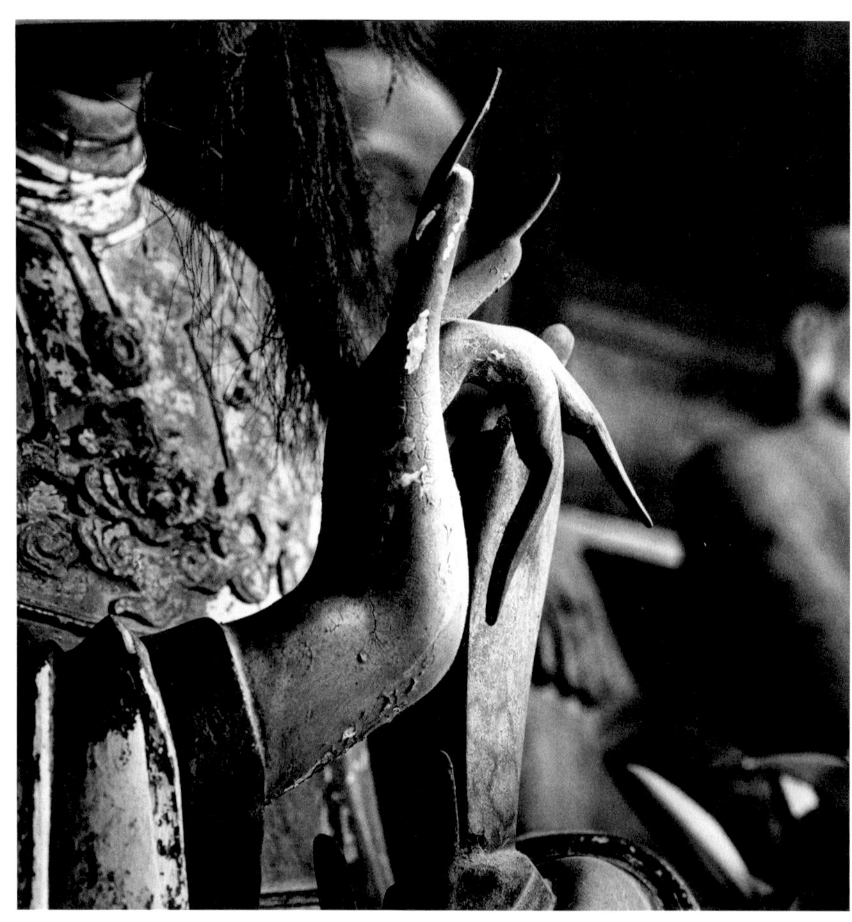

Long-Nailed Mudrā,
Hanoi, 2019

Lily Offerings, Tay Pagoda,
Hanoi, 2019

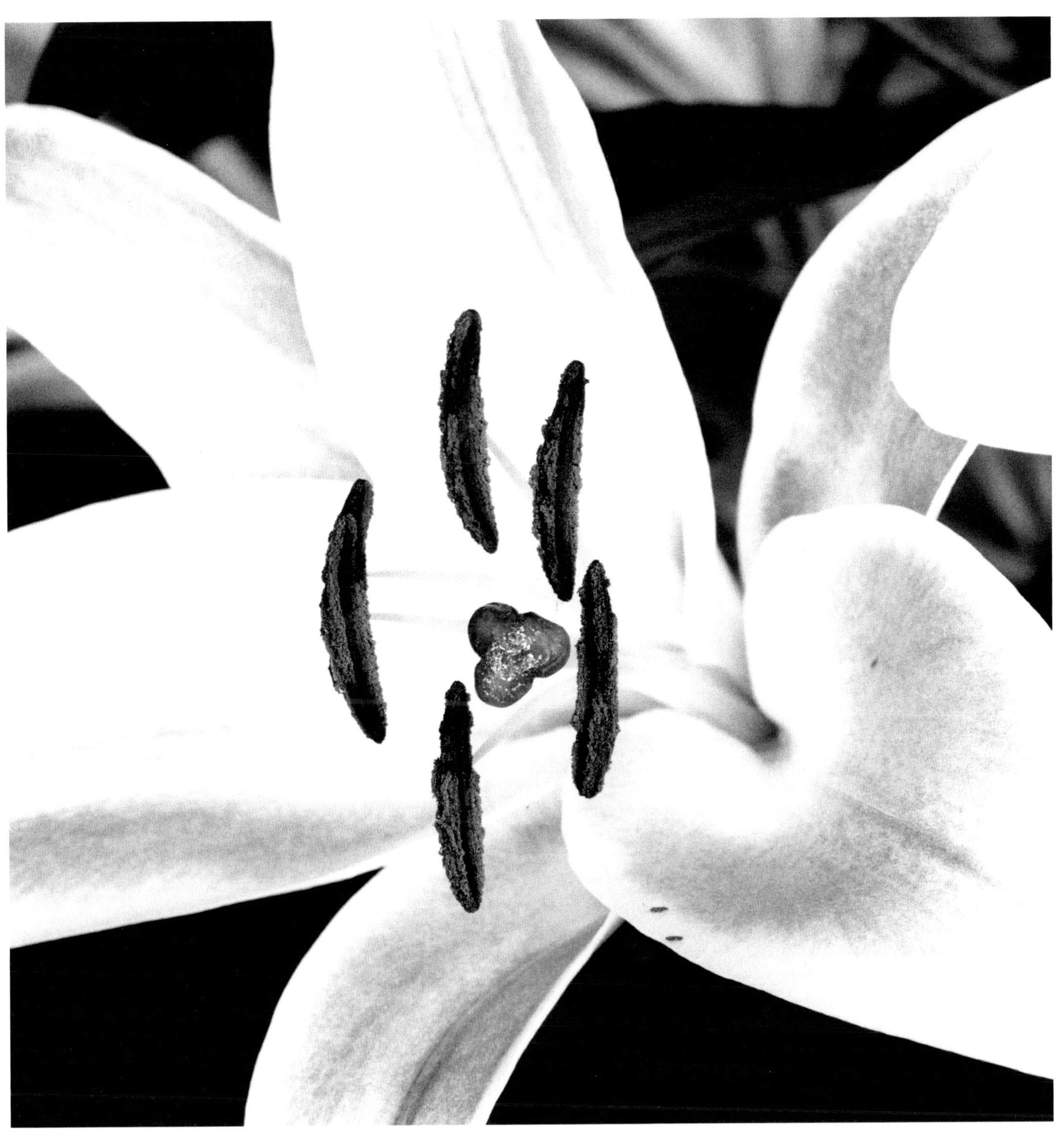

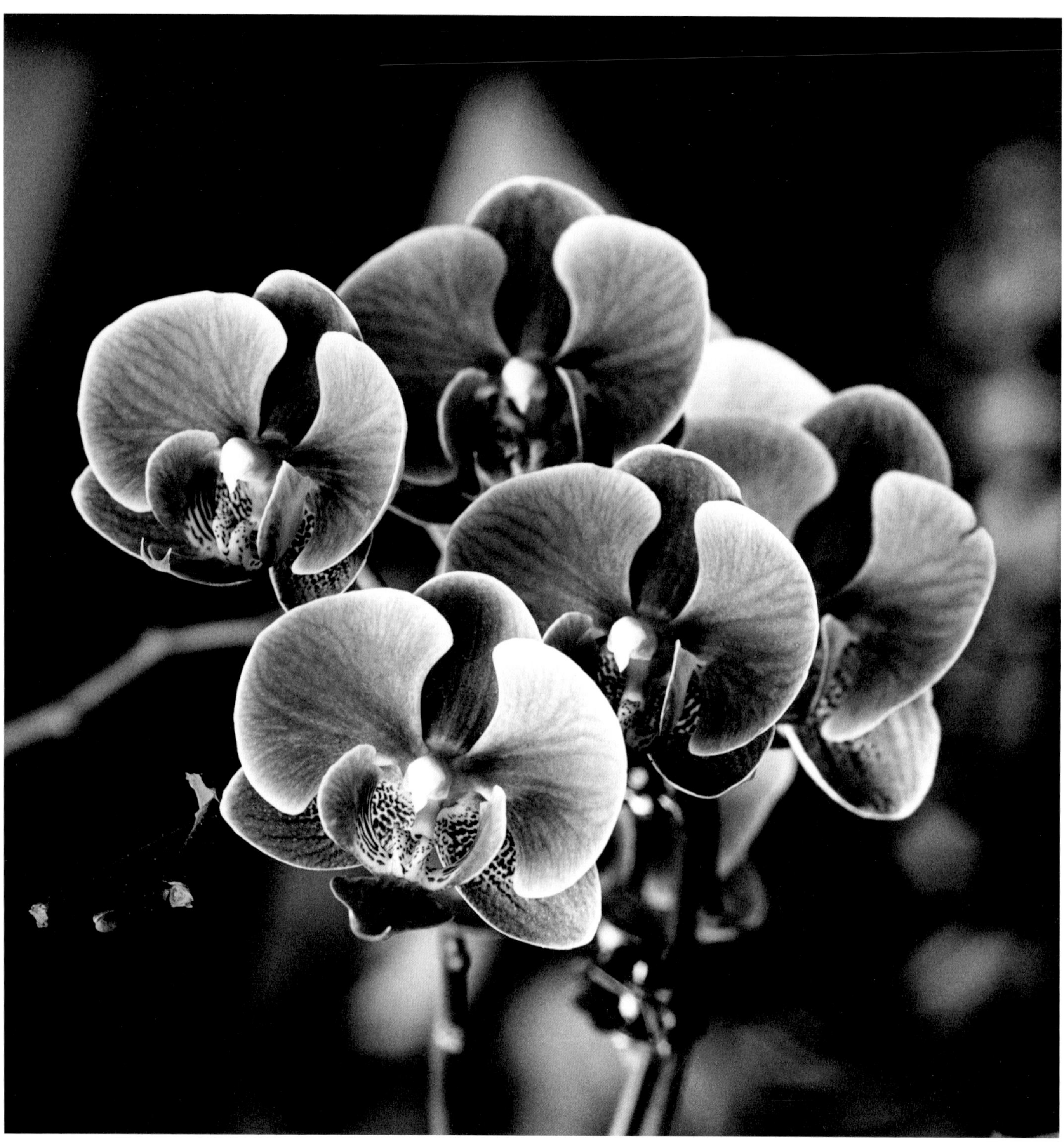

Orchid Offerings, But That Pagoda,
Bak Ninh, 2019

Phuac Hoa White Buddha,
Hue, 2019

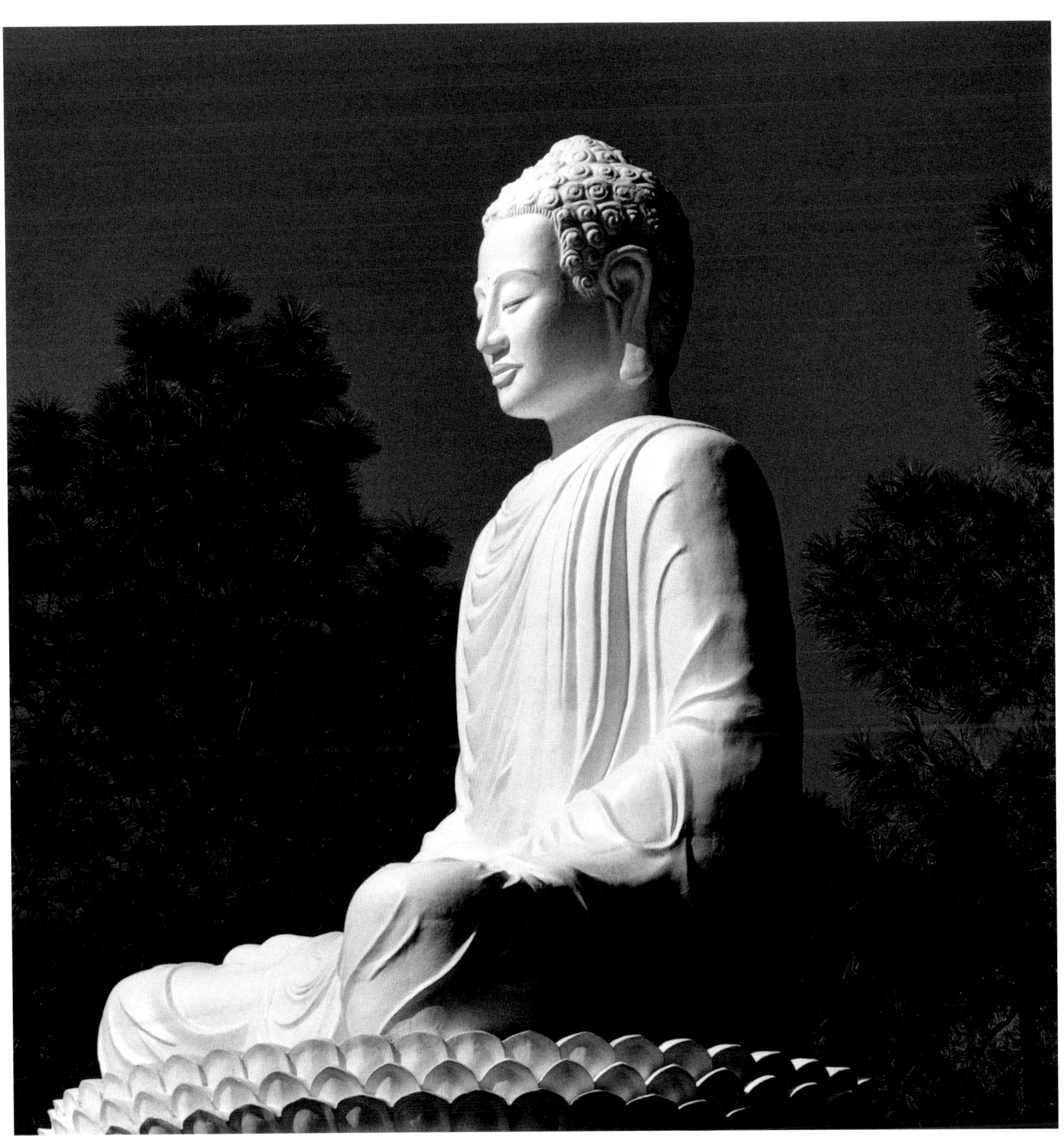

A PILGRIM'S PROGRESS

Visiting eighty-eight Buddhist temples throughout Shikoku, Japan, was a fiftieth-birthday gift to myself. The journey I took followed one taken more than twelve centuries previously by Kōbō-Daishi (aka Kūkai), the founder of the Shingon sect of Esoteric Buddhism. I suppose one might consider a Buddhist pilgrimage to be quite an odd birthday choice for someone raised in a rather strict Catholic family in northern England. I will therefore attempt to explain this decision.

In my younger days, as soon as I was old enough, I became an altar boy at my local church of St Bede's, Widnes. I learnt the duties and responses required, and served at baptisms, confirmations, first holy communions, masses, weddings and funerals. All these services were in Latin, which meant that I had no real idea what was being said. I had to use my imagination, which added several extra layers of mystery and intrigue to these rituals. St Bede's also drew me back between services. I spent many solitary hours there, sitting, kneeling, walking, praying or just listening, absorbed by the atmosphere and interior architecture of the church. A faint scent of incense from earlier services usually lingered in the air, and a lit candle over the altar symbolized that an unseen but present God was at home, hidden in the tabernacle in the form of the host, a wafer of consecrated bread.

At the age of ten, my most fervent wish, other than to become a rugby league player, was to be a priest myself, so that I could continue to explore the mysterious rituals embedded in the Catholic religion. I subsequently applied to and was accepted at St Joseph's College, Upholland, a seminary boarding school. I lived and studied there for the next seven years and learnt more about prayer, meditation, silence, patience and discipline, as well as other more academic subjects. For various reasons, which is a whole other story, I did not become a priest. I chose instead the path of an artist.

In 1987, I visited Tokyo for an exhibition opening of my photographic work. I subsequently travelled on to Kyoto and Nara to photograph. This is when I first experienced Buddhist temples and Shinto shrines. I was immediately mesmerized by the complex and imaginative statuary and imagery, particularly the enormous Vairocana Buddha at the Tōdaiji temple complex in Nara. There was something so powerful, awe-inspiring and yet calmly peaceful and serene about this massive Buddha, and it kindled an immense curiosity in me. Up to this point, I had been indifferent and quite ignorant about Buddhism. This now changed and I felt the need to educate myself. Over the following years, whenever I revisited Japan, I sought out temples, shrines and museums which had Buddhist content. The temples I wandered into often turned out to be seductively atmospheric places, fragrant with exotic incense and replete with offerings of fruit, flowers and singular imagery. Chants and incantations, again in a language I did not understand, were punctuated by the ringing of bells, and in the Shinto shrines, by the clapping of hands. These spaces held a fascination and attraction closely akin to how I had felt in the churches of my youth. They touched a certain note in my being and I was captivated. I began to read about Siddhārtha Gautama and the origins of Buddhism, and I continued to photograph.

In 2003, I made the month-long birthday pilgrimage through Shikoku. I did not know what to expect, but it proved to be a memorable and deeply felt experience. In each temple, I prayed, meditated, photographed and recited in Japanese a specific heart mantra. Some of the photographs in this book were made during that journey. I have found that, while engaged in a spiritual practice and/or photographing, silence greatly helps one's concentration and creativity. Eliminating noise from our everyday lives can be cathartic. It may be one of the reasons why I still enjoy spending long hours in a darkroom, printing. As a young seminarian, I would look forward to the three-day silent retreats in our school calendar. I regarded them as opportunities to recharge and regenerate. Since then, I have had the good fortune to participate in comparable retreats with Benedictine monks at Mont St Michel in France and Buddhist monks at Kōyasan, Japan. The experiences were remarkably similar—simple food and accommodation, no talking, attendance at services required, and chanting with the monks highly encouraged, yet still optional.

From Japan, I ventured to China, Hong Kong and Korea, primarily to photograph landscapes and cityscapes, yet I could not resist visiting and photographing in Buddhist temples during those travels. Later, I also photographed Buddhas in Cambodia, Laos, Myanmar, Thailand and Vietnam. The idea to compile the studies into a book came about only recently and the stimulus for that was a visit to the Guimet National Museum of Asian Arts in Paris, which has an astonishing collection of Asian artefacts. I was graciously given permission to photograph there, enabling me to add imagery from countries such as Afghanistan, India, Nepal, Pakistan and Tibet, which happily complemented my own collection of photographs.

I should state unequivocally that I am not an expert in Buddhist iconography and that this group of images is a personal selection, not a comprehensive survey. Beauty is in the mind of any individual beholder. The reaction each of us has when face to face with a Buddha is similarly personal. Feelings of serenity, calm, protection, acceptance, kindness, respect, reverence and curiosity may be evoked, or they may not. I suspect enlightenment should be added to this list, but I would certainly not presume so far. I rather like William Shakespeare's suggestion via Hamlet that human knowledge is limited: "There are more things in heaven and earth, Horatio, than are dreamt of in your philosophy."

Many years have passed since the days of my boyhood fixation with the Catholic religion. Having been exposed to other faiths, I can no longer subscribe to any one religious dogma. I married my lovely wife, Mamta, who was raised Hindu, in a Buddhist ceremony in Thailand. Our family home is decidedly multi-denominational, with a wide assortment of artworks and artefacts from many different religions scattered and displayed throughout. One of the Buddha studies in this book is from our private collection. At my current young age of sixty-six, I feel that I now know just enough about life and religion to appreciate how little I actually do know. Despite my lack of definitive understanding, I continue to be fascinated by, and love to visit, places of worship, reverence and prayer.

I hope that you will enjoy the images compiled in this book. I have thoroughly enjoyed making them. Thank you.

Michael Kenna
Asahikawa, Hokkaido
February, 2020

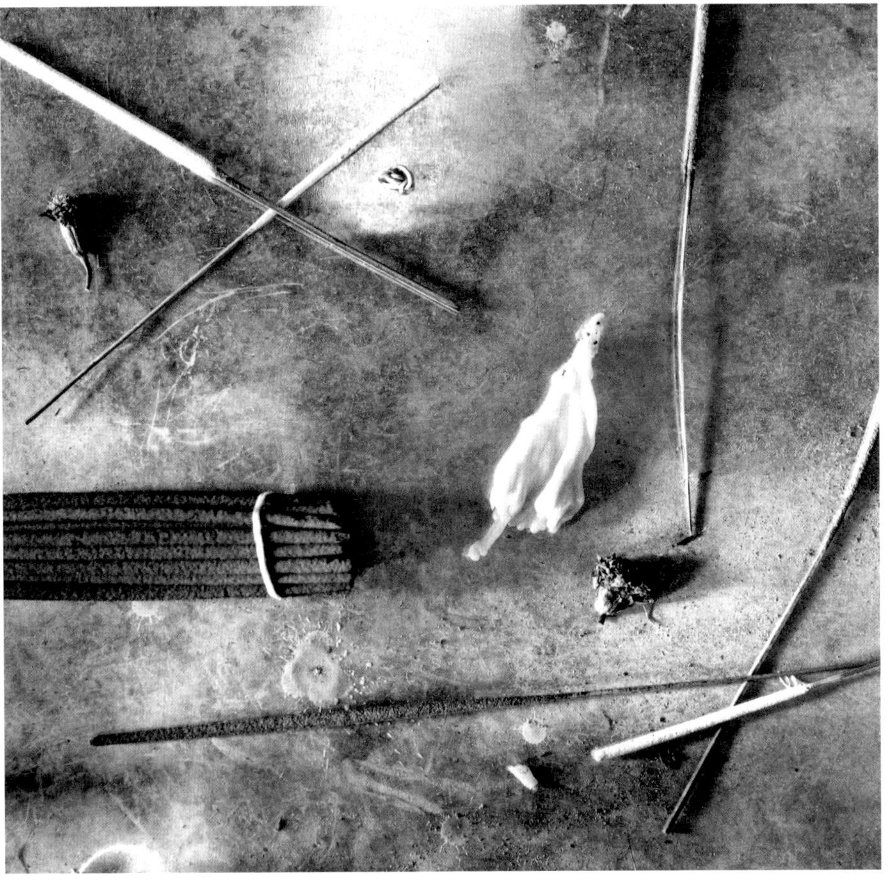

Incense Offerings,
Luang Prabang, Laos, 2015

BIOGRAPHIES

MICHAEL KENNA is widely recognized as one of the world's greatest and most influential living photographers. Born in Widnes, England, in 1953, he studied at St Joseph's College, Upholland, with a view to becoming a Catholic priest. At 18, he changed direction and attended the Banbury School of Art, Oxfordshire, before concentrating on photography at the London College of Printing, where he graduated with distinction in 1976.

Kenna then moved to San Francisco, where he worked for ten years as a photographic printer for the renowned photographer Ruth Bernhard. Kenna adopted many of Bernhard's ways of creative working and has developed his own distinctive and often emulated style of photographing and printing. Kenna's personal, handmade, non-digital photographic prints have been shown in more than 600 gallery and museum exhibitions throughout the world.

More than 70 monographs and exhibition catalogues have been published on Kenna's work. His limited-edition fine art prints are in the permanent collections of over 100 institutions, such as the The National Art Museum of China, Beijing, The National Museum of Modern Art, Paris, The Museum of Modern Art, New York, and The Victoria and Albert Museum, London. Michael Kenna lives in Seattle, USA, and continues to photograph around the globe.

JENS-UWE HARTMANN studied Indology, Tibetology and Sinology in Munich. After his habilitation in Göttingen, Germany, he was appointed professor for Tibetology at Berlin's Humboldt University in 1995. In 1999, he became professor of Indology at the Ludwig Maximilian University of Munich, a position he held until his retirement in 2018. In 2001, he was elected to the Bavarian Academy of Sciences and Humanities.

Hartmann's research focuses on the literature and history of Indian Buddhism, especially old and lost manuscripts and early translations into Tibetan and Chinese. Most of his books and articles are dedicated to the research of manuscript collections and the publication and translation of works on Indian Buddhism. He has held visiting professorships in Paris, Tokyo, Berkeley and Stanford.

GUDRUN MELZER studied Indian art history, Indology and Tibetology in Berlin and Munich. She was awarded her doctorate in 2007 at the Ludwig Maximilian University of Munich, which included the translation and publication of several sermons of the Buddha from a unique birch-bark manuscript in Sanskrit. Melzer has extensively studied ancient Buddhist manuscripts in Indian languages, some of which date back to the first century.

Since 2002, she has taught at the Free University of Berlin as well as at the universities of Vienna, Leipzig and Munich. Since 2012, Melzer has been involved in the long-term project on the publication of Buddhist manuscripts from the Gandhāra region (present-day Pakistan and Afghanistan), which are among the oldest-known manuscripts of Buddhism.

IRA STEHMANN is a photography expert, freelance curator and art advisor. She has curated exhibitions of contemporary art—specializing in photography—for museums, galleries and companies for almost thirty years and runs a project space for art and photography in Munich. Since 2005, she has advised the Nicola Erni Collection, Switzerland, in the field of contemporary photography.

Stehmann has edited and co-edited numerous publications on contemporary photography, including major monographs on Cathleen Naundorf, Jeanloup Sieff and Christopher Thomas.

GRATITUDE

This Prestel book on the Buddha would not exist without the kindness of many people. I am truly grateful to all who have contributed to this publication. I have tried to acknowledge as many of them as possible and I apologize to those I have inadvertently left out.

First and foremost, my deepest thanks go to my late mother and father, Eva and Walter Kenna, for their unconditional love. They raised me safe and secure in a close family, fostered in me a sense of the sacred at a very early age, and supported my unusual request to leave home and train to become a Catholic priest. I have so much to be grateful for and will always be indebted to them. I feel they still watch over our family. My sister, Patricia, and brothers, Peter, Francis, Anthony and Vincent, have always been an integral part of the journey. I would like to express appreciation for my late stepmother, Kathleen, for her love and support. I thank the priests at St Bede's, Widnes, for encouraging me to be an altar boy, thereby sowing important seeds for my spiritual journey. I thank the teachers, priests and staff at St Joseph's College, Upholland, for furthering both my secular and religious education, and I thank the teachers at the Banbury School of Art and the London College of Printing for their instruction and encouragement to follow a creative path.

The photographer Ruth Bernhard remains a powerful influence in my life. In the early 1980s, she introduced me to Zen Buddhist teachings, and her enthusiasm regarding everything Japanese turned out to be highly contagious. While I was working with Ruth, Minoru Shirota, owner of Gallery Min, Tokyo, invited me to visit Japan for the first time. Connie and Stephen Wirtz, owners of the Stephen Wirtz Gallery, San Francisco, organized the trip from the US. Maya Ishiwata, who had worked with Gallery Min, coordinated from Japan. Later, Maya became my agent for Japan and represented me for almost three decades until she retired last year. Maya travelled with me throughout Japan and specifically to Shikoku where she introduced me to the eighty-eight-temple pilgrimage. She guided me to many Buddhas, including the Amida Buddha in Kamakura featured on the cover of this book. Her work has been extraordinary and critical to my Asian experience. I continue to work with her partners, Emiko Harada and Hideyuki Taguchi, owners of Office Ram, Tokyo, on many projects, including the recent *45 Year Odyssey* exhibition, and with Miwako Takasuna, the owner of Gallery Art Unlimited, Tokyo, who has exhibited my work many times. Japan would not be Japan without these wonderful people, whom I regard more as family than work associates. My guides in Japan have included Satoshi Tanaka who accompanied me on part of the Shikoku pilgrimage, Tsuyoshi Kato, who took me to the Buddhist temples of Osorizan and Kōyasan in Honshu, and has guided me on many winter travels in Hokkaido over the past sixteen years, and Kaori Kodama, who also guided me in Kōyasan.

I first visited South Korea in 2005 for an exhibition at Whitewall Gallery, Seoul. Youn Sun Park, the gallery owner, organized a tour, guided by Young-Ju Baik, which included a visit to Woljeongsa Temple, Gangwondo. I was extremely fortunate to experience a snowstorm there and recently printed some of those photographs for this book. I have worked with several other guides in South Korea since, in particular Mina Shin, who has guided me to many Buddhist temples and has kindly watched out for me ever since we first started to work together in 2007. Jai W. Lee, Taek-ki Min, Andy Mooyo Kim, Eni Kim, Neo Kim, Saeho Kim, Jonghyun Nam and Munjeoung Kim have all accompanied me on various travels. For the past ten years, I have been represented in South Korea by Grace Kong, owner of Gallery KONG, Seoul. She has published three books of my work and has held many exhibitions. A huge thank you to all my kind Korean friends.

In 2006, I began to photograph in Hong Kong and China. My guides there were Nancy Lau and Miranda Zhuang. Later, Wang Zhao, Liu Ruirui and Vincent Zhen also guided me. I have worked closely with Lu Xiao, the owner of Timeless Gallery, Beijing, for the past ten years. He and his family, along with associates Can Haidong and Zhao Xia, have very graciously taken me to many locations throughout China. I greatly appreciate their continued friendship and support. More recently, I have travelled with them to Cambodia and Myanmar, where I was able to photograph a wide range of fascinating Buddha statues, many of which are included in this book.

The photographer Kenro Izu contacted me in 2015 about photographing in Laos to aid a children's hospital he had helped to set up there. I was delighted to be able to contribute to this worthy venture and worked with Adri Berger and Nouvanh Nconcotali. I visited many temples on my travels around this beautiful country. My wife and I have travelled to Thailand for the past eleven years. The Thai Buddhas in this book were primarily photographed in Ayutthaya, Bangkok and Phuket. I would like to thank Surin Banyatpiyaphod, Bheema Jotikabukkana and Akarapol Luksanakoses for their guidance. My most recent trip to photograph Buddhas was in 2019, to Vietnam. I thank Suzanne Lecht, the owner of Art Vietnam Gallery, Hanoi, for her kind encouragement and logistical support. She introduced me to Quynh Xuan Nguyen, who organized a specific itinerary concentrating on Buddhist pagodas. His associates, Hue Hong La and Tho Hoang Truong, spared no effort to show me many beautiful Buddhas. It was a thoroughly inspiring tour.

Much as I love to travel, I have not been able to photograph Buddha's in a number of countries represented in this book. Very fortunately, I was given access to the marvelous collection at the National Museum of Asian Arts – Guimet, Paris. I would like to sincerely thank Sophie Makariou the president of the museum, Jérôme Ghesquière who is responsible for the photographic collections, and Dominique Fayolle-Reninger who has kindly researched and fact checked the museum image titles for this book. I feel very proud and honored to have an association with this prestigious museum. I am extremely grateful to my irrepressible and energetic agent for Europe, Sabine Troncin-Denis, who is chiefly responsible for this timely collaboration.

Ira Stehmann, owner of Ira Stehmann Fine Art, Munich, exhibits my work. I did not know, until we fortuitously met at Paris Photo 2018, that she also has a great interest in Buddhas. She agreed to sift through the pool of images I had made as a selection for this book. It has been a joy to work with her. Curt Holtz, at Prestel Publishers, has been unreservedly enthusiastic about this project since it first came up in an email exchange a few years ago. Although he supports the wrong football team, our working relationship over this, our fifth book together, has been seamless, and I am very thankful for his constant optimism and confidence. I am grateful to Jens-Uwe Hartmann and Gudrun Melzer, who have contributed a very knowledgeable text, and also helped to guide the selection of images in this book. My sincere thanks to Andreas and Kathrin

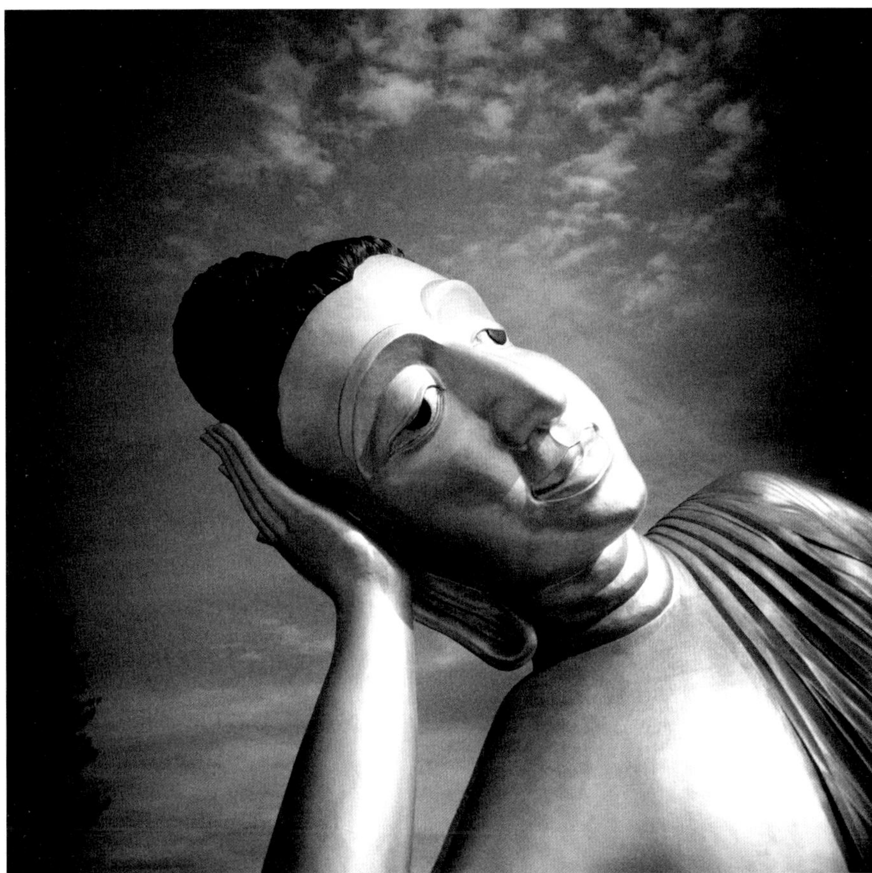

Lindner for sharing their unique knowledge about Buddha imagery. Thanks go to the designer of this publication, Florian Frohnholzer, who patiently built and rebuilt the book over the past year. I am extremely grateful to Mark Silva, who has been my diligent assistant, studio manager, friend and overall right-hand man for some eighteen years. I cannot express enough my thankfulness for all he does.

Much, much love and appreciation goes to my children, Olivia, Anika and Akul, for their kind patience and understanding while I am away photographing, and for their consistently warm and happy welcome when I return. I give my sincere and heartfelt thanks to my wonderful wife, Mamta, who makes it all happen. Our life together has been truly magnificent and our journey continues to include churches, mosques, shrines, synagogues and temples. Her unwavering love and support give me the freedom to pursue my dreams.

I would like to express my appreciation and respect for my late father-in-law, Shri Shobhachand Chintamani-ji, whom I never actually met, but who, I am absolutely sure, watches over our family. Finally, I thank my mother-in-law, Mithilesh Kumari Gupta, (fondly known as Ma), who lives with us. Her daily prayers and chanting, ringing of bells and burning of fragrant incense, help our home to be a temple, where reverence, respect, curiosity and love can flourish.

Michael Kenna
Seattle, Washington
March, 2020

Wat Sri Sunthon Buddha,
Phuket, Thailand, 2018

A member of Verlagsgruppe Random House GmbH
Neumarkter Straße 28 · 81673 Munich

Front cover: Amida Buddha, Kotoku-in, Kamakura,
Honshu, Japan, 2007 (see page 26)
Frontispiece: Gilded Buddhist protector deity,
Lama Temple, Beijing, China, 2016
Back cover: Mamta's Lotus Flower, Ban Viengkeo,
Luang Prabang, Laos, 2015 (see page 151)

Prestel Publishing Ltd.
16–18 Berners Street
London W1T 3LN

Prestel Publishing
900 Broadway, Suite 603
New York, NY 10003

Library of Congress Control Number is available;
British Library Cataloguing-in-Publication Data:
a catalogue record for this book is available from the
British Library.

Editorial direction: Curt Holtz with
Josephine Fehrenz
Translation from the German: Marielle Sutherland
Copy-editing: Danko Szabó
Design, layout and typesetting:
Sofarobotnik, Augsburg & Munich
Production management: Corinna Pickart
Printing, separations and binding: Longo AG, Bolzano
Paper: Arctic Volume White

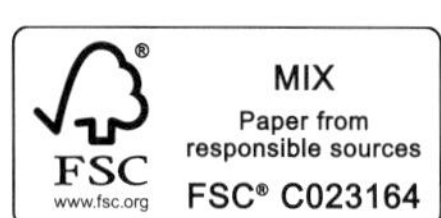

Verlagsgruppe Random House FSC® N001967

Printed in Italy

ISBN 978-3-7913-8508-2